SUPPORTING THE MENTAL HEALTH OF CHILDREN IN CARE

by the same editors

Understanding Looked After Children
An Introduction to Psychology for Foster Care
Jeune Guishard-Pine, Suzanne McCall and Lloyd Hamilton
Foreword by Andrew Wiener
ISBN 978 1 84310 370 7
eISBN 978 1 84642 684 1

of related interest

Healing Child Trauma Through Restorative Parenting
A Model for Supporting Children and Young People
Chris Robinson and Terry Philpot
Foreword by Andrew Constable and Karen Mitchell-Mellor
ISBN 978 1 84905 699 1
eISBN 978 1 78450 215 7

Educating Children and Young People in Care
Learning Placements and Caring Schools
Claire Cameron, Graham Connelly and Sonia Jackson
ISBN 978 1 84905 365 5
eISBN 978 0 85700 719 3

Therapeutic Residential Care For Children and Youth
Developing Evidence-Based International Practice
Edited by James K. Whittaker, Jorge F. del Valle and Lisa Holmes
Foreword by Robbie Gilligan
ISBN 978 1 84905 963 3 (Hardback)
ISBN 978 1 84905 792 9 (Paperback)
eISBN 978 0 85700 833 6

Team Parenting for Children in Foster Care
A Model for Integrated Therapeutic Care
Jeanette Caw with Judy Sebba
ISBN 978 1 84905 445 4
eISBN 978 0 85700 820 6

Responding to Self-Harm in Children and Adolescents
A Professional's Guide to Identification, Intervention and Support
Steven Walker
ISBN 978 1 84905 172 9
eISBN 978 0 85700 306 5

Empathic Care for Children with Disorganized Attachments
A Model for Mentalizing, Attachment and Trauma-Informed Care
Chris Taylor
Foreword by Professor Peter Fonagy
ISBN 978 1 84905 182 8
eISBN 978 0 85700 398 0

SUPPORTING THE MENTAL HEALTH OF CHILDREN IN CARE

EVIDENCE-BASED PRACTICE

EDITED BY JEUNE GUISHARD-PINE OBE,
GAIL COLEMAN-OLUWABUSOLA
AND SUZANNE MCCALL

FOREWORD BY JENNY PEARCE OBE

Jessica Kingsley *Publishers*
London and Philadelphia

First published in 2017
by Jessica Kingsley Publishers
73 Collier Street
London N1 9BE, UK
and
400 Market Street, Suite 400
Philadelphia, PA 19106, USA

www.jkp.com

Library of Congress Cataloging in Publication Data
Names: Guishard-Pine, Jeune, editor. | Coleman-Oluwabusola, Gail, editor. | McCall, Suzanne, editor.
Title: Supporting the mental health of children in care : evidence for practice / edited by Jeune Guishard-Pine, Gail Coleman-Oluwabusola and Suzanne McCall.
Description: London ; Philadelphia : Jessica Kingsley Publishers, 2017. | Includes bibliographical references and index.
Identifiers: LCCN 2016007166 | ISBN 9781849056687 (alk. paper)
Subjects: | MESH: Child Behavior Disorders--therapy | Foster Home Care--psychology | Mental Health Services
Classification: LCC RJ503 | NLM WS 350.6 | DDC 616.8900835--dc23 LC record available at
http://lccn.loc.gov/2016007166

British Library Cataloguing in Publication Data
A CIP catalogue record for this book is available from the British Library

ISBN 978 1 84905 668 7
eISBN 978 1 78450 172 3

Printed and bound in Great Britain

Contents

Foreword

This is an exciting and innovative book, exploring some of the complex questions facing foster carers as well as childcare practitioners and policy makers today. For example, how do we support the sustained provision of nuanced and appropriate foster care for children who might say they do not want a 'new' family and how do we overcome a simplified notion that all children, including older teenagers, have similar needs and interests? How do we best explore and communicate about details of previous trauma and loss that children entering foster care might have experienced? Are our systems fully equipped to provide training and support for foster carers and their families as they try to understand the mental health needs of children in their care and provide healthy attachments? How do we support foster carers to manage the significant impacts that caring for foster children have on their existing family networks? How child centred are we when we are making decisions about future care and support for, and with, foster children? These and many other questions are touched on within this book, which is essential reading for those working in this field.

The reason this is important is that as we increasingly rely on foster carers to support children in local authority care, we need evaluations and research in the area to extend our knowledge of helpful, evolving and good practice. While it is appreciated that a blanket acceptance of so called 'truths' giving 'objective' assertions of what is good needs to be questioned, it is also important that we do engage with critical reviews of foster carers' and children's experiences. We need to understand trends and themes that give us messages of what is important to consider, what seems to have positive impacts on children, and what best supports those who care for them. For too long it might have been assumed that providing a caring environment was just a 'natural' attribute of family members. While the commitment and compassion of many families who provide foster care is without question (indeed, both are essential features that help sustain engagement with a range of sometimes very difficult and damaged foster children), it cannot be assumed that all approaches to 'safe' family life are based on the same understandings of effective parenting or that training and support of foster carers is not needed.

My own experience of engaging with research with practitioners exploring their views about the needs of trafficked children (Pearce, Hynes and Bovarnick 2013) showed how essential it was for foster carers to be provided with information about the mental, physical and sexual health needs of the children they were providing for. It also showed how important it was for carers to have training and support about child mental health and attachment theory, and about the variety of forms of exploitation and abuse experienced by some children in their care. The research revealed how foster carers needed supervised networks around them to help manage the various challenges facing both them and the children they cared for. Other areas of work on child sexual abuse and exploitation show how difficult it can be for children to report their experiences of abuse, and how important it is for practitioners and carers to be equipped to identify the indicators of abuse so that they can help children to disclose (Melrose and Pearce 2013). The National Society for the Prevention of Cruelty to Children (NSPCC) (Radford *et al.* 2011) notes that at least one in 20 children are affected by sexual abuse, recognizing that this is an underestimation of the numbers concerned. As many children entering foster care will have experienced family breakdown it is possible that disclosure of previous forms of abuse may well occur while the child is in foster care. Managing this and supporting the child is a complex process (Beckett and Warrington 2015). It is not until we create learning environments for carers, practitioners and researchers to share information about best practice that we will begin to create forums for these challenges to be worked with collaboratively. The Economic and Social Research Council (ESRC) recently funded a seminar series run through joint collaboration between The Rees Centre at the University of Oxford, the International Centre, researching child sexual exploitation, violence and trafficking at the University of Bedfordshire and the University of Gothenburg.[1] This series gave foster children, foster carers, non-governmental organizations (NGOs) working in the field, academics, practitioners and policy makers the rare opportunity to

1 http://reescentre.education.ox.ac.uk/research/teenagers-in-foster-care

meet and discuss a range of issues similar to those raised in this book. Although the series was focused on a particular age group, the mere fact that discussion was taking place between a number of service users, service providers and service evaluators provided unusual scope for different voices and perspectives to be heard. While there are many excellent NGOs leading in this area, the Fostering Network being one example,[2] we need more books like this one here to inform such debates with research findings.

This book is also of critical importance because it extends our awareness and understanding of the significant role that children's metal health services can play for looked after children. When children are experiencing loss and bereavement, problems with drug or alcohol misuse, interpersonal violence, eating disorders, and/or sexual violence, abuse and neglect, they could be supported by sensitive, appropriate and accessible mental health services. There are significant questions to be raised and addressed about thresholds for children's access to services, the scope and role of talking therapies with children, and foster carers' own role in engaging with children's mental health problems. As said often within this text, if we can assume from research that a caring and helping relationship is an important part of a mental health intervention for children, then the role of the foster carer is of central importance. To underestimate the significance of this relationship and to overlook the mental health needs of children who have been affected by family breakdown is to undermine the potential of so many children in care. We must not ever underestimate the achievements that children in care can make, and how many create fulfilling lives for themselves. Neither must we underestimate the role that foster carers can play in helping this to occur. This book gives us the opportunity to bring research findings into these debates and offers valuable insights into the important role of research informed practice.

Jenny Pearce OBE
Professor of Young People and Public Policy
University of Bedfordshire

2 www.fostering.net

Acknowledgements

Jeune

First of all I would like to thank my co-editors who both in their own way and with their own strengths took each of my arms and pulled me firmly up and out of the quicksand! I have never been as fortunate as I am today to be surrounded by the creative energies that went into the production of this book. Thanks to Professor Jenny Pearce OBE for generously contributing her time to write this foreword; she is both an inspiration and a sage. Lastly, I have been lucky enough to be part of not one but two 'A-teams'. First of all my family who have supported me in all of my journeys as a researcher and author, and second the awesome Service to Children Requiring Intensive Psychological Therapies (SCRIPT) which has given service to over 500 children in care – never faltering or failing in its passion and commitment to these children, many of whom have had the most appalling introduction to their lives. Thank you for being part of the tremendous work that refreshed their childhood.

Gail

The basic meaning of the Igbo and Yoruba (Nigeria) proverb 'It takes a village to raise a child' is that child rearing is a communal effort, and responsibility is shared with the larger family. Without a doubt, in my case I can say, 'It takes a village...to edit a book!' As such, I would like to say thank you to my co-editors who kept me focused and were extremely patient with me. I would like to thank my husband, Victor Oluwabusola, my children, my parents and my siblings, for their encouragement and support. Furthermore, for me, part of my village includes my faith. I am thankful for my faith which keeps me hopeful in my work with children and adolescents who have had their lives torn apart. Their experiences inspire me to write, ever hopeful of change.

Suzanne

Thanks to all in involved in bringing this book to fruition, including my patient co-editors and my long-suffering family. But special thanks go to those who taught me over many years, the adolescents.

Introduction

In 2007, Jessica Kingsley Publishers published our first book, *Understanding Looked After Children: An Introduction to Psychology for Foster Care.* It summarized our immediate learning at that time, which was that foster carers need to have an accessible book in order to develop their understanding about the psychological needs of children in care.

Since this time, the number of children looked after by their local authorities has risen and now in England stands at 69,540 (British Association of Adoption and Fostering 2014). It is currently at a higher point than at any time since 1985. Importantly, also 60 per cent of these are children subject to care orders. This 60 per cent, at the very least, will represent the most abused and neglected young people in England. While statistics vary depending on the year and source, it can be said that at least a third of these young people will have a mental health problem, and many studies suggest a higher percentage (Zayed and Harker 2015). The statutory guidance on promoting the health and well-being of children in care revealed that:

> A further source of information on the prevalence of emotional and behavioural difficulties among looked after children is the Looking After Children longitudinal study of children and young people who remained in care for at least a year. This considered the needs of children at the point of first entry into care and identified emotional and behavioural problems from information recorded in case files by social workers and subsequently assessed by psychologists. Using these methods, it was found that 72 per cent of looked after children aged 5 to 15 had a mental or behavioural problem compared to 45 per cent in the ONS survey. Among children starting to be looked after under the age of five (this age group was not included in the ONS survey), nearly one in five showed signs of emotional or behavioural problems. (Department for Children, Schools and Families 2009, p.12)

The evidence for an urgent need to continue developing practice to deliver specialist services for children in care is irrefutable. The National Institute for Health and Care Excellence (NICE) guidance (2010, updated 2015) follows a number of government papers over the past ten years examining the poor outcomes for children in care and directions for local authority service provision. It recommends that dedicated services to children in care should be commissioned that are 'informed by the views of children, national evidence, guidance and performance data, the corporate parenting board, local knowledge and experts, local audits, the JSNA and local plans for meeting their health needs'. The guidance also recommends that these services have 'expert resources' to address emotional health needs, offer greater choice and quality of service, and prioritize the needs of children in care. An ever-widening professional group will have to gain the knowledge and skills to meet such guidance.

This book aims to contribute to the continued development of the specialist knowledge base required to work therapeutically with children in care and the networks around them. This is achieved as we share the lessons from the last 13 years of our therapeutic work and research within a specialist child mental health service (CAMHS) established to provide intensive interventions for children in care – the Service to Children Requiring Intensive Psychological Therapies (SCRIPT). The service was led by Professor Jeune Guishard-Pine. The book also incorporates contributions from the research and writings from other colleagues actively practising with children in care. It is primarily based on the direct work of practitioners, rather than academics.

The title of this book reflects our journey as practitioners from 'discovery' through research and learning to 'recovery', through intervention and therapeutic work in progress. 'Discovery' in the context of the service, included the outcomes of three doctoral theses. For all research supervised, there was a stipulation that the direct implications for the work of child mental health services with children in care should form a focal point. As stated, there is specific focus on the practice-based evidence of clinicians specializing in working with looked after children for the most part within a targeted children in care team.

As a team, a critical message that we hope emanates from this book is that professionals working with children in care need to engage in open and reflective discussions with each other in order to understand the young person's communication of distress and to address this in a useful way. However experienced, the wisdom of a single individual needs to be balanced with the contributions of all those around the young person, especially in the face of the unknown and the complex. Without this mechanism for understanding, processing and containing the immense pain and damage historically inflicted on a child in care, this trauma simply ricochets around and repeats throughout the system.

The specialist child mental health service happened to be in the UK. However, the mental health issues of children in care largely transcend race and culture, for example the trauma of non-consensual sex, neglect and physical abuse. As such, the chapters cite relevant research regardless of which part of the world it was conducted in. Such evidence suggests that the increased vulnerability to mental health difficulties for children in care in Europe, North America and Australia is fairly consistent cross-culturally (Cicchetti and Carlson 1989; Tarren-Sweeney 2008).

However, the evidence base is relatively small and there are a number of factors that contribute to this. For example, frequent changes of placement and in social work staff, poor school attendance and young people's mistrust of formal initiatives all present problems for researchers. Additionally, evaluating mental health outcomes for children in care is a complex process, as it is very hard to disentangle the effects of family and social and environmental factors when trying to measure the impact of their having been in the care system (Baron 2012). Also, as with all children who access mental health services, particularly traumatized children, an increase in symptoms at significant points such as puberty, important anniversaries or working through the process of therapy itself is not uncommon. This presents an important consideration when there is a political focus on outcomes in terms of symptom reduction. Hence research in this field benefits significantly from 'practice-based evidence', a complementary paradigm to improve clinical effectiveness and the associated positive outcomes (Margison *et al.* 2000), in addition to the traditional, 'evidence-based practice' for psychological interventions.

The chapters have been written with a wide range of readers in mind but typically those already practising or undertaking training in working directly with children in care. We believe, however, that for those whose work may include children in care from time to time this will also provide useful reading. Above and beyond any other hopes for this book, we have endeavoured to present throughout the clinical work undertaken with the voice of the child and its potential as a powerful educational resource.

In the first chapter, Siobain Bonfield and Professor Jeune Guishard-Pine remind us why this book is needed. Specifically, as stated, this is because of the higher rates of emotional and mental health needs of children in care, together with an underuse of services. Evidence exploring barriers to accessing child and adolescent mental health services is presented. Consequently, the role of the foster carer and the number of help-seeking steps he has taken becomes an important focus of this chapter. The need for foster carers to be explicitly and continually sensitized and informed about the mental health needs of children in care so that this counterbalances their often relatively high threshold of tolerance is postulated. This sets the tone of the book, which continues in detail to inform the reader of the mental health needs of children in care and what works in practice, drawing successfully on a diverse and robust evidence base throughout.

In Chapter 2, Christine Cork, a highly experienced childcare practitioner, invites us to think about the way that the lived, negative experience of the individual child can potentially permeate the entire care network. She describes a number of themes that emerge for children who enter the care system in the early years and the behaviours that bring them to the attention of child mental health services. It is a bold, insightful piece that questions whether the experience of shame can influence neurological development and the dynamic of shame in relationships between child, carer and the rest of the network.

In Chapter 3, Sam Warner and Clare Shaw contribute to a child-focused view of self-harm. This includes excerpts from the second author's early history, as an expert by experience. The importance of formulating the function and socio-cultural context of self-harm for the individual child is highlighted. Higher rates of self-harm and suicide for children in care are usefully linked to disproportionate experiences of abuse, neglect, exploitation and loss. Some of the common methods available to children in care are identified and the negative impact of over reliance on a harm cessation approach is discussed. However, the need to understand where coping ends and suicide begins is emphasized, with the point that each requires different strategies. Examples of such strategies are usefully outlined, including an important discussion on the role of harm-minimization as a way to survive while working towards recovery. Finally, there is a discussion about the secondary trauma of working with young people who self-harm and the need for a shared understanding about self-harm across providers.

Specific case material becomes the focus of the next four chapters. This begins with Chapter 4, which summarizes the risk factors associated with substance misuse from an international perspective. Lisa Robinson and Professor Jeune Guishard-Pine discuss substance misuse as a way some young people communicate and cope with the pain of neglect and abuse. As such, there is recognition of the fact that there is a need for interventions that do not solely focus on substance misuse. Examples are given of good practice in both NHS and voluntary sector services in the UK.

In Chapter 5, child and adolescent psychoanalytic psychotherapist, Olatayo Afuape, presents the psychotherapeutic assessment of two siblings in foster care and provides detailed insights into the complexities of this work. Working with ideas of safe therapy, she outlines the role of containing and mindful specialist teams in supporting therapists to usefully process difficult and disruptive feelings emanating from the work. Themes of splitting, omnipotence and paralysis endemic to the assessment can be seen to be reflected in the experience of the therapist experiencing organizational upheaval and change. Importantly, the author asks us to reflect on how organizational issues may skew how we conceptualize the work.

In Chapter 6, Tonie Lawrence-Mahrra, CAMH practitioner and transpersonal therapist, presents through images her work with Lauren, who was sexually abused from a young age. Sexual abuse most often inflicts a very particular wound for a young child whose sense of themselves can be annihilated at a very fundamental level. Of course, it is also always accompanied by other forms of abuse, such as physical, emotional and neglect. Tonie provides us with an insight into her sand-tray work with Lauren and how the worlds she created in it were received and understood by the therapist.

In Chapter 7, Eleanor Havsteen-Franklin presents two case studies exploring the role of art psychotherapy with children in care who are returning home. She explores how the nature of previous trauma shapes each child's engagement with the art materials and importantly also how the therapist may be experienced by the child. In planning for and returning home, Eleanor describes the vital work that is done in therapy to assist this often difficult transition back to the care of a parent/s and how this joint work is pivotal to successful transition.

Moving towards a focus on outcome and intervention, in Chapter 8 Professor Jeune Guishard-Pine and Hannah Baron draw on the second author's research and the evidence base to challenge the focus on technique within current attachment-based therapies. This highlights the loss of focus on actual 'attachment' or relationships and instead a push towards a one-size-fits-all approach to therapy in mainstream services. The reader is reminded of the importance of the therapeutic relationship. Then, more specifically, the authors highlight the importance of the co-created therapeutic relationship for children in care with lives dominated by a lack of control. The concepts of anarchy and ecstasy of co-created relationships are discussed and proposed as a powerful and important approach to therapy with the potential for continuing bonds.

Chapter 9 presents a strong argument in support of increasing the professionalization of foster carers. The definition of professionalization in this chapter is particularly concerned with increasing communication skills and more specifically the application of counselling skills to the foster carer's relationship with the child. Hence delivery of an accredited course in child and adolescent mental health created by Professor Guishard-Pine and Suzanne McCall is described, together with the positive outcomes foster carers assigned to the training. In an innovative step, the creation of the skills-based course is seen as a way to bridge the divide between the lack of higher education among foster carers and an agenda around professionalism potentially focused primarily on pay associated with formal education. Furthermore, the real need for such training is linked to evidence which demonstrates that a staggering percentage of children in care are not having their mental health needs met by relevant services, due to limited resources. Hence this progressive training is also presented as a way that foster carers can safely support the mental health needs of the children in their care, and reduce the cumulative impact of unmet mental health needs. This includes the impact on the carers themselves.

Chapter 10 is essentially about boundaries, context and outreach and the ethical issues they can challenge. Without thorough reflection and evolution of practice, the traditional therapeutic practice in terms of frequently applied boundaries can represent a glass ceiling for children in care. In this way the most vulnerable young people living chaotic and fragmented lives receive either no therapy or 'ricochet' off a system that regards them as unsuitable or unable to engage. Recent research confirms what we have known for a long time: children in care often feel they are in the middle of a 'pass the parcel' game and their experience of professional services can be one of secondary abuse. Suzanne McCall argues that to minimize therapy being experienced in this way, we must re-examine therapeutic boundaries for their usefulness with this client group. Organizations, too, need to shift some 'service boundaries' to enable an efficient and effective service for children in care.

In Chapter 11, Professor Jeune Guishard-Pine and Emily Wilkens emphasize the point that individual services cannot support a child in care in isolation. Furthermore, the child has to be at the centre rather than being caught up in inter-agency rivalries with their needs not being met if the child is to benefit from a protective shield composed of services, the foster carers and, when appropriate, birth family members. Without such a shield, recovery for the child can be subconsciously or more openly sabotaged. The authors propose that the key is to understand one's role as a professional within the protective shield as part of integrative working. Furthermore, just as a kaleidoscope operates on the principle of multiple reflection, professionals all bring multiple perspectives through which they view the child in care and the various networks around them. Hence it is convincingly argued that an essential component of recovery is for intervention to be provided specifically for the network around the child, in addition to proposed individual psychotherapy for children in care or individualized input for foster carers.

In Chapter 12, Zoë Lander describes her journey in working with looked after children, discussing the anxieties and pressures this process has entailed for her in arriving at a place where she feels competent in her work with this group of young people. She provides us with an open and human account of how she has experienced this journey and her reflections on how becoming identified as a 'specialist' entails building a resilience as a practitioner. Zoë also directs us to understand that the work often most needed is to support and contain those who are directly caring for the young person and the emotional cost of caring for those who foster.

Cultural competence is a core construct within the domains of both psychology and psychotherapy (Sue *et al.* 1982). This original theory suggests that the racial and ethnic identity of an individual in distress cannot be ignored if he is to be truly helped to recover from his presenting distress. Carter (2001, p.787) puts this succinctly:

> The traditional and standard principles of helping are culturally bound and are at odds with the cultural norms and expectations of racially and ethnically different people. Sue posits that cultural competence must be understood and acquired from many dimensions. He argues that it is imperative that the social and organizational context in which cultural competence is learned becomes a part of competence training (e.g., Carter 2000).

Thus, culture not only influences the motivation to seek help but also impacts on how mental illness is experienced. One aspect of culture is ethnicity, and there are trends with regards to children in care in the UK:

> The ethnic breakdown for children looked after has varied little since 2011. The majority of children looked after at 31 March 2015 (73%) are from a White British background: similar to the general population of all children. Children of mixed ethnicity continue to be slightly over-represented, and children of Asian ethnicity slightly underrepresented in the looked after children population. (Department for Education 2015a)

In terms of the over-representation described above and actual numbers, 2320 were of mixed ethnicity but this was closely followed by Black African children who made up 2200 of the children in care population in 2015 (Department for Education 2015a, Table A1, National Tables).

Gail Coleman-Oluwabusola, who has had a clinical focus on working with Black and 'ethnic' minority communities in the UK, challenges us in Chapter 13 to consider whether a 'culture' exists for children in care. Multi-dimensional aspects of culture dominate the world of children in care. Gail Coleman-Oluwabusola refers to pertinent research that describes the major issues and themes that overlay the 'culture' of children in care, based on the voice of child. The main lessons that need to be learnt about understanding the many cultural layers of a child in care's existence (birth family, fostering family, the community, local authority, education and health services) are explored. How they interrelate and how they repel each other to the benefit or detriment of children in care is one of the main discussion points of the chapter.

Chapter 14 discusses qualitative research on how therapy assisted service users' recovery to mental health. Sidra Aslam cleverly reveals layer upon layer of the service users' experiences to highlight the strategies and devices that need to be employed to ensure that the patient can remain on the road to recovery. She goes on to make recommendations for what individual clinicians and child mental health services can do to provide a 'safe space' for children in care to have their mental health needs adequately addressed.

With a strong focus on a largely qualitative research, in Chapter 15 Olatayo Afuape provides an important platform and voice for a specific group intervention with kinship carers. The status of kinship carers internationally is discussed with recognition of the low status often accorded this in the west, specifically in comparison to foster carers and adoptive parents, in addition to wider society. As such they present as invisible and the chapter gives voice to their significant, often unrecognized, input and the emotional journeys associated with this. The detailed format and reflective analysis of the group intervention described is pioneering and highlights the dearth of research in this area. The successful outcomes for the children impacted by this intervention are outlined together with implications for this important area of research.

Chapter 16 stands alone as the only contribution from the world of academia. Lucie Shuker is one of the country's leading experts on the risks of child sexual exploitation of children in care. She discusses her research conducted on the multi-dimensional approaches to safety for children in care and the various change theories that potentially complement the approaches to encourage sustained change in the protective behaviours of children in care at risk of child sexual exploitation.

Can we take this opportunity to say that this process has been a stimulating one! This is a very well researched book that draws on research from every level: from personal communications to doctoral theses, to national reviews around the world. Being able to scope what is happening on an international level and how it synthesizes with what has been happening in the UK has been particularly satisfying. We are very proud of the work that has been produced and hope you will be too.

Chapter 1

'I Try Hard Not to Scream'

Responding to the Distress of Children in Care

SIOBAIN BONFIELD AND JEUNE GUISHARD-PINE

Introduction

Following the implementation of the Children Act 1989, the Department of Health in England started to record the needs of the child that led to referrals and interventions from social services. For the most part, her needs and difficulties emanated from the adverse environment created by socio-economic disadvantage, poverty and homelessness and the impact of these factors on family life. Some of these families cannot overcome such disadvantages and their children may be placed in care due to family breakdown or dysfunction (Department for Education 2014e).

The grim statistic is that there are currently over 93,000 children in care in the UK (CoramBAAF 2015). The most recent evidence is that as many as 62 per cent of these children were physically, emotionally and/or sexually abused and neglected (Department for Education 2014e). As the spirit of the Children Act 1989 is to keep birth families together, it is unsurprising that children who enter the care system will have suffered abuse or neglect for a prolonged period. Many others will have experienced significant losses such as those that arise from bereavement or disability or have had to live with or become young carers for one or both parents with serious mental or physical health conditions. Most disabled children who are in foster care are looked after not because of their disability, although this may be a contributing factor, but for the same reasons as other children in care, namely reasons associated with family breakdown or dysfunction or abuse and neglect (Sinclair *et al.* 2005).

These cumulative factors predispose children to mental health problems (Meltzer *et al.* 2003; Utting *et al.* 1997), thus children in care are a group of particularly vulnerable young people whose mental health needs are known to be greater than those of the general population (Jütte *et al.* 2015). Research in the USA and Canada has also indicated that, even when compared to the most disadvantaged children residing with their birth family, children in care have higher rates of psychopathology (DosReis *et al.* 2001; Farmer, Burns and Chapman 2001; Ford *et al.* 2007; Stein *et al.* 1996). Despite their significant profile of deprivation and disadvantage, they have been found to underuse mental health services (Minnis *et al.* 2006; Richardson 2015). Services for these young people are problematic as they have complex needs and can be a mobile population. Consequently, their problems are also often undiagnosed and therefore remain untreated (Bonfield *et al.* 2010; McCann *et al.* 1996).

What is also clear as a reason for why some children in care do not use mental health services is the influential role that significant others have in determining whether or not they receive help from mental health services for their mental health problems. This chapter discusses the implications of a study of the mental health literacy of a group of 113 foster carers and the extent to which this skill promoted or inhibited the use of child mental health services for the children in their care.

How do children in care show their distress?

Many children feel a sense of relief when they are taken into care. However, there may be many feelings elicited around being taken into care, rooted in the sorrow and disappointment that children in care might have when they finally accept the idea of no longer residing with their parents (Selwyn *et al.* 2008; Sinclair *et al.* 2005). These confusing – and often competing – feelings are evident despite them having had significant trauma and difficulties over and above those experienced by most of their peers. It is because of this uncomfortable combination of their history of trauma and these conflictual feelings that they can show severe distress.

The title of this chapter reflects a comment made to the second author. The child, who was aged nine years at the time, wanted to communicate the frustration that the invisibility of her distress could cause. Earliest research has shown that emotional and behavioural difficulties in female pupils in co-educational schools masked a history of sexual abuse (e.g. Guishard and Malcolm 1993). More extensive research has produced similar findings: that abused children bring attention to their distress through their behaviour (Kay 2003; Roesch-Marsh 2012). Roesch-Marsh (2012) comments that:

> Practitioners need to be curious about what young people are communicating through their behaviour and should not simply focus on 'managing' behaviours. Practitioners must remember that the young person may be communicating their distress in relation to an experience of on-going neglect and abuse. (p.6)

The distress of children in care typically manifests as a range of mental health disorders (Meltzer *et al.* 2003) (see Tables 1.1 and 1.2). The prevalence of mental disorders differs between the survey of children in care to local authorities and the 2000 survey of those living in private households.

Table 1.1 Mental health disorders for children aged 5–10 years

	Meltzer *et al.* (2000)	Meltzer *et al.* (2003)
Mental health disorder	**Private households (% aged 5–10 years)**	**Children in care (% aged 5–10 years)**
All	8.0	42.0
Emotional disorders	3.3	11.0
Conduct disorders	4.6	36.5
Hyperkinetic disorders	1.5	11.5

Table 1.2 Mental health disorders for young people aged 11–15 years

	Meltzer *et al.* (2000)	Meltzer *et al.* (2003)
Mental health disorder	**Private households (% aged 11–15 years)**	**Children in care (% aged 11–15 years)**
All	8.0	42.0
Emotional disorders	11.9	40.5
Conduct disorders	7.1	5.6
Hyperkinetic disorders	6.2	1.5

In Meltzer *et al.*'s (2003) survey of the mental health needs of children in care, one of the conclusions was that the application of diagnostic categorization was fundamentally flawed because it does not sufficiently take into account the magnitude of the impact that children's distress has, not just on themselves but on those who care for them.

Barriers to children in care getting help for their distress

Phillips (1997) conducted research on the views of social workers on the mental health needs of children in care. The survey revealed that the social worker perceived that 80 per cent of the children needed treatment from mental health services, whereas only 27 per cent received it. The reasons given for the gap were found to be placement instability, inadequate child mental health resources and insufficient local authority funding. Saunders and Broad (1997) in their study found that 17 (35%) of the children in care had engaged in deliberate self-harm since the age of 15 years; 29 (60%) had thought about taking their own life and four out of ten had actually attempted suicide. In addition to this, they found a further 17 (31%) of the children in care had referred themselves for mental health problems, of whom sadly 12 (77%) did not find the service useful. These statistics in relation to the use of mental health services may go some way towards explaining why these children escalate their needs and difficulties in order to bring attention to not having their needs adequately responded to. To cite Leon Russell (1972): 'They tried to talk it over but the words got in the way.'

Reasons why some children in care may not access mental health services

It is also important to highlight that recurrent disruptions in relationships, loss and vulnerability to mental health difficulties are not the case for all children in care. Between 2013 and 2014, according to the Strengths and Difficulties Questionnaire (SDQ) (Goodman 1997), approximately half of all children in care aged 5–16 years were deemed to have emotional and behavioural health that is considered normal. This compares with 90 per cent of children who live with their parents (Department for Education 2014a).

Just why as many as 50 per cent of children in care might have normal emotional and behavioural health has been the subject of much research. Research that has debated the impact of early life experiences on later development indicates that resilience may play a preventive role in children in care developing mental health disorders. Resilience refers to a person having the capacity to resist or recoup from adverse experiences (Gilligan 2000). Developmental psychologists have shown that resilience is common among children growing up in disadvantaged conditions (Masten 2001).

Schofield and Beek's (2005a, 2005b) longitudinal studies revealed that a range of factors and processes appear to enhance or threaten the stability, progress and resilience of children in long-term foster care and that this was independent of adverse early experiences. The findings as to which factors may actively hinder access to mental health services for children in care are inconsistent. Some evidence suggests that children in care may lack resilience because of their high levels of need, while recent research has demonstrated that children in care hold more positive self-perceptions than children in their birth families (Honey, Rees and Griffey 2011).

While most of the reasons are linked to the child, there are also factors related to the foster carer and the mental health service that deter children in care from accessing mental health services. Foster carers who were having difficulty coping and experiencing burden may be more likely to seek help from specialist services (Verhulst and van der Ende 1997). In the study to be expanded on in this chapter, the foster carers had a higher level of coping skills.

How can we improve access to mental health services for children in care who need it?

The practical reality is that carers often have sparse information on the recurrent traumas of the child and consequently have a limited perspective on how these specific traumas are manifesting. Hence such youngsters often elude a clear diagnostic label when using diagnostic tools in isolation from a complementary qualitative assessment (Angold, Costello and Erkanli 1999; Goodman *et al.* 2000). Meltzer *et al.* (2003) recommended that the antidote to this is to give a higher profile to the clinical judgement of the child's expressed distress and to the social impairments this produces within her and in her relationships with others.

Latterly, it is often the burden of the child's problem on others, rather than the burden of the symptoms on the child itself, that is a measure of the scale of the problem. This leads to the 'problem' being defined in terms of whether the child's difficulties cause distress to the carer/family by making them worried, depressed, tired or physically ill. Therefore, the impact that her distress has on her support network – specifically her carers – also needs to be scrutinized.

Maguire (2005) was a pioneering study that sought to inform more widely what processes need to be established so that the mental health needs of children in care are adequately addressed within mental health services. Yet to be replicated, her research zoomed in on the skills and competences that foster carers need to enhance in order to respond to the children's distress. Her research has been extended (Bonfield *et al.* 2010) and was followed up only very recently in the USA with mental health practitioners estimating the mental health literacy of parents and carers (Frauenholtz, Conrad-Hiebner and Mendenhall 2015).

Cited in numerous national reviews (e.g. NSPCC 2014; O'Neill, Holland and Rees 2013; Parliament UK 2015; Public Health England 2015; Social Care Institute for Excellence 2010) as Bonfield *et al.* (2010), this seminal study accessed a cross-sectional study of 113 foster carers. It was undertaken to explore the factors that influence the use of mental health services by children in care with mental health problems. The mental health literacy (MHL) and attitudes toward seeking psychological help among a group of foster carers were examined, as were other factors that have previously been found to significantly influence the help-seeking process for children.

The role of mental health literacy and help-seeking attitudes in children in care accessing mental health services

Primarily, MHL refers to the ability to recognize specific disorders or different types of psychological distress, but also includes knowledge of services available, attitudes that promote problem recognition, and appropriate help-seeking behaviour (Jorm *et al.* 1997). In general, foster carers have little guidance on the recognition of early warning signs of psychological distress and this too may underlie an inability to recognize child mental health problems (Logan and King 2001). In contrast, studies using the general population reported that adults have a poor ability to detect specific disorders or different types of psychological distress (Goldney, Dal Grande and Fisher 2002). As well as facilitating specialist service use, Jorm *et al.* (1997) believed that high levels of MHL would aid advancements in the prevention of, and earlier intervention in, most mental health problems.

The questions that examined the MHL of these carers covered the following five inhibited and five disinhibited characteristics in their children:

Inhibited:

- I1. Reacts to other people's or his/her own distress by hitting out.
- I2. Avoids emotional closeness with familiar adults.
- I3. Avoids emotional closeness with familiar children/teenagers.
- I4. Has difficulty trusting familiar adults.
- I5. Has difficulty trusting familiar children/teenagers.

Disinhibited:

- D1. Too friendly with strangers.
- D2. Tries to make friends with everyone, persisting despite obvious rejection.
- D3. Too cuddly with people she/he doesn't know well.
- D4. Forms many shallow relationships with adults.
- D5. Over-independent, for example wandering off or exploring without checking.

In order to further explore whether different coping strategies adopted by carers influenced the 'burden' of the mental health needs of children in care on them, each foster carer was given a measure of coping skills. This self-report scale indicated how many overall coping strategies were used by each foster carer.

Attitudes towards help seeking among foster carers

Help-seeking attitudes have been the most consistent and strongest predictor of intention to seek psychological help (Cepeda-Benito and Short 1998; Kelly and Achter 1995; Morgan, Ness and Robinson 2003; Vogel and Wester 2003). Prior help seeking and psychological distress have been shown to affect intention in some adult studies (such as Cepeda-Benito and Short 1998; Morgan *et al.* 2003). People possess basically positive or negative help-seeking attitudes. An example of a negative help-seeking attitude would be a dismissive or contemptuous view of the efficacy of professional treatment (Zahner and Daskalakis 1997) or fears of labelling (Arcelus, Bellerby and Vostanis 1999). An example of a positive help-seeking attitude may follow a previously successful episode of mental health care (Ciarrochi and Deane 2001; Gonzalez, Alegria and Prihoda 2005). However, Minnis and Del Priori (2001) suggest that it is possible that foster carers have become habituated to working with 'disturbed' children in care, which impacts on their ability to recognize when specialist services are needed. The fact that individual children rarely seek help with their distress complicates the help-seeking process where children are concerned.

There is a formalized model of help seeking that describes five stages of activity:

Step 1 Identification/detection

Step 2 Attitude to need for support

Step 3 Contact with support service

Step 4 Referral

Step 5 Service use.

A help-seeking pathway model for children in care has been established using a population from the USA (Zima *et al.* 2000). This five-step model, therefore, was used as both an organizing and a descriptive framework for this study, and other factors not previously explored in their study were incorporated.

In the fostering agency that represented all of the foster carers in this study, referrals of children in care were only made by social workers, general practitioners (GPs) or teaching staff. Foster carers therefore did not have the responsibility for making referrals for the youngster to access mental health services. However, they did have some responsibility for supporting the children with attending their appointments (service use).

Her original study examined a wide range of factors such as: MHL, coping skills, child age, education level of the carer, help-seeking attitudes, number of social worker visits and the nature and impact of a mental health problem and how they influenced the help-seeking steps (Maguire 2005).

Meeting the mental health needs of children in care: the help-seeking model

Maguire (2005) found the following (see Figure 1.1):

- A relatively high percentage of the children in care were perceived to have a mental health problem (80%) (detection).
- There was a lower percentage of children where it was felt that it was a problem that needed an intervention from a specialist mental health service (58%) (perceived need).
- An even lower percentage of these children with mental health needs were actually referred to a specialist mental health service by a social worker, teacher or GP (48%) (referral).
- And even fewer of these children used the service (32%) (service use).

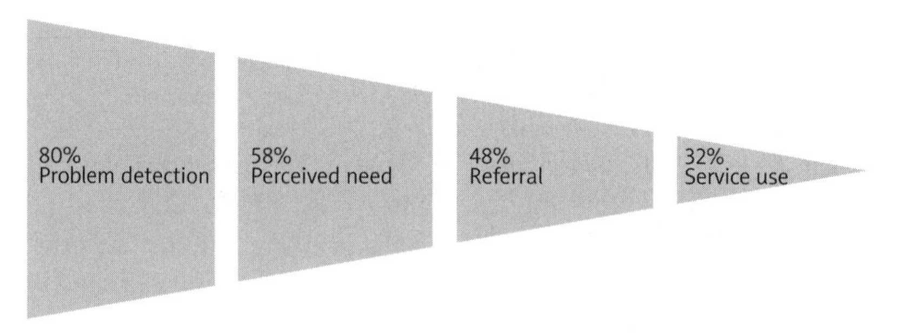

Figure 1.1 The percentages of children in care recorded at each help-seeking step (adapted from Maguire 2005)

This finding provided preliminary support for the discrepancy highlighted earlier in this chapter between high prevalence rates of mental health problems in children in care and underutilization of mental health services. These higher scores on diagnostic tools commonly used to record mental health are already well documented. Ultimately, however, what is useful to take from this study is that children in care whose foster carer had gone through all of the help-seeking steps were significantly more likely to use mental health services than foster carers who had not taken each of the help-seeking steps.

The risk of untreated mental health problems

In Maguire's (2005) research, despite the foster carers identifying a high level of children in care with mental health problems (80%) there was a lower level of mental health service use (32%). This finding raises additional questions about early intervention for mental health disorders that may initially go undetected by foster carers.

There are numerous implications of untreated mental health problems (Ward *et al.* 2002) and several studies have examined factors that predict the use of mental health services using factors such as child age (Garland *et al.* 1996; Halfron, Berkowitz and Klee 1992; Leslie *et al.* 2000; Meltzer *et al.* 2003), child gender (Leslie *et al.* 2000; Meltzer *et al.* 2003), child ethnicity (Leslie *et al.* 2000), length of time within a care placement (Meltzer *et al.* 2003), and placement type (Leslie *et al.* 2000). All of these studies predicted uptake of mental health services, but similarly found underutilization.

While it is encouraging that foster carers in Maguire's study recognized more severe mental health problems, it is important to consider that many children in care would have been experiencing high levels of distress and placement-related difficulties before receiving the services from which they may benefit. Overall, this suggests that many children in care who have not grasped how to tolerate and manage difficult feelings may employ maladaptive coping strategies instead, (Singer, Doornenbal and Okma 2004).

What has been learnt about helping children in care when they communicate distress?

In Maguire's study, two facts combined led to the conclusion that if a foster carer is habituated to working with 'disturbed' children in care this may mean that their threshold of tolerance may be higher and therefore the children in care's distress may have less of an impact on them (Minnis and Del Priore 2001). The presence of a mental health problem in children in care was defined by scores that were in the abnormal or borderline ranges of the SDQ (Goodman 1997). These foster carers also had coping skills that were higher than would be expected.

Although this phenomenon potentially links to the prevention of placement breakdown, the other side of the coin is that this higher threshold of tolerance may mean that these children are not adequately supported to access the mental health services that they need in a timely way. Recent research indicates that there needs to be a 'whole system' approach to address the poor outcomes for children in care. Consistent with the spirit of the 'everybody's business' (Public Health England 2008) agenda, this suggests, that foster carers and referrers together need to be able to respond to the distress of children in care by sourcing help to adequately support the child with relieving their distress, and mental health services need to provide an appropriate service (Bazalgette, Rahilly and Treveleyan 2015). The argument going forward is potentially a circular one. For therapists to do their work, the child needs to be referred and supported in accessing mental health services. Therefore, when a child is utilizing child mental health services, it is essential that the work of therapists explicitly and continually sensitizes and informs foster carers about the mental health needs of children in care so that this counterbalances their relatively high threshold of tolerance. By doing this, not only are foster carers able to better understand the child's communication of her anguish, but they will also be equipped to make more refined and appropriate responses.

Chapter 2

Children Under Five In Care

What a Shame!

CHRISTINE CORK

Most children under the age of five years who enter the care system have already lived through significant frightening experiences of abuse, neglect and insensitive parenting. In all likelihood, they will have had experiences of shame, as this is believed to be a core aspect of child maltreatment, especially of physical abuse (Loader 1998). As a result, their development is likely to be compromised on a number of paradigms: physiologically, psychologically, socially, neurologically and relational. They will have difficulties in feeling safe and will have developed defences to cope with the uncertainty and anxiety in their lives.

In my work as a primary mental health worker in a child and adolescent mental health service, I am often requested, by referring social workers, to support foster carers with strategies to manage behaviour difficulties in order to prevent placement breakdown. Just as children can be overwhelmed by their experiences of loss, fear and abandonment, similarly foster carers can experience overwhelming feelings that can make it difficult for them to hold on to their strengths and abilities. However, it is crucial for foster carers to understand the children's communication and not feel disempowered. This will allow them to empathize with the children's distress, while providing an environment where recovery from failed and disrupted attachments can begin. In this chapter, I will consider the psychosocial and neurodevelopmental evidence that has helped me to understand some of the extreme behaviour, such as withdrawal and rages, reported by foster carers. I will evaluate the influence of shame, which adds to the complexity of the relationship and behaviour of both child and carer. Finally, I will examine how issues of shame might permeate the professional network and interfere with the capacity to consistently negotiate what is in the best interest of the child.

Psychosocial and neurodevelopmental underpinnings

For most children under five in care, the sometimes sudden and distressing physical separation of being taken into care is unlikely to be their first experience of separation and loss. Their past experiences of maltreatment will have been traumatic and a threat to their survival. Each represents an experience of a loss of feeling safe, and of having their emotional needs met by an available, sensitive caregiver, both of which are essential for the development of healthy attachments. Their repeated fearful experiences and the excessive activation of their stress response systems will lead to insecure attachment patterns together with altered neurological development, which can have long-lasting repercussions affecting their ability to learn, self-regulate, use impulse control and form trusting relationships possibly into adulthood (Brown and Ward 2013; Davidson and Smith 1990; Famularo, Kinscherff and Fenton 1991; Shonkoff *et al.* 2012).

Scientists have been able to demonstrate robustly that the structure of babies' brains is altered by the experiences they receive. For example, experiences during the critical periods of early childhood organize brain systems and create neural networks through which all new input is filtered (Goelet and Kandel 1986). These neural networks become increasingly fixed with repeated activation and die when not used. From birth to three years, most of the neural connectivity occurs in the right hemisphere, which is the only part of the brain fully functioning at birth (Schore 2000). The brain structures activated when a child experiences stress are in the lower right hemisphere, while the regions and networks which help to modify the effects of stress and for adjusting thinking and behaviour are in the right prefrontal cortex (Carmichael and Price 1995; Schnider and Ptak 1999). Schore (1994) explains that the right hemisphere is therefore central in the activation and moderation of vital functions needed for survival, such as the primitive flight, fight or freeze response system. Unfortunately, the control systems in the prefrontal cortex are inhibited when children are exposed to social environments that foster insecure attachments (for example, domestic violence) or if the child is in a repeated state of hyper-arousal. The brain circuitry is altered (Schore 1997). Babies and young children are therefore more vulnerable to the effects of stress and need the adult caregiver's brain to help reduce the damaging effects of stress on brain development (Schore 2012). Without this buffering, the prolonged activation of the stress response system often experienced in children exposed to stressors such as abuse, neglect, parental substance abuse and maternal depression (Felitti *et al.* 1998) can become toxic and damaging.

Dawson (1994) demonstrated that parenting directly influenced the developing patterns of neuronal connectivity. If a child is not soothed and helped to calm down when his stress response system is activated, the result over time is that his biological stress response system becomes sensitized and remains permanently on high alert. Once sensitized, the same neural activation can be elicited by decreasingly intense external stimuli (Kalivas and Kuffy 1989).

In addition, research shows that prolonged activation of the stress hormone in early childhood can actually reduce neural connections in the brain, at just the time when neural connections should be forming, which has long-term implications for physical and mental health (McEwen 2006; McEwen and Gianaros 2010).

I wonder whether similar neurological pathways, patterned responses and sensitization can result from repeated shame experiences?

Research on the complex self-conscious emotion of shame has also expanded in recent years, although theorists do not concur on the age of onset of shame or on its definition. Most agree that shame is a most painful, distressing and least tolerable negative affect, associated with social withdrawal and negative self-attributions (Barrett, Zahn-Waxler and Cole 1993; Tangney *et al.* 1996a). Shame's aversive quality motivates efforts to terminate it with the desire to hide the damaged self from others (Tangney 1999).

Nevertheless, the experience of shame is necessary for development and has some beneficial impact, i.e. to create inhibitions that keep children safe. As in the co-regulation of the stress response, what is important is for the child to have the intense negative and painful feelings of shame modulated by the parent or caregiver. Schore (1994) points out that in a nurturing relationship, the process of re-integrative shame enables the child to develop strong beneficial brain connections to regulate impulse. Children with unmet attachment needs, however, might have great difficulty in managing both impulse and shame.

For some authors, shame is first experienced between the ages of two and three years, (Lewis, Alessandri and Sullivan 1992; Stipek 1995) when a child has developed objective self-awareness and self-evaluation, can compare his behaviour to a standard and can perceive that the self has failed because a rule has been violated.

However, Schore (1998) indicates that shame can develop as early as 14–16 months when the child develops mobility and the parent becomes a socializing agent thwarting the natural desire to explore with negative feedback. Lewis (1992) points out that when infants see a disgusted face, they turn sharply away and seem inhibited for a moment. He suggests that it is likely that such behaviour reflects shame.

Babies are born seeking social contact and are ready to relate. The infant first begins to learn about himself in the context of the relationship with his primary caregiver, more often through the mother's eyes. In mis-attuned face-to-face interactions, when there is an abrupt break in the anticipated increase in positive affect, shame may be experienced (Kaufman 1989; Schore 1998). In psycho-dynamic theory, the 'primary disappointment' (Emanuel 1984) that infants suffer when there is a failure of the parental object to meet his innate expectations to be held in mind, possibly describes an experience of shame. In addition, Meltzer (1998) describes 'aesthetic reciprocity', which is the experience felt by both mother and baby of being blown over by the aesthetic beauty of the other. The baby is overwhelmed by the visual impact of his world and the mother's beauty, but is saved through the reciprocal beauty as seen through her eyes on him. When this fails, perhaps when babies are perceived as too demanding or ugly, the baby is left with a sense of being defective, a disappointment and unworthy of love (Emanuel 1997). These feelings also connect with a sense of shame developed through an un-reflected look in the mother's eyes (Ayers 2003).

But what about young children who in addition suffer from abuse?

Many studies have found that maltreatment and harsh, negative or authoritarian parenting are associated with shame among preschool children (Alessandri and Lewis 1993; Belsky and Domitrovich 1997; Mills 2003) and shame has been found to be related to increased anger (Bennett, Sullivan and Lewis 2005; Tangney *et al.* 1996b). Research suggests that if children are severely punished, criticized, treated with hostile rejection or ignored by their primary caregiver, they are likely to believe that they are unwanted and unlovable and these negative self-beliefs are primary elicitors of shame (Lewis 1992).

To summarize, from early infancy, children can experience shame, which is associated with anger and feelings of being deeply flawed, exposed and helpless. Children who have suffered from repeated experiences of abuse or neglect are likely to have poorer neural connections, which may hinder their use of the 'thinking part' of the brain to moderate their hyper-aroused negative feelings. They are also likely to have fewer opportunities for interactive repair with their primary carer to alleviate stress and shame and this may leave them vulnerable to even more intense toxic feelings. Just as sensitized neural pathways can be triggered by decreasingly intense external stimuli or by seemingly minor events, so too the shame response can become sensitized and be triggered more readily. The neurological and relational deficits compounded with shame can account for difficulties in emotional regulation and the extremes of behaviour so often witnessed by foster carers.

It is therefore important for those living and working with traumatized children to be aware of these contributing factors, all of which impact on the child's physiological, cognitive, emotional and behavioural functioning. With understanding, foster carers could then be supported to use their own experiences of shame to develop skills that help infants or young children in their care to reintegrate their emotional experiences without 'losing face'.

Adaptive–maladaptive stress responses and shame

The human body and mind respond to threats by deeply ingrained physical and mental neuronal patterns. Two major response patterns, important for the traumatized child, the hyper-arousal continuum (fight or flight response) and the dissociative continuum (freeze or surrender response) are described by Perry *et al.* (1995). Each of these response patterns activates a unique combination of neural systems located in the right brain hemisphere (Schore 2001). For infants, the dissociative pattern is more common as they are unable to fight or flee. This was illustrated in the experience of a foster carer who described an eight-week-old baby who came into her care as a result of neglect due to her mother's drug abuse. This baby was unresponsive and did not cry. It was not possible to determine her physical state of hunger and she seemed to withdraw when touched or cuddled. This depressed baby who made little demands required her carer to be particularly attentive to her mental state, to capture her mind in a welcoming and sensitive way, to reduce her anxiety and enliven her expectations of the world. The foster carer reported that the baby did not cry for the first six weeks in her care and slept for most of the contact sessions with her mother.

Another foster carer described a three-year-old girl who appeared unaffected by an acute separation from her mother following a long history of neglect and domestic violence. She was brought to the foster carer by the social worker from the police station. On entering her home, the child seemed more interested in the toys available in the room and seemed to adapt readily, making little eye contact with the foster carer and showing no emotion when the social worker left. She became overly compliant.

We can understand that both these children had developed patterns of behaviour to cope with their anxieties. It is as if they had mastered how to numb their own natural stress response and appeared to have developed a sense of having to look after themselves and take control. Perry *et al.* (1995) explains that with infants and young children the behaviours exhibited in the acute and post-acute trauma include numbing, compliance, avoidance and restricted affect, all consistent with a primary dissociative response pattern. It is possible that the children in both these examples perhaps were displaying shame responses of withdrawal (for the baby, it was as if there was a wish to withdraw from life) and a wish not to be seen (the three-year-old). Over time, these adaptive responses can become detrimental to their emotional well-being.

The other stress response pattern to threat – the fight or flight response – can also be seen in young children, more commonly boys. Perry *et al.* (1995) explains that when one system of the brain becomes sensitized, other functions mediated by that system also become sensitized and this results in a total body response. The traumatized child is left in a persistent fear state when everyday stressors that previously may not have elicited any response now elicit an exaggerated reaction. The child will very easily be moved from being mildly anxious, to feeling threatened, to being terrorized. The extreme rages can therefore be understood as neurological maladaptive emotional and behavioural responses. These rages can also be understood as shame rages (Lewis 1971), involving extreme dysregulation, when there is an intensity in feelings created by the shift in emotion from shame to anger, and the desire to retaliate and use aggression (Tangney *et al.* 1996b).

Shame permeating the professional network

Foster carers find these alarming outbursts in young children very difficult to manage. The child is perceived as being severely damaged, attention seeking or dramatizing. Foster carers sometimes feel inadequately trained to meet such children's needs. They also have to consider the impact of the child on other children in their household and on their own children and themselves. One foster carer described feelings of exhaustion and how she dreaded waking up to another day with the child. She felt unable to take the child out because of the unpredictability of his behaviour. As a result of not feeling able to contain the child and the frightening feelings that are generated, it is not uncommon for foster carers to begin to lose confidence in their own abilities and feel a generalized sense of dissatisfaction. This might lead them to feel negative or ambivalent towards the child and perceive the difficulty to be grounded in the child. This dynamic can become self-perpetuating; the less the child feels understood, the more likely the rages will occur and the less the foster carer will feel able to contain the child and to provide the safety that is so essential for recovery. To cope with the anxiety held by the foster carer and social worker, these young children are referred to child and adolescent mental health services with an expressed wish for the child to have therapy.

In my experience, as the relationship between the child and the foster carer deteriorates, it becomes harder for the foster carer to reflect or make links between his daily experience of the child and his own emotive and difficult feelings, sometimes rooted in his own past experiences, beliefs and values – in other words, to reflect on what belongs to him and what belongs to the child. As an example, one foster mother described an incident when the child, aged four years, asked her to hold her school bag while walking to the car from school. She said no, as it was no more than a few paces away and she felt the child was able to wait. A sudden explosion of rage followed. The child explained that she had wanted to open a packet of sweets that she had been given and felt that she had only asked the carer 'to hold her bag'. The foster mother, who was disabled, had felt justified in her response but defeated by the experience. Trying to explore the miscommunication other than in terms of an example of the child's dysfunction was more difficult.

When I meet foster carers, they sometimes feel blamed and threatened by my attempts to explore their feelings, attitudes and responses in relation to the child. They are unsure and naturally hesitant about why this should be of relevance in helping to understand the child's difficulties and need for therapy. My efforts at psycho-education of the child's emotional needs or empathic behaviour management strategies are sometimes rejected or perceived as ineffective. As in the above example of miscommunication that triggered a shame-rage response, I suggest that this difficult dynamic between carer and therapist is also linked to feelings of shame, with a wish to withdraw and avoid unpleasant exposure.

The life of a looked after child is one filled with shaming experiences. Multiple frustrations arise from being let down and having expectations crushed, for example when parents do not show up for contact, or do not phone when expected or when decision-making meetings about them are cancelled. He experiences being looked at, monitored intensely and treated differently by numerous agencies, professionals and his peers. Shame is typically accompanied by a sense of worthlessness and powerlessness (Lewis 1971).

As a way of managing and avoiding the impact of these destructive and unbearable feelings, they are projected unconsciously into his carers who in turn experience shame perhaps arising from their feelings of insecurity in the face of trying to manage intimidating and frustrating behaviours. They might seek help from the supervising social worker, who might feel undermined in turn. The social worker might experience shame in trying to meet the foster carer's needs due to internal or external demands within the care system. The cumulative experience of shame then manifests in the relationship with the therapist, who is shamed through their apparent lack of understanding of the foster carer and social worker's positions. From a humanistic and cultural perspective, I also wonder if children in care elicit more collective feelings of shame, in that society also has failed to protect these children from harm.

Perhaps my view of the multi-layered experiences of shame within the network is too simplistic. Nevertheless, as shame is a hidden subject that is hard to face, let alone acknowledge, I wonder whether it can lead to absences in mindfulness and interfere with the ability to attend thoughtfully to the needs of traumatized children, for example, when contact arrangements are made with a mother who is unable to provide emotional containment due to mental illness or when placements are agreed which have the potential to re-enact the child's original traumatic experiences. Potter-Efron and Potter-Efron (1989) indicate that toxic shame causes paralysis, escapism, withdrawal, people pleasing, perfectionism, criticism and rage. Paralysis in the system's ability to think clearly about the child's need is also described by Emanuel (2002) as an unconscious defence against the powerful projections of disturbing emotional states of children in care and their families. These result in inter-departmental and inter-agency conflict and difficulties in decision making. Can this process be associated with shame?

Are good outcomes possible?

Studies have demonstrated that young foster children have the possibility to form enduring secure attachments when placed in stable and well-functioning foster homes (Jacobsen *et al.* 2014; Stovall-McClough and Dozier 2004). Stability in the placement with a committed caregiver is crucial.

Just as children need to feel safe through a relationship with an attuned caregiver, all those involved with severely damaged infants and young children also need to feel safe within their working environment. With this ensured, integration within the extensive network of carers (including social workers, foster carers, birth families, schools, managers and therapists) can perhaps be facilitated within consultative relationships providing a space for reflection and containment as demonstrated by Sprince (2000) and Emanuel (2002).

It might then be possible to mitigate the toxicity of shame, not only to find solutions but also to find ways of promoting the children's ability to integrate aspects of themselves that are felt to be so undesirable or unforgivable.

As Dan Siegel and Mary Hartzell states: 'The integration of our own self-knowledge facilitates our being open to the process of becoming emotionally connected... Coherent self-knowledge and interpersonal joining go hand in hand' (Siegel and Hartzell 2014, p.68).

Chapter 3

Working with Looked After Children Who Self-Harm

Understanding Coping, Communication and Suicide[1]

SAM WARNER AND CLARE SHAW

Introduction: defining our knowledge base and focus

Self-harm is a complex issue that affects a great many young people. In the last 20 years there have been significant attempts to capture children's own perspectives on self-harm (Spandler 1996) and to develop a child-focused knowledge base (Spandler and Warner 2007). This chapter is situated within that tradition. We draw on a wide array of sources in order to inform our approach, actively soliciting information from service users/experts by experience and using this to challenge, theorize, elaborate and reflect on more formal research findings. Specifically, in this chapter Clare draws on her own personal history of self-harm to provide a rich account of what it is like to be a young person struggling to survive with abuse and neglect in an often hostile world. As yet, there is limited research on looked after children as a specific group who self-harm, although this is changing (see Evans *et al.* in press). However, there is considerable research on the issues children in care often face. Children in care come from backgrounds that are typified by abuse and neglect at home, and/or exploitation, violence and criminality on the street; such traumatized children are at increased risk of hurting themselves and completing suicide (IRISS 2013).

1 This chapter is based on a training course on self-harm developed and delivered by Clare and Sam that was commissioned by Lancashire Care Foundation Trust for their entire mental health workforce – that was inclusive of those who work with children in social and mental health care.

In this chapter we identify some of the common self-harm methods available to children in care. We explore the socio-cultural context to self-harm and identify key experiences and underlying issues that are associated with self-harm for children who may end up being cared for away from their families. We then explicate how self-harm functions to manage emotional distress. We consider the relationship between coping, communication and suicide, and identify key factors associated with increased risk of self-inflicted death. We describe a harm-cessation approach designed for working with children who are at high risk of suicide or serious self-injury and consider the negative impacts of over-extending this approach. We then describe core elements of a harm-minimization approach. We discuss the impact on those who work with children in care who self-injure and conclude by identifying principles for practice and policy that are best able to safeguard these children and the people who work with them.

Throughout this chapter, self-harm is used as a generic term to describe any action that by omission or commission causes physical harm to the body (anything from cutting or drug and alcohol use to self-neglect and tattooing). Self-injury is understood as a specific form of self-harm that is distinguished by being directly physically harmful, with a relatively immediate (vis à vis cumulative) impact, and which is heavily stigmatized (e.g. cutting, taking an overdose). Suicide is also a specific form of self-harm and self-injury which is distinguished by the intention to end life.

How children self-harm: prevalence and underlying issues

Children (and adults) self-harm for many different reasons and use very many different methods. The types of methods utilized by children are indicative of the socio-cultural context of their lives. This means that although individuals utilize methods that have particular *salience* for them, choice of method will be mediated by demographic factors including age, gender, ethnicity, geography, class, ability and institutional/residential setting. For example, scratching, cutting, hitting the self and head banging are common methods of self-harm for younger children, children and adults in institutional care and those with learning difficulties (e.g. Heslop and MacCaulay 2009). Although diverse in nature, all of these groups have carers who limit *access to* and *opportunity to use* a wider repertoire of self-harm methods (scratching and hitting the self require no tools, and head banging only requires a wall or floor).

Recognizing demographic differences is helpful, therefore, because such differences point to key issues (indicated here in italics) that are highly indicative in self-harm. *Identity*, particularly sex/gender identity, is highly significant. In the UK, men are three times more likely to kill themselves than women (Harker *et al.* 2013), although women are three times more likely to attempt suicide, with some groups of women being at particular risk – for example, South Asian, Indian and East African women (Ineichen 2008). By contrast, in serious case reviews, at least, suicide in the 8–18 age range is fairly evenly spread across boys and girls (Brandon *et al.* 2011). Here all children who died had been maltreated (the reason for a serious case review) and two-thirds were open to children's social care – with one third being looked after and another third having been on a child protection plan.

Between 2012 and 2014, a 70 per cent increase in 10–14-year-olds attending A&E for self-harm related reasons was recorded over the preceding two years, with a threefold increase over the last decade in teenagers who self-harm in England (World Health Organization 2014). Indeed, self-harm can be understood to be a particular issue for adolescents – the majority of people who self-harm are aged between 11 and 25 years, with a peak in mid adolescence (Hagell 2013). At least 13 per cent of young people may try to hurt themselves on purpose at some point between the ages of 11 and 16, but the actual figure could be much higher (Self-harm UK 2015). Lesbian, gay, bisexual and transgendered (LGBT) people have a higher than average rate of suicide and self-harm, with one in two LGBT youth reporting self-harm at some point in their lives. The gap is even higher for ethnic minority LGBT people and those with disabilities (Guerra 2015). It is not insignificant that LGBT children are more at risk of being bullied than their heterosexual peers (Guerra 2015). Hence we can assume that issues concerning helplessness and exclusion are particularly acute for minoritized, ostracized and powerless young people.

Why children self-harm: underlying issues, core experiences and the management of emotional distress

For most young people, self-harm and suicide are associated with difficult and distressing life experiences that leave them feeling powerless, excluded, invalidated, frustrated, lost, isolated and hopeless. It is little wonder then that looked after children, who suffer disproportionate experiences of abuse, neglect, exploitation and loss resulting in increased mental health and social problems, exhibit higher rates of self-harm and suicide than their peers.

To understand self-harm it is necessary, therefore, to look beyond the behaviour to make sense of the thoughts and feelings that instigate the need to self-harm (see Figure 3.1). Self-harm is not random, but is an adaptive response to distressing feelings and specific and difficult situations.

In order to understand how self-harm functions for children in care it helps to consider specific instances of self-harm – using a functional analysis that identifies core issues in terms of general setting conditions, specific triggers and consequences – both immediate and longer term (see Figure 3.2).

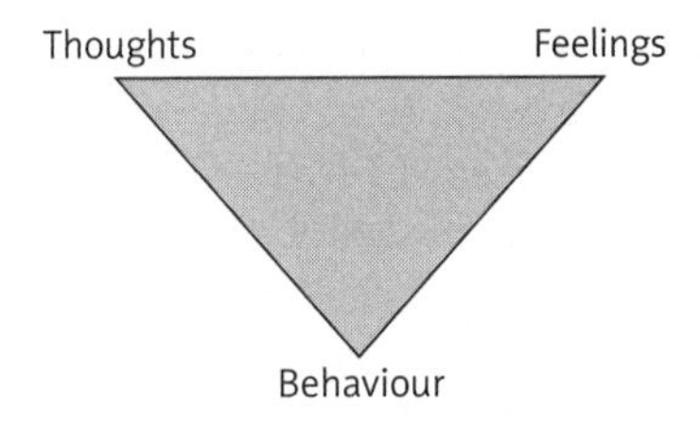

Figure 3.1 Communication[2]

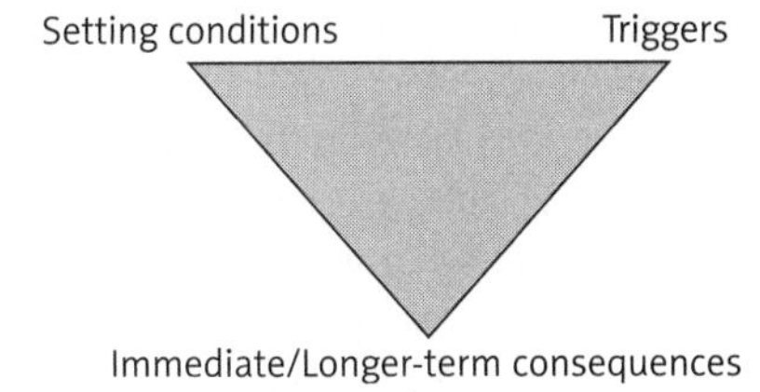

Figure 3.2 Self-harm functions

2 All diagrams in this chapter taken from Warner (in press) unless otherwise stated.

Below Clare writes about some of her own experiences of self-harm to illustrate and illuminate this process.

CLARE'S STORY: FEELING ALONE

Setting conditions and background

Life had not been easy. I was the youngest of six in a single-parent family where money and attention were in short supply. My visits to my father's house were characterized by alcoholic and predatory adults; I was unsafe there but could do nothing about it. At the age of ten, I was raped. I passed through the police and court systems with no support. I began to self-harm as a way of trying to attract the recognition and care I wanted.

But I didn't tell anyone about it. I'd been brought up not to express difficult emotions or to communicate difficult experiences. My sense of shame was huge. By the age of 13, when I started to get crushes on girls, that shame intensified. I had been brought up in the Catholic tradition and on the right wing of British politics and I could tell no one about how I felt. Self-harm helped me cope with often unbearable feelings of despair, hurt and anger.

Triggers and consequences

By 15, my distress and my sense of isolation had increased. My hidden sexuality was a huge source of anxiety and shame. I began to harm myself more frequently: starving myself, cutting myself with razors and taking overdoses. If I was visibly thin, ill, wounded and sleep-starved, surely someone would notice?

It was at this age that I first needed hospital treatment. Everyone was out of the house and I felt profoundly and completely alone. I cut myself on the palm of my hand. I could explain this away as an accident – my mum had new kitchen knives and had warned me to be careful with them. I preferred to present my injuries as accidental – I didn't want anyone to know that I was hurting myself deliberately.

The immediate consequence: I lost a lot of blood. Watching it flow helped me feel alive, connected to myself at least. It spoke to me about how I felt: wounded, hurt, in pain, but surviving. A secondary consequence was that I needed to go to hospital for stitches, where, as a young person with an 'accidental' injury I received the care, compassion and understanding I desperately needed. Over time, self-harm became the primary means through which I survived my life. It was an effective way of temporarily alleviating my distress and expressing to myself and the people around me how much I was hurting.

Institutionalized care and suicidal thoughts – what didn't help

Eventually I was admitted onto a psychiatric ward. Six years of spending time in and out of psychiatric hospital is hard to summarize: fear, hopelessness, boredom and powerlessness are just a brief reflection; those feelings, of course, ran alongside the distress and despair that had taken me into the system in the first place. My self-harm escalated to life-threatening proportions.

The more that my distress was dismissed, the more I tried to communicate it through more severe acts of self-harm. I felt – and I was told – that there was no hope, and it was hard to maintain any sense of myself as someone defined by anything other than difficulty and madness. Ironically, I inflicted all of my most dangerous self-harm in institutions where self-injury was not allowed – in places I felt least understood, most controlled and where I had to use whatever method of self-harm was available before someone could stop me.

Eventually my desire for death outweighed any impulse towards life and I made several attempts to end my life. Ultimately, this time marked a distinct change in my approach. What came before was a struggle with pain, but having survived my suicide attempts, what came afterwards was a struggle towards happiness.

Transforming my life – what helped

Suddenly, it seemed, life could improve. I rediscovered small pleasures, like looking at the trees outside the ward. I began to make positive plans. I found myself re-rooted in a physical world, noticing sensations in my own body. I began making choices for myself, including the decision to leave hospital and never go back. I began to take small steps towards the future.

What helped? In the short term, people were there when I reached for them. I was not alone. If I had been, I would not have survived. Friends and staff were there when I needed them; a crisis team worked out crisis plans with me, negotiating with me, step by step, the hours ahead. I left enough space in my consciousness for doubt to creep in when I did not die as planned. I allowed that doubt to grow. I reached out. I held on. I was hungry for change and for my life to improve. I noticed what things made me feel better and I tried to do them again. I realized that I was capable of happiness – and I wanted more of it.

Through therapy and reading, I opened myself to the possibility that there were more helpful ways of viewing the world than seeing myself as ill or disordered. I began to move away from the passive 'patient' role I'd occupied so unhappily. In times of distress, I attended to the small and necessary details of surviving and thriving. Though I still harmed and starved myself, I dramatically reduced the damage I did to myself.

Over the long term, I have made – and continue to make – large scale, holistic change, addressing the causes of distress in my life at every level. I have a strong sense of connection with the people I have in my life and I engage with life with a passion and appetite that might only be shared by those of us who have looked death in the face.

Learning from Clare's story

Clare's story is deeply personal, but speaks to important themes that structure the lives of many children in care. Like them, Clare experienced neglect, abuse and sexual violence. She suffered from a profound lack of safety at home and on the streets. Like very many children in care, she was made to feel shame around her identity and was pathologized for her self-harm when she was desperately trying to survive. She was frequently given no permission to voice her hurts and concerns. Like other young people living away from their families, Clare was most hurt within institutions that sought to control her rather than to listen and understand (Shaw and Shaw 2007).

Young people in care use self-harm like Clare for three reasons: mostly to manage their distress, to communicate to themselves and others about their distress, and only sometimes as a means to end life (see Figure 3.3).

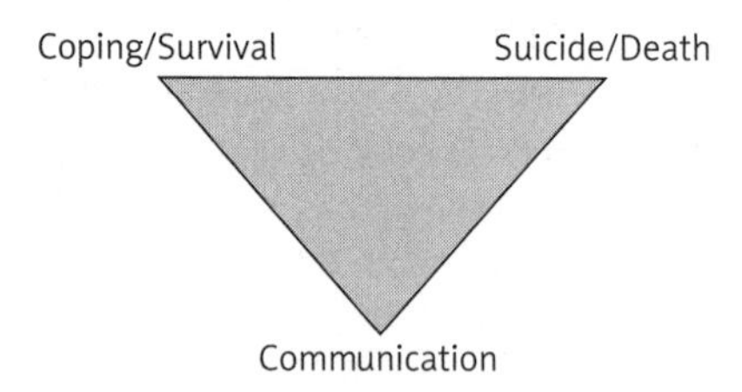

Figure 3.3 The primary functions of self-harm

Whether self-injury is a survival strategy or a means to end life, something is always being communicated – even when this is not the main function of the injury. It is vital to help children untangle the meaning of self-harm as this helps to identify what is troubling them;

and what, specifically, they need. As noted, self-injury helps people manage their emotional world. It does this by helping individuals cope with the emotional pain or numbness that is a result of psychological distress (Lancashire Care Foundation Trust 2012). In effect, self-harm helps children manage their emotional arousal (see Figure 3.4).

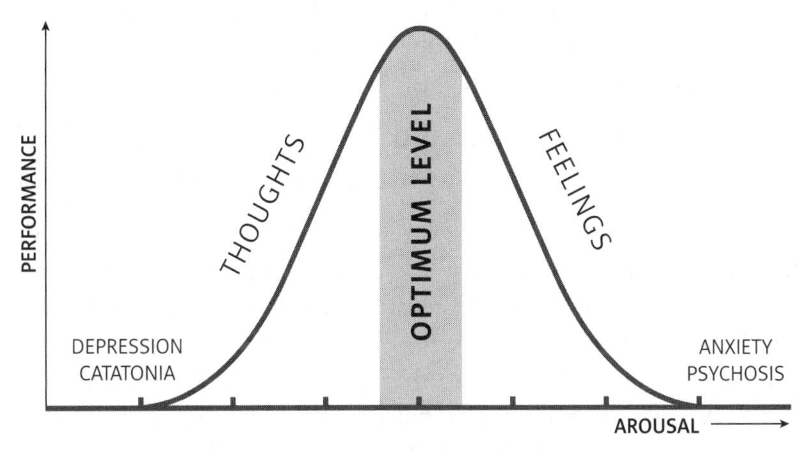

Figure 3.4 The relationship between performance and arousal (Warner in press, adapted from Yerkes-Dodson's Law 1908)

This model provides a means through which the relationship between arousal and performance can be understood, and through this, illuminates how self-harm works. Simply put, in order to perform people must be aroused/awake. As arousal increases, so does performance until an optimum level is reached after which the ability to perform well decreases. When people become over-aroused they are overwhelmed by their feelings and if pushed to extreme emotional levels they become highly anxious and eventually may start to see visions, hear voices or have flashbacks. People can retreat from extreme emotionality back to the other side of arousal where thoughts dominate. Too many negative thoughts push people into depressive states where they shut down emotionally, becoming numb, disengaged, dissociated and, in extreme circumstances, catatonic. Self-harm 'works' because it enables people to manage their arousal: if they feel too much it can move them away from their feelings, through distraction or self-punishment, for example; or if they feel too numb, self-injury can help people to feel alive and connected, as Clare did when she cut her hand.

Self-injury can only help to manage emotional arousal. It does not solve underlying problems. For some children in care, their emotional pain may be too overwhelming, their disengagement from life too strong, and self-harm simply does not bring enough relief. At this point they may, as Clare did, become actively suicidal. It is crucial, therefore, to understand where coping ends and suicide begins, as coping and suicidal self-harm require very different strategies.

Coping, communication and suicide: identifying distinctions and understanding how to work with risk

Self-injury has a clear relationship with suicide, but they are not equivalent. Only a small proportion of people who self-harm kill themselves thereafter. For example, Hawton, Zahl and Weatherall (2003a) found that 0.7 per cent of people who were seen in hospital for self-harm die by suicide within a year of that self-harm. This figure increases to 2.4 per cent after ten years. Nevertheless, over half of those who go on to complete suicide will have self-harmed at some point in the past (NICE 2002). Following an act of self-harm, the rate of suicide increases to between 50 to 100 times the rate of suicide in the general population (Hawton, Hall, Simkin and Bale 2003b; Owens, Horrocks and House 2002) (see Figure 3.5).

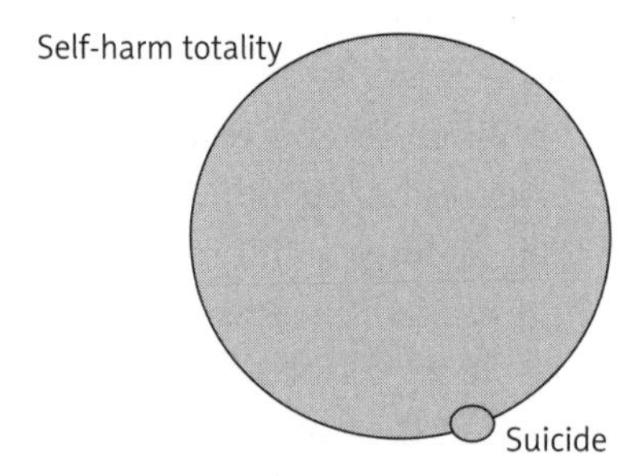

Figure 3.5 The relationship between self-harm and suicide

As this figure illustrates, although the vast majority of people who self-harm do not go on to kill themselves, it is very important to consider the potential for suicidality because a history of self-harm is highly indicative in suicide. The first step, therefore, is to assess the risk of suicide. Children and adults with diagnosable mental health problems are at high risk of suicide: the diagnosis, per se, indicates very little. Rather, we should be concerned with any change that has occurred in respect of thoughts (e.g. stated intention to die); feelings (e.g. an elevation in mood in the context of nothing changing in circumstance); and/or behaviour/circumstance (e.g. negative life event or anniversary of negative life event). In summary, change must occur in at least one of these three dimensions. The child must feel hopeless and believe that things will not get better or will not get better in a time frame he can tolerate. Additionally, the child must have access to lethal methods of self-harm and have the opportunity to use them. In the short term there are a number of psychological and physical measures that can be taken to reduce the risk of suicide.

Stopping suicide and restricting risk: safe certainty and harm cessation

Risk assessment should lead to a formulation (based on setting conditions, triggers and consequences) that informs the risk management plan. At times of high risk, more restrictive safety plans must be in place. There are two main psychological methods that are designed to stop suicide. These are both designed to build *a pause* between the desire to end life and the suicidal act. In the short term psychological barriers are useful. This may simply involve saying, 'Can we talk about this first?' to someone who has expressed a desire to die. It is the same principle that underpins the use of safety nets and the provision of the Samaritan's contact details at places where people could kill themselves (high bridges, buildings or cliffs, for example). Psychological barriers cannot physically stop someone trying to kill themselves but may provide enough of a pause for the small voice of survival inside to be heard (as happened with Clare). Longer-term services can develop *advance agreements* with young people that can help staff identify when the child is starting to become hopeless, what triggers are around and what helps and hinders in such circumstances. In this way children are enabled to take their thinking into their most out-of-control moments. Advance directives can be further developed over time as services get to know the young person and her needs better.

Practical restriction may involve removing a child into care, or moving an already looked after child into a more restricted environment such as a secure unit or hospital. Anything that may be used to cause harm to the body (CDs, knives, tablets, belts etc.) may be removed.

Conversely, children may be encouraged or even forced to take increased medication (when detained under the Mental Health Act). Children may be physically restrained, secluded and/or placed on 'constant observation' by one or more carers. Such measures may be necessary to keep the child alive, but they have very many negative consequences. The child may feel controlled, hurt, violated, scared and angry. Her relationship with her carers may be undermined. As Clare's story indicates, restricting opportunities to self-harm can paradoxically increase risk (Shaw and Shaw 2007). As such, any decision to restrict access and opportunity to self-harm should not be taken lightly and a less restrictive approach should be adopted as soon as possible.

Enabling change through positive risk taking: safe uncertainty and harm minimization

When children are not engaged in highly risky self-injury and are not actively suicidal, then a less restrictive approach is indicated (c.f. Mason 1993). This involves positive risk taking in which children are enabled to change, but not overly restricted in their behaviour. This may mean they continue to self-harm. Indeed, from a harm-minimization perspective stopping self-harm ceases to be the primary aim of intervention – rather recovery becomes a more individualized, self-defined process. Pembroke (2007, p.166) argues that 'harm-minimisation is about accepting the need to self-harm as a valid method of survival until survival is possible by other means'. There are three main aspects to a harm minimization approach: behavioural, cognitive and emotional.

In behavioural terms, there are a number of measures that can be used to reduce the risks associated with self-injury (see Pembroke 2000, 2007). These include: using sterilized/new blades to minimize the risk of infection, having first aid kits and having someone around to look after the person who is self-harming if needed or desired etc.

In cognitive terms, children need to know about how their body works and the impact of self-injury on different injury sites, the immediate and longer-term effects of self-poisoning and burns and so on and the impact of infection. They may need to know they are not alone and that self-harm is not indicative of madness, but rather something people sometimes do when they are unable to cope in less damaging ways. They may need therapeutic help to make sense of their own relationship with self-harm: the underlying issues that provide the backdrop to their self-injury, the triggers that instigate their self-injury and the maintaining factors that keep them self-harming. Although children may be aware that self-harm helps them feel better, they may feel ashamed about what they do (this is unsurprising when it is so highly stigmatized) and they may not fully understand how it works for them.

Finally, in emotional terms, children's desire to self-harm is reduced when they are treated with respect by sympathetic, supportive and warm staff (Arnold 1995); when they have opportunity to talk about their feelings about self-injury and have someone to listen to them (Heslop and Macaulay 2009); when they are treated like whole human beings rather than seen purely through the lens of self-harm (Shaw 2006); and when they have choice, control, safety and dignity in their lives (Warner 2009).

In practice, services have differing abilities to engage in the full range of harm-minimization approaches with looked after children. Our duty of care to looked after children is to reduce risk and to safeguard their best interests. This may be best achieved by operating a harm-minimization approach, rather than too quickly trying to stop young people's self-harm. This is best achieved by all colleagues adopting a shared understanding of the child, within a context of multi-disciplinary cooperation, utilizing our different skill sets. For example, as a clinical psychologist Sam does not have the medical knowledge to offer advice regarding self-harm and the biological body. However, she is well placed to help children make sense of their lives (the abuse, neglect and loss they may have suffered prior to and during their time in care) and how self-harm works for them psychologically (how it helps manage negative thoughts and feelings). All workers have a duty to act with respect, warmth and care while being mindful to listen to young people, to treat them with dignity, and to recognize their multiple identities beyond the self-harm.

The impact of self-harm and suicide on professionals and carers: practice and policy implications

Staff experience secondary trauma when working with young people who self-harm. For example, Arnold and Magill (2005) found that staff who worked with people who self-harm report feeling shock, horror and disgust, incomprehension, fear and anxiety, distress and sadness, anger and frustration, powerlessness and inadequacy – the same feelings that children who self-harm feel. If staff and carers are to use their feelings to help them empathize with their clients, and thereby continue to work compassionately and creatively and in a child-centred way, they need robust support from the services they work within. Safe services provide access to training as well as ongoing opportunities to offload and reflect. Staff also benefit from having opportunities for teamwork and to network with other agencies and having access to peer support groups and effective management and external supervision. Finally, workers (like clients) benefit from acknowledgement and appreciation (Arnold and Magill 2005).

Compassionate and safe services are supported by clear and comprehensive policies and guidance that are inclusive of strategies for preventing suicide as well as identifying strategies for working with children who use self-harm to cope and communicate. There should be shared understanding about self-harm across care providers, while recognizing and valuing the different roles different professionals and foster carers play in respect to children in care. Service providers should have developed accessible means for evaluating interventions that provide meaningful information for clients and providers as well as commissioners of services. If behavioural methods are to be used to evaluate intervention, then a more finessed understanding of behaviour should be adopted. Noting whether someone has stopped self-harming is too blunt; it is more meaningful to consider the frequency, intensity, number and duration (FIND) of different methods of self-harm (see Warner and Spandler 2012). There should be clear understanding of how to assess, formulate and work with risk at different levels, encompassing a clear appreciation that risk is never static but is mediated by past events and current concerns.

Ultimately, a framework is required for deciding what will work best with each particular child, and identifying when change of method or focus is needed. This involves a functional analysis of changing needs. It is based on a holistic approach that recognizes self-harm is best understood in terms of a child's whole life, and that understanding what brings children into care, and facilitating positive relationships thereafter, will reduce children's need to self-harm not just in the present but also in the future.

Chapter 4

Drugs and Alcohol as a Form of Self-Medication from Trauma and Past Abuse Among Children in Care

LISA ROBINSON AND JEUNE GUISHARD-PINE

Introduction

The risk factors associated with the onset of problem substance use as distinct from experimental use among young people is a growing interest for psychologists. The term 'substance' refers to both drugs and alcohol but not tobacco. There is no single theory that explains what motivates a youngster to begin to abuse substances.

The NHS Health Advisory Service (HAS) report (1996) states 'one off and experimental use of drugs and alcohol cannot in itself be seen as indicative of having caused actual harm or being related to any personal disorder' (p.3). This suggests that although it is recognized that all substance taking carries the potential of harm, a youngster taking a substance should not lead to an automatic conclusion that there is a problem or condition to be treated. A useful definition of substance misuse is 'substance taking which harms health or social functioning' – substance misuse may be dependency (physical or psychological) or substance taking that is part of a wider spectrum of problematic or harmful behaviour (Aarons *et al.* 1999).

Lloyd (1998) cited a panorama of risk factors for substance misuse, including a range of family, school and mental health problems.[1] He refers to these factors as an 'interactive "web of causation"'. Annexed to this, the literature points to the vulnerable groups of 'marginalized'

1 Having parents or siblings with problem drug use, family disruption, poor attachment or communication with parents; child abuse, low school grades, truancy, exclusion from school, childhood conduct disorder, crime, mental disorder (in particular depression and suicidal behaviour during adolescence), social deprivation (although evidence is limited) and a young age of drug use onset (Lloyd 1998).

youngsters such as children in care, those excluded from school, some with specific mental health disorders and those who have become part of the youth justice services who are at increased risk of substance misuse (Hawkins, Catalano and Miller 1992). Such findings are echoed in subsequent research. For example, Ward *et al.* (2003) and Newburn and Pearson (2002) found that children in care who have witnessed parental drug and alcohol misuse may have a skewed perception of excessive drug and alcohol use as 'normal'. Recent statistics indicated that as many as ten per cent of children in care aged 16–17 years had substance problems (Department for Education 2014a, 2014b), but that figure is decreasing. In the UK, Lewis (2015) reported on national statistics that showed that five per cent of young people reported to be receiving drug interventions stated that their accommodation status was living in care as a child in care or living independently as a child in care. The majority of young people entering specialist drug and alcohol services (58%) reported two to four vulnerable factors, which included experiencing abuse and neglect, truanting from school, offending, early sexual activity, antisocial behaviour and being exposed to parental substance misuse. The evidence is that the more risk factors young people have, the more likely they are to misuse substances, be harmed by them and misuse drugs and alcohol as adults.

Young people can enter specialist substance misuse services with a range of problems either relating to their substance use (such as poly drug use, drinking alcohol daily) or wider factors which may impact on their substance use (such as pregnancy, self-harming or offending), as follows:

- young person began using primary substance aged under 15
- young person reports involvement in offending behaviour
- young person reports self-harming
- young person is a child in care
- young person reports using opiates and/or crack
- young person is not in education or employment
- young person reports unsettled accommodation status or has no fixed abode

- young person reports using two or more drugs in combination (poly drug use)
- young person is pregnant or a parent
- young person reports almost daily drinking or drinking in excess of eight units (males) or six units (females) on an average drinking day when drinking, and drinks 13 or more days of the month.

Hence, children in care are more likely to have higher rates of prevalence than those living with their birth parents to smoke, drink and take drugs (Edmonds *et al.* 2005; Fendrich *et al.* 2011; Ford *et al.* 2007; Meltzer *et al.* 2003; NICE 2007b; Solis *et al.* 2012; Williams *et al.* 2001). There is also evidence to show that children in care tend to start using drugs at an earlier age, and use them at higher levels and more regularly than their peers who live with their birth parent/s. This has led to preventative steps to avert their drug use from becoming more entrenched (Big Step Social Inclusion Partnership 2002; National Treatment Agency 2012; Newburn and Pearson 2002; Ostrea, Chavez and Strauss 1976; Save the Children 1995; Weinberg *et al.* 1998).

However, there is an alternative, yet parallel story of the potential misuse of drugs and alcohol as a means of self-medicating following experiences of trauma and/or abuse to cope with painful emotions and to escape from problems (Harrison, Fulkerson and Beebe 1997; Khantzian 1997; Stewart 1996), while researchers such as Bensley *et al.* (1999); Boyd (1993); Briere and Runtz (1987); Briere and Elliott (1994); Dembo *et al.* (1989); Harrison *et al.* (1997); Herrenkohl *et al.* (2013); Kilpatrick *et al.* (2003); Mirza *et al.* (2008); Mulvihill (2005); Teets (1990); Singer, Petchers and Hussey (1989); and Young (1990) go further to investigate the specific long-term effects of childhood abuse and trauma on substance and alcohol misuse in adulthood. Singer, Petchers and Hussey (1989) explicitly identified substance misuse as a coping strategy.

Substance misuse and associated problems harm children and young people's welfare and prevent them from achieving their full potential (Aarons *et al.* 1999; Currie, Small and Currie 2002; Johnson and Richter 2002; McAuley and Davis 2009; Moroz 2005; Newbury-Birch *et al.* 2009; Pavis, Cunningham-Burley and Amos 1997). It is for this reason that policy recommends that screening and assessing children in care for substance misuse should be a core part of care planning. Lloyd (1998) indicated that delivering successful preventive interventions to these groups was challenging but despite this, there should be ongoing attempts to embed drug work within the work already delivered by youth-focused agencies. His views are reiterated in subsequent policy and legislation. In the Every Child Matters (2003) policy, for example, 'choose not to take illegal drugs' is a core objective of the 'be healthy' outcomes framework and integral to the improvement cycle for local authorities, including the Annual Performance Assessment and the Joint Area Reviews. In addition to this *Promoting the Health of Children in Care* guidance was first published in November 2002. The guidance includes a section on young people and drugs as it is a key issue for consideration when assessing the health, well-being and safety of children in care. The most recent guidance from the Department for Education and the Department of Health (2015) directs health assessments for those aged 11–18 years to include an assessment of whether a referral to a specialist centre for substance misuse is appropriate.

This chapter looks at the themes of the relatively high prevalence of drug and alcohol abuse among children in care, including the issue of self-medication as both a facilitator and inhibitor of communication. It concludes with messages about how the joining up of mental and physical health services can assist with recovery and specifically the combined learning of a child mental health service and specialist youth drug and alcohol service in addressing the needs of children in care who have drug and alcohol problems.

Child sexual abuse and substance misuse

In the USA, the research into aetiology of substance misuse has been a subject of research for several decades (Deykin, Levy and Wells 1987; Goeders 2003). In the main, this has been on the adult population that are using rehabilitation services (Briere and Runtz 1987; Kendall-Tackett 2002). Over the years, what has been spotlighted is prior experience of childhood sexual abuse (Benward and Densen-Gerber 1971; Davis 1990; Dube *et al.* 2003; Rohsenow, Corbett and Devine 1988; Simpson and Miller 2002). Reviews have shown that approximately two out of three female substance abusers have had a prior sexual abuse experience, usually before the age of 16 years (Boyd 1993). Subsequently, Boyd (1993) found that 44 per cent of women who presented for drug rehabilitation reported child sexual abuse. Such overwhelming research indicates that working with post abuse recovery is an integral part of drugs work, particularly with females who misuse substances (Bensley *et al.* 1999; Rohsenow *et al.* 1988). It is recommended that the sex of the therapist and the composition of therapy groups should be carefully considered when treating females recovering from sexual abuse as well as the addiction.

Liebschutz *et al.* (2002) found that as many as 81 per cent of their female participants and 69 per cent of their male participants reported experience of physical and/or sexual abuse in their childhood, starting from as young as 11 years. They found that for males, if they were abused before the age of 17 years, their substance misuse was more entrenched than if the abuse started after the age of 17 years. However, substance misuse was indicated for all ages of their female participants. The inference is that substance misuse among girls is potentially a communication of child sexual abuse. Consistent evidence of the comorbidity of trauma and substance misuse prevails (e.g. Kilpatrick *et al.* 2003).

Early intervention for substance misusing children in care

In the UK, the strong link between the experience of abuse and neglect and substance misuse has meant that the rate of substance misuse among children in care is a matter that has been scrutinized by the government. The most recent statistics available show that although the current rate of substance misuse is lower than in 2012, of the total 47,670 children continuously in care for 12 months at 31 March 2014, 1680 children (3.5%) were identified as having a substance misuse problem during the year. In 2012, the rate was 4.1 per cent. Comparable rates for all children are not available.

Children in care all have a history of 'significant harm' (Department of Health 1989). What they also have in common is that they are deemed as having no birth family members to care for them. Despite this, children in care are far from being a homogenous group. In recognition of this potential complexity, NICE has recommended specialist child mental health services for children in care

(NICE 2010), although in the UK, specialist services to children have colloquially been seen as the 'Cinderella services'.[2] The SCRIPT team was developed in 2002 and over that time accumulated knowledge and experience of this vulnerable group of youngsters. Though limited in resources, the restrictions enabled the team to become more creative in meeting the diverse needs of this group. One such method was to provide a balance between long-term individual psychotherapy and preventative work via consultation, support and training to social workers and foster carers.

Fierce Commitment (Guishard-Pine *et al.* 2013) was a two-day course that was devised specifically for the needs of foster carers who specialize in adolescent placements. It was so named to reflect the potential *white-knuckle* turbulence that foster carers experience while caring for adolescents in foster care. The course explicitly connected the first-hand experiences of foster carers – both as adolescents and as carers of adolescents – to the complex mental health issues of the abused and neglected adolescents that they care for.

The course was devised in partnership with colleagues in physical health namely the specialist nurse for children in care. The uncharted territory for these carers was the adolescent world of substance misuse. They learnt, for example, that a small proportion of the clients engaging with the Luton Drug and Alcohol Partnership – about 15–20 per cent – show class A drug abuse, mostly heroin and cocaine. As a result of the Fierce Commitment course, dedicated courses for foster carers were devised and delivered by the Drug and Alcohol Partnership as a rolling programme.

This course provides delegates with the knowledge and skills to talk to young people about alcohol and drugs including:

- increasing awareness and knowledge about drug and alcohol use and effects
- increasing awareness and knowledge about new psychoactive substance use and effects
- understanding current trends in young people's alcohol and drug use

2 'A Cinderella service within the NHS' is one of the most common phrases people hear when using the term, meaning 'neglected, ignored or something that is given little attention or care' (www.kgbanswers.co.uk/what-does-the-expression-a-cindarella-service-mean/18350993).

- exploring how different types of alcohol and drug use impact on young people
- examining what you can do and when to refer
- examining the effects of living with parental use of alcohol and/or drugs
- how to refer to the Luton Drug and Alcohol Partnership and how they can support the child in care.

The Luton Drug and Alcohol Partnership provides a range of holistic interventions[3] to service users.

The foster carer in the case study below had attended the Luton Drug and Alcohol Training that was designed specifically for the needs of foster carers. From the knowledge and skills that she acquired at the training, she was able to identify behaviours that were indicators of possibly more serious substance use. Consequently, she felt this training was paramount for her, and had enabled her to make contact with the Luton Drug and Alcohol Partnership for more intensive support.

NATALYA'S STORY

There are many theories that attempt to explain why young people abuse drugs and alcohol. Consequently, different hypotheses can provide an understanding of what is going on for the young person. One of the main perspectives is the self-medication theory. This theory suggests that young people who use substances problematically do this as a way of escaping memories of unpleasant experiences such as trauma or abuse, as in the case of Natalya.

Natalya is 15 years old and had been in foster care since the age of two years. Her foster carer found cannabis paraphernalia in the placement and was concerned about the impact this might have on the relationships and also on the well-being of other children within the home. Natalya was referred to the Luton Drug and Alcohol Partnership due to concerns with cannabis use.

---

3 Full drug and alcohol assessment, alternative therapies – auricular acupuncture and electro stimulation therapy, cognitive behaviour therapy, motivational interviewing, mapping, mindfulness, care planning, risk assessing, psychotherapy/counselling, prescribing, sexual health interventions (including blood borne virus testing), relapse prevention and harm reduction, group work (relapse prevention, emotional well-being), working with significant others (children who are affected by family drug/alcohol use), multi-agency working (including health, mental health teams, police, probation, youth offending services, social care, GPs, sexual health services, local safeguarding children boards).

An appointment for a comprehensive assessment was made for Natalya, and her foster carer was invited to attend and support her at the appointment. In addition to this, the Luton Drug and Alcohol Partnership advised the foster carer and offered support to both the carer and Natalya.

At the assessment Natalya disclosed her history of sexual abuse by a family member. She was able to chat with her allocated specialist drug and alcohol worker about a range of issues, including her experience of being in foster care and the support she had received from her foster carer. Natalya was positive about her relationship with her foster carer and wanted her to be closely involved with the assessment. Later in the assessment, Natalya further disclosed that although it did not occur on a daily basis, she had smoked cannabis. She continued that she sometimes used cannabis to assist with sleep. Natalya recognized that she was self-medicating and wanted support to achieve abstinence.

Natalya's treatment plan followed a holistic approach involving a range of statutory and voluntary services to which she had been referred. The specific interventions that were employed to address her substance abuse included a variety of drug interventions including harm reduction, relapse prevention, alternative therapies and therapeutic counselling. As a significant other, her foster carer was offered support including interventions on how she could support Natalya to reduce her cannabis use.

The National Delivery Plan for young people and substance misuse

The National Delivery Plan was developed across government departments in the UK to ensure that every young person with increased vulnerability to developing substance misuse problems had early identification of his substance misuse and received an appropriate service or intervention to prevent the problems escalating. It is important to reiterate here that those who use drugs or alcohol problematically are likely to be experiencing a range of problems, of which substance misuse is one. The aim is that all needs are met, rather than addressing substance misuse in isolation and that intervention is successful before problematic use becomes entrenched. The relevant contribution of child mental health services became even more important when the then National Institute for Health and Clinical Excellence published two guidance documents on public health (NICE 2007a) and psychosocial interventions (NICE 2007b). These documents highlighted the need for young drug and alcohol users to be able to access competent family-focused workers (NHS 2007).

Family-based interventions to treat substance misuse

Young people who are substance misusing have different needs from their adult counterparts. The majority of young people accessing specialist drug and alcohol interventions require psychosocial and family interventions, rather than treatment for addiction per se. The benefits of an integrated young people's care plan for the majority of youngsters are that they can access specialist drug and alcohol services for a few weeks, before extending their support within another agency.

For youngsters in the care system, problems with drugs and substance misuse usually occur within a complex matrix of multiple chronic stressors. A review of the literature confirms that many of the substance-abusing young people have had a very chaotic and disrupted early childhood with significant levels of bereavement, loss, neglect and abuse in addition to being in care to social services (Cleaver, Unell and Aldgate 2011; Davies and Ward 2012). Many have had unsuccessful school careers, sometimes because their learning disabilities have been masked by their emotional and behavioural needs, thus many of the boys and some of the girls who are substance misusing lack basic literacy skills. Many others are involved with crime and are in care to the local authority (Prior and Paris 2005). The evidence also indicates that many young substance-abusing or dependent young women are sexually exploited (Department for Children, Schools and Families and Department of Health 2009). Specialist resources have been produced to support this growing problem (Barnardo's Scotland 2014).

Young women who are or have been in the care system also have a relatively high rate of teenage pregnancy (Haydon 2003; Social Care Institute for Excellence 2005). Unsurprisingly, there are a number of risk factors associated with being a teenage mother in the care system, including mental instability and substance misuse. The most common substances that they are misusing are alcohol, tobacco, cannabis or combinations of the three. This has emerged from research in the USA and Scandinavia as well as the UK (Bebbington and Miles 1989; Christoffersen and Soothill 2003; Franzén, Vinnerljung and Hjern 2008; Friedlaender *et al.* 2005; Kalland *et al.* 2006; Needell and Barth

1998; Simkiss *et al.* 2012). The Luton Drug and Alcohol Partnership has managed to engage some of these pregnant and young mothers and has found that close liaison with maternity services and subsequent aftercare is essential.

Final comment

There is a dominant view that the most useful approach to deterring or reducing drug and alcohol misuse is to provide early intervention, information and awareness to young people (Butcher and Ryan 2006). The Fostering Network has produced a leaflet for foster carers in collaboration with FRANK, a national drug education service established by the UK government in 2003. It is helpful to remember that education is only one aspect of reducing harmful drug use. Other equally important tactics are to encourage positive relationships and to suggest that the youngster changes his social networks to include more young people who are not abusing drugs. Most importantly developing a healthy relationship with the child in care enables him to invest in a more positive, drug-free future.

Chapter 5

'Run Run as Fast as You Can, You Can't Catch Me I'm the Gingerbread Man'

An Assessment of Brothers in Care within the Context of 'Safe Therapy'

OLATAYO AFUAPE

Introduction

The purpose of using this case study is to highlight the importance of psychotherapeutic assessments, which as well as evaluating clients' suitability and readiness for psychotherapy (Hinshelwood 1991) can also be crucial in determining their state of mind. In addition, a psychotherapeutic assessment can provide a short, discrete piece of therapeutic intervention in its own right (Rustin and Quagliata 1994; Winnicott 1971). Certainly in the cases of 'hard to place' children in care, who regularly change placements, a comprehensive assessment may be their only opportunity to experience an intervention through to completion.

The Gingerbread Man as a symbol of omnipotent fantasy

The fairytale of the Gingerbread Man is an allegory about the loss of omnipotence. The Gingerbread Man's omnipotent fantasy that he is not made of gingerbread and can outrun those that want to catch him is ousted when he is outwitted by a fox that carries him across a river only to eat him when they reach the other side.

The Gingerbread Man is a useful analogy for thinking about the assessment of Thomas and Charlie, two brothers in care. Their unusual behaviour, which entailed demonstrations of, and comments about, their powerfulness, seemed to disguise their catastrophic anxieties and fears of separation during the breakdown of their placement. In this case study, making sense of the brothers' communication of powerfulness provided a deeper understanding of their state of mind and enabled us to make better sense of their systems' and our own sense of powerlessness.

For the purpose of this case study I will think about the brothers' communication of powerfulness in terms of their omnipotence. Omnipotence, as defined by Freud (1918) and Winnicott (1965), is an illusion of 'all powerfulness', which is seen as an intrinsic part of early childhood, but also according to Winnicott (1965), identified as essential to a child's emotional well-being. Winnicott proposed that the role of the good enough mother is to uphold the fiction of omnipotence through her attunement and responsiveness to her child's needs. A mother's emotional or physical disconnection leads to catastrophic anxieties and feelings of fragmentation within the child. Without the illusion of omnipotence the child's external and internal world becomes a dangerous, terrifying and persecuting place.

Thomas and Charlie

Thomas and Charlie were removed from their birth mother when Thomas was four and Charlie two. Their mother, who had a history of severe mental illness, was sectioned after abducting her 22-month-old nephew and causing Thomas actual bodily harm. As well as being physically aggressive towards her children she was a survivor of domestic violence. She was unable to keep her sons physically safe and when the neighbours complained that Thomas was found wandering the street on several occasions, and the brothers were found in their home, alone, soiled and in squalid conditions, they were placed in care. They had been in their present placement for two years and this was their seventh placement.

Assessment as a transitional space during organizational change

Thomas and Charlie's assessment was conducted by my colleague (a clinical specialist counsellor) and I in response to an urgent referral by social services. They were referred at a time of organizational change and upheaval within the specialist mental health service we worked in. My colleague and I were members of a long-term specialist team for the most complex cases of children in care, but we were in the process of being disbanded and incorporated into a short-term team where the focus was on generic support and early intervention. Some members of the long-term core team (who would be now required to work with children in longer term care) had expressed concerns that they did not have the clinical expertise to manage the complexity and high risk associated with children in care. Their concerns were dismissed by managers who disputed that clinicians needed specialist skills to work with this client group, and also demanded a clear explanation for long-term work with this vulnerable group, which they questioned the need for.

We offered a comprehensive assessment of Thomas and Charlie's needs as a short-term intervention, which would support the systems that supported the children while providing evidence that would justify the need for long-term work. We felt that given the level of deprivation they experienced they would initially benefit from an intervention that was structured and had a sense of completion. The organizational change process had weakened and blurred the internal systems for allocating, referring and co-working and we were especially worried that there were 'structural gaps' through which these children might fall. We took advantage of the transitional period, where we as clinicians were not yet one thing or another, to negotiate the nature of our role, fearing that once the assessment was completed the brothers could languish on a waiting list.

Thomas and Charlie's assessment, which consisted of a series of consultation meetings with the professional network, individual sessions with the brothers, and consultation with the long-term and short-term specialist mental health teams, became a transitional space bridging the gap between long-and short-term work. This work equally exposed another gap between assessment and intervention as the short-term team protocol defined assessment as pre-intervention. More importantly, it exposed the gap between long-term specialist work with children in care and short-term, early intervention work with children in care by begging the question, could the former really be replaced by the latter?

Falling through the gap: the need for safe therapy for children in care

The unique trauma and losses of children in care have been highlighted by Gianna Williams (1974) and Louise Emanuel (2002). Williams (1974) identified the child's experience of abuse and neglect, and then separation from her family and home, as a 'double deprivation'. Emanuel proposed that the child experiences a third deprivation when the family and professional systems are disabled by the child's projections. These projections impact on the systems' decision-making capacities and management and containment of the child, and they begin to mirror the child's internal dysfunction and chaos.

A child whose external world can quickly become dysfunctional and chaotic needs more than the therapeutic alliance to feel safe. The child also needs the systems that surround her to be containing and mindful. The idea of having a 'handle' on the child's internal and external reality or having 'two minds' is the basic tenet of safe therapy. However, it is not left to the child's therapist to have two minds but it is a responsibility that is shared within the therapist's team and among the systems that support the child. This promotes the idea that no one person can be responsible, and no one person can support the child on their own (see also Chapter 11).

Within the safe therapy structure, therefore, each case has a therapist working with the child and a second therapist working with the systems that surround and support the child. Guishard-Pine, McCall and Hamilton (2007) propose that the systems (family, school, social care, community etc.) can guard against the child's mental ill health and become protective shields which are well-informed, interconnected units that can link up their thinking in order to process the child's anxieties.

The need for safe therapy was even more necessary given the brothers' impact on their systems. In our team meetings, thinking about the needs of Thomas and Charlie generally resulted in the managers ending the discussion prematurely without making a decision. This paralysis in thinking, feeling and acting seemed a very important aspect of the brothers' internal narrative.

Assessment process: meetings with the network

The assessment of Charlie and Thomas began long before they were seen, contextualized by reports of an almost biblical nature of the older brother attempting to kill the younger brother. During the first consultation meeting, which consisted of the brothers' foster carer, her supervising social worker and the brothers' social worker, the foster carer reported that Thomas had barricaded his bedroom door, which she managed to force open just in time to prevent him from crushing Charlie's windpipe with his knee.

She struggled to say anything positive about Thomas, but Charlie was portrayed as the gentle, respectful and vulnerable younger brother. Thomas was portrayed as having always detested his brother and being extremely envious of him. She strongly believed that Thomas would have succeeded in killing Charlie had she not opened the door in time and did not want this on her conscience. At the time of the consultation meeting Thomas was in respite care while Charlie remained in the foster placement, and support from our service seemed to hinge on whether Thomas could return.

The idea that Thomas had always hated his brother seemed inconsistent with social services reports that presented Thomas as his brother's protector both from the violence between his parents and from his mother's rage. When Thomas was taken into care he reported that he would take blows for his brother as well as dodge his mother's blows by running between her legs and out of the house. Given this relationship one wonders what could have happened between them to make Thomas attempt to seriously harm his brother.

Even though the supervising social worker and brothers' social worker attempted to present a more balanced view of the boys, they both referred to a mental health assessment which highlighted that Thomas was at high risk of developing mental health issues while Charlie's mental health risk was minimal. The divergent perceptions of Charlie and Thomas seemed curious, worrying and convenient. My colleague and I hypothesized that the identification of the brothers as essentially good or bad could serve an important function for them and their systems by placing all the unbearable feelings and anxieties onto the bad object. There seemed to be an alarming demonstration of this during our first meeting with the professional network at the brothers' school.

School staff were in full attendance; Thomas's class teacher attended, the head of behaviour support, two members of staff who supported Thomas, his mentor, a teacher from the pupil exclusion unit where he had spent his fixed-term exclusions, and Thomas's respite carer. For Charlie, his class teacher's feedback came via the headteacher and the brothers' foster carer (who still cared for Charlie) did not attend. The brothers' social worker also attended. My colleague and I entered a room filled with what we experienced as stony faces, and were met with accusations of incompetence and inaction even though we had responded promptly to the referral. Charlie, we were informed, was well behaved and high achieving in school but was becoming increasing embarrassed by his brother's behaviour. They felt our specialist intervention was needed for Thomas as a matter of urgency.

Thomas was presented as a disturbed and destructive child who could be charming and endearing especially when given individual attention but had no friends, was feared by his peers (and members of staff), and was extremely disruptive in class. Thomas's class teachers reported that he was unpredictable and manipulative, and when he became disruptive he could trash the classroom and she had no option other than to evacuate the class in order to keep the other children safe. The head of behaviour support detailed how, after these destructive outbursts, Thomas would regress to a much younger self and whimper like a baby. The headteacher further described him as a danger to himself. Thomas hated being touched or reasoned with when he was in his vulnerable state. He knew no boundaries or restraint. Thomas had bitten and kicked her to escape her grasp when she had tried to prevent him from running out into the playground. On one occasion Thomas had found the school gate unlocked and run onto a busy street almost getting himself killed. In their desperation to keep him safe the teachers would run after him but he would outrun them or avoid them by dodging past them or running in between their legs: 'Run, run as fast as you can, you can't catch me I'm the Gingerbread Man.'

My colleague and I attempted to make links between Thomas's past childhood experience and his present behaviour, to wonder how brothers sharing the same experience could function so differently and we offered some strategies for managing Thomas's hyper-vigilant defences. We expressed our concern that it seemed difficult for Charlie to be anything other than good when Thomas was seen as so bad. We warned that Charlie might internalize and repress his anxieties, causing him to develop emotional and behavioural difficulties at a later stage. These thoughts were *thoroughly* dismissed.

Later, when my colleague and I reflected on the network meeting we deduced that we had become the bad but omnipotent object. The network, despite making us the 'all powerful' mental health professionals – the only ones who could address their concerns about Thomas – at the same time rendered our knowledge and opinions useless.

Individual sessions with Thomas

My colleague and I agreed to see Thomas together because we wanted to have as broad and as varied a perspective of him (and his brother) as possible.

Thomas took us both by surprise; not only was he an attractive, charming and intriguing child but he was diminutive in stature. His physical presentation seemed at odds with the boy who could trash a classroom, intimidate his teachers and peers and would bite and kick a headteacher. As we initially sat and spoke with his respite carer, my colleague noticed through a gap in the door that he had crept out of his room and quietly was sitting on the top of the stairs. When called by his respite carer he came down the stairs eagerly but with an air of caution.

Thomas sat upright on the sofa with one leg over the other and his back straight. We both shared afterwards that it felt as though we were in the presence of an elderly gentleman. He pronounced his words carefully and precisely and often corrected our comments and use of language. Sometimes his tone was frustrated and impatient.

Thomas seemed encouraged rather than deterred by the presence of two new adults, as if our combined presence gave him more kudos and credibility. He seemed very relaxed and open in his 'home' environment and eager to discuss his concerns and grievances. His tone was insistent as he described how the 'pranks' he played on his teacher with the collusion of his peers would go horribly wrong and result in him being accused of disrupting the class. The injustice of being singled out incensed him and he would refuse to leave the class, becoming even more irate if the teachers attempted to 'manhandle' him. Thomas further conveyed his sense of claustrophobia and fear of restraint through the descriptions of himself as a tiger being trapped by poachers and a free-runner who – when chased by teachers – would run so fast that he would get carried by the wind and become uncatchable.

He seemed to lack any compassion for his peers, teachers, or his brother, who he accused of standing by while he was 'physically and emotionally assaulted' by a previous respite carer. Charlie had also continually taunted him before the incident that had him removed from their placement. He refused to say anything further about his brother and said he did not want to speak about him ever again. This made us wonder whether underneath Thomas's calm and controlled persona he was full of fear and trepidation as to what would come out of our visit and his present respite placement. We also wondered if it was better for Charlie not to exist in Thomas's mind rather than him to acknowledge their separation.

Individual sessions with Charlie

Charlie was seen a few days after Thomas. Despite being the younger brother Charlie looked much older and was much bigger. Also attractive and charming, Charlie presented as gentle and more overtly vulnerable. He was very polite and seemed eager to please, responding to questions rather than leading the discussion. He was also an articulate child but seemed cautious and reserved in his use and choice of language.

Charlie reported that he did not know that we were coming although his foster carer had reminded him. He waited until he heard his foster carer go up the stairs and opened the door a few times before settling down to speak to us. He displayed a similar level of trepidation and hyper-vigilance as his brother; for Charlie it seemed as though there was something about adults having and/or sharing information that made him anxious.

Although Charlie also seemed eager to speak to us he spoke about his secrets and prefaced his comments with 'No, I can't say that'. His first secret was about having a girlfriend and the second about missing his brother. It seemed that Charlie's secrets and 'I can't say that' comments were his way of seeking permission from the adults before he could say what was on his mind. Charlie's hyper-vigilance seemed to be expressed through his need to pacify adults, and his guarded approach. He seemed to retain many worries and concerns and we wondered if he would feel safe enough to air his grievances, especially since the brothers' separation.

Charlie could admit his fear of Thomas when he became aggressive towards him, but also admitted to instigating situations that Thomas would often take the blame for. He said that he was very much missing his brother and reminisced about the brotherly chats they would share when they were together and how close they had been. Charlie seemed to hold the regret, sadness and loss (of his brother) that Thomas had disconnected from. His obvious feelings of guilt were paralleled by an anxiety that if he did not pacify adults he would also be rejected by them.

Towards the end of the session he wanted to show us handstands, stating that he could also do one-handed handstands. He desperately attempted to demonstrate this but was unsuccessful, falling over in quite awkward positions. Despite our concern that he would hurt himself, which was expressed by us recognizing how much he had to do to get the adults' attention and to let them know how unsafe he felt at times, he became determined. He told us that he had to be strong and seemed mortified when eventually he had to concede this endeavour. We wondered whether he wanted us to know how difficult it was without his brother and how much he felt that there was something missing.

It seemed to us that Charlie's unspoken worry and concern was being expressed through this final communication – the pain and frustration of having to stand on his own – and how precarious and unpredictable this could be.

Discussion

The assessment of Thomas and Charlie concluded that they had been severely traumatized by their early experience. They had endured and survived severe abuse and neglect and several placement breakdowns, but had always been together. Their displays of omnipotence seemed to be designed to stave off their fear of falling apart, which was verified in a very concrete way by their separation. Their internal anxiety and sense of powerlessness – which was reflected back to them via the adult systems around them – intensified their sense of catastrophe that their separation would be permanent.

Although Thomas held the stigma of being the bad child, it seems that Charlie was the sad child, connected to the loss of his brother and his guilt that he may be responsible for their separation.

This was further complicated by our service's organizational upheaval which constrained our approach; we would have normally recommended that we worked with the brothers individually and in the longer term, while supporting the foster carer and offering regular meetings with the network. Our sense of powerlessness and anxiety that, against our best efforts, our intervention was not safe enough may have influenced our judgements and identifications. No matter how reflective and mindful one is as a therapist, it is always likely that organizational issues impact the work that we do. Additionally, both my colleague and I were so identified with how devastating it would be for the brothers to separate that we had not considered that they might also be expressing a need to separate, no matter how painful.

The assessment had been invaluable in terms of providing a state-of-mind assessment for the brothers during their transitional period of changes in placement. It also provided a cautionary tale about ignoring the needs of Charlie who, while still in his previous placement, began to mimic some of Thomas's challenging behaviour.

A final thought on the paralysis in thinking, feeling and acting within our service might also have provided us with some insight into the brothers' early experience. I wondered if paralysis or omnipotence were the only options available to a much younger Thomas and Charlie in order to survive living with a terrifying, persecuting and aggressive mother. I felt that while my colleague and I had been experienced as omnipotent professionals, we had also had a paralysis in thinking and acting during the network meetings. On reflection, we could have resisted the network's insistence to see these boys and offered consultation to the network and foster carer until they were both seen for long-term work.

Chapter 6

Working with Sexually Inappropriate Behaviour and Incest

A Case Study

TONIE LAWRENCE-MAHRRA

Introduction

The negative outcomes for children in care are well documented by my colleagues in this book. It is a sad testimony to the impact of active and residual memories of abuse that what can follow being placed in care is a downwards spiral involving drug abuse, self-loathing and also a tendency to go on to have another generation of children that are placed into care (Department for Education 2015a).

Early traumatic experiences are those that occur from birth to six years. Infants and young children tend to react differently to traumatic experiences from older children and adults because they are less able to describe the traumatic or dangerous incident/s verbally. It is because of this fact that people often assume that their developmental stage protects them from the severe impact of traumatic experiences. Consequently, adults may presume that the child is 'too young' to understand or to remember and discourage or otherwise inhibit him from talking about the event. However, there are far-reaching ramifications of early childhood trauma even though he may not understand what happened (Allen and Johnson 2011; Cohen, Berliner and Mannarino 2010; Courtois, Ford and Cloitre 2009; Widom 1989). It is important for a traumatized child to engage in therapy as early as possible, so that he can be supported through these difficult circumstances at the time of suffering. In order to reach and soothe childhood trauma, one essentially has to rework and, it is hoped, reverse the mental health problems that have developed from a flawed foundation. In promoting early intervention, practitioners have to also seek to prevent re-traumatization – thus working through the trauma as early as possible (Cohen and Mannarino 1996) will mean that there will be less of a long-term impact on the child (Goodyear-Brown 2012). Successfully breaking this spiral places a huge responsibility onto therapists who aim to break generational patterns of neglect. Also, studies show that 30 per cent of sexualized children will go on to commit sexual offences as adults, but for those who receive timely therapeutic intervention, this drops to 5–14 per cent (Rich 2011).

First, this chapter chronicles the case study of a six-year-old girl who I have called Lauren. A combination of factors led to Lauren being placed in care: she was a victim of sexual violation and was physically and emotionally deprived and neglected. Like so many children, this abuse occurred within her own family system, a system that society entrusts and relies on to raise and protect the nation's children. These children in turn can show predatory behaviour towards their siblings and other relatives (Hackett, Masson and Phillips 2006). Alongside this story, the chapter describes through images the themes that often dominate work with children who have been sexually abused. The inner world and torment of Lauren after she was admitted for therapy to her local child mental health service is highlighted. The challenge for the therapist is to contribute to the multi-professional approaches to reduce the likelihood of re-enactment.

The story of *Charlotte's Web*

Charlotte's Web (White 1952) is an allegory of friendship, loyalty, courage, real love and the natural cycle of life and death. Through the characters, it illustrates qualities of innocence, trust and determination that are needed to encounter the challenges and feelings experienced in relationships. However, like many children's stories, *Charlotte's Web* also documents the darker costs of relationships and life:

> What is a life anyway? We're born, we live a little, we die. A spider's life can't help being something of a mess with all it's trapping and eating flies. (White 1952, p.154)

Throughout my therapy with Lauren, I found this story a constant companion in our sand play work particularly: themes of entrapment, enmeshment and death.

> I have come to realize that sexual assault is an imposed death experience for the victim. That is, the victim experiences her life as having been taken by somebody else. (Kane 1989, p.33)

Charlotte's promise was to save the instinctual innocence represented by Wilbur the pig. Being the runt of the litter, Wilbur was unaware of his impending slaughter. Not once, but twice, he was saved from this ordeal. Fern, the farmer's daughter, displays her love for Wilbur and pleads for her pet's life. Meanwhile, Charlotte weaves inscriptions of praise for Wilbur in her web, attracting much publicity and this praise is attributed to divine intervention, which increases Wilbur's celebrity. Wilbur is entered into a country fair where he is celebrated by visitors and thus his prestige prevents the farmer from killing him.

Therapy with the sexualized child

One vulnerability of the sexualized child can be his need to be liked. Inadvertently he may continually endanger himself because of a lack of sufficient and adequate personal boundaries. Such learnt experiences are powerful and repetitively drive him towards unsafe people whom he believes are trustworthy and reliable due to his need to maintain what had been experienced as normal. Lauren was initially referred because she exhibited inappropriate, sexualized behaviours and language well beyond her years. Lauren had disclosed sexual abuse by her father when she was brought in to care, as her mother could not protect her. A previous referral was made by Lauren's school when she was four because she displayed sexualized behaviour. Her mother also shared concern and claimed a boy they knew had got on top of her and moved up and down. Lauren had formerly lived with her maternal aunt when her mother was sectioned for a few weeks. Lauren disclosed that the aunt tried to strangle her, but her mother said that Lauren sometimes lied.

The case brings to light the difficulties of working with sexually abused children, including the ethical decisions involved when meeting these children's needs. Prioritizing a safe working practice – including regular supervision – in order to work through the therapists' countertransference is of vital importance.

The emotional and psychological impact of sexual violation on a child is so disorientating that the child internalizes the blame of the other who violated him, and develops a lack of self-boundaries (Goodyear-Brown 2012). Through a need to be close, he confuses sensuality with sexuality, which can lead to future violation. In her placement Lauren displayed a fascination towards exposing the genitals of her dolls and made them explicitly sexually interact. During these interactions Lauren could become highly anxious, aroused and excited, with an increase in her giggling and her masturbating. She was often witnessed moving up and down on top of her teddies in a sexualized way. Lauren displayed a lack of personal boundaries, being intrusive of others' personal space, hugging and kissing others repeatedly. At school, Lauren frequently refused to do what people asked and became inexplicably angry and aggressive. Furthermore, she interacted aggressively and punitively with peers, was often controlling and lacked any empathy after pinching and hurting them.

Lauren's therapeutic process through imagery

Figure 6.1 The fragmented self

Lauren created the character 'Chloe' perhaps to represent Lauren's sexualized self. In this sand tray, 'Chloe' was buried beneath the sand in the middle of the circle. Once 'Chloe' was hidden, the fairy was brought out, possibly as a representation of Lauren's innocence. This 'fairyland' existence denies the painful, sexualized aspect of her to create an innocent, polite persona. While the other symbols – all animals – sat outside, Lauren's fairy saw no danger and went straight into the circle, like Lauren in her innocence, willing to attach to potentially unsafe adults. The symbols may link to Miller's (2008) ideas of the interplay of the *animal soul and the angelic souls.* According to Grubbs (1994, 1995), the burying of objects into the sand suggests a regression and possible sadistic attitude towards oneself and others.

Figure 6.2 Scattered self

Lauren left a trail of mess around the room, taking out random toys that she did not use. The mess possibly mirrored her chaotic life story. Lauren placed more toys outside the box than inside and this I feel reflected Lauren's unfulfilled potential of her innate qualities; they were not a part of the tray but a part of her psyche (Daly 1984). As she had not integrated them into the tray my hypothesis would be that she did not recognize these parts of herself, suggesting a split on the self-ego axis (Neumann 1988). Lauren verbalized that 'Chloe' (on the horse) was being attacked by two females. She added: 'Chloe does not like me', suggesting that the sexualized aspect of herself blamed her helpless innocent self, as represented by the fairy that lay face down in the sand. These instinctual, innate aspects of herself, represented by the animals excluded from the tray, perhaps failed to protect 'Chloe' from the two negative female objects.

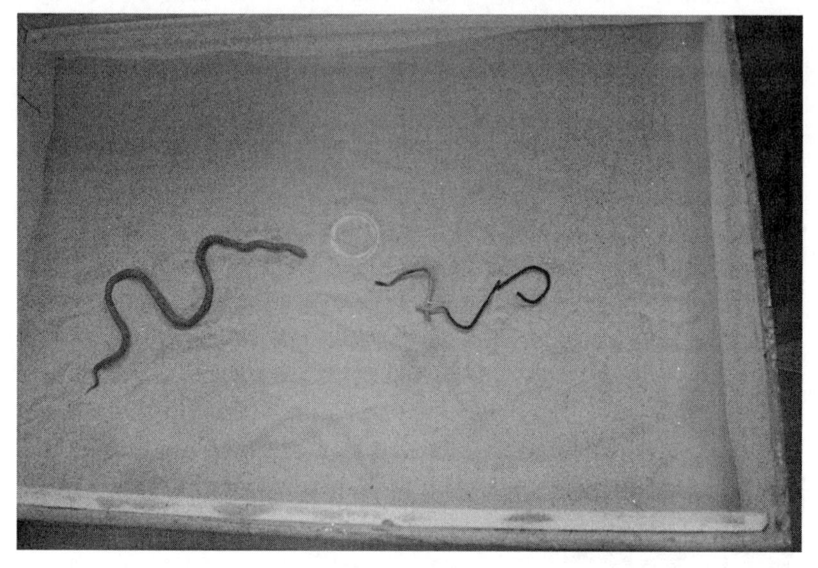

Figure 6.3 Violation

Snakes symbolically represent violation (Daly 1984), which led to an interpretation of this display as penetration of the womb by two perpetrators – or more than once.

When Lauren's mother was pregnant with her there had been allegations of incest between her father and grandmother. There was known domestic violence between her father and mother. If a womb is 'toxic', as well as being part of a chaotic wider world, the child may construe that they, too, are 'toxic' through intrauterine bonding (Verny and Weintraub 2002).

Figure 6.4 Ambiguity

This sand tray in session 10 showed Lauren's self-abusing aspect through the monster threatening the innocence of the butterfly. It further highlighted Lauren's inability to hold personal protective boundaries. For me, very powerfully, it also represents the idea of the presence of both the benign and the dangerous being in the same space. This co-existence is, of course, a facet of familial sexual abuse and incest and can represent one of the hardest elements to be worked through in later life.

In thinking about permanency plans the local authority proposed a move for Lauren and her brother to reside in a paternal kinship care placement abroad. My colleagues and I were extremely concerned that this had not been thoroughly researched and that her safety was being compromised with the possibility of re-generational patterns of abuse being enacted. It was proposed that inexperienced kinship carers with minimal training and understanding of traumatized children might be her source of care and trust. At the point in which these considerations were being explored, Lauren's father still paid frequent visits to the family members involved.

Figure 6.5 Desolation

This sand tray reflected the potential move. Lauren's projective identification of defencelessness is evident here; the soldiers were all dead, so there was no one fighting for her. The spider represented the negative mother aspect (Daly 1984), and was not aiding any progression. The turtle perhaps represented her father – who protects only himself; it is on the opposite side to the spider perhaps representing the parents' relationship, living in different countries. He was facing towards the tree, symbolic of the nurturance of the positive static feminine (Hill 1992), hidden behind a fence for some protection from him.

Figure 6.6 Decline

In Figure 6.6 Lauren's drawing of grid-like bars perhaps represented imprisonment, where she is hemmed in by their circumstances and powerless to do anything. The black, somewhat phallic, downward spiral suggests a fear and terror, highlighting a potential decline into the unknown (Daly 1984). As though in an attempt to escape from the situation, the gashes might symbolize Lauren's lashing out. Lauren, in her defence and to avoid feelings of such intolerable rejection, made an allegation against her carer, which eventually resulted in her placement breaking down rather than a planned move being achieved. For me, this displayed a re-enactment of historic trauma when she made the original disclosure resulting in her and her siblings being taken into care. So far the consistency of the placement and the therapy had helped her to gain basic trust in the world that she did not learn in the trust verses mistrust stage (Erikson 1950). Thus, when rejection was imminent, Lauren jeopardized the trust that had been built up, and her long-term therapeutic intervention in exchange for an experience of re-abandonment.

Lauren allowed her nose to run, too, and declined offers of a tissue. I felt the mucus represented the pain she wanted others to see rather than being ashamed of it. Lauren expressed that she did not like it when people laughed at her, but she liked the feeling of her nose running as though, through her bodily sensations, she was connecting to her vulnerability. She could still deny this vulnerability by refusing tissues as this fuelled her need to remain isolated from others for fear of depending on them. Throughout the therapy I had never seen Lauren cry, so it was as though she was 'crying through her nose' and did not want it to be cleared away and ignored. Regressive behaviours acted as an unconscious defence mechanism (Lear 2005). As well as toddler-like tantrums, Lauren rocked and sucked her thumb at this time, too.

Figure 6.7 Desertion

In the next session, Lauren's rather barren sand tray showed the aspects of two homes, one negative, represented by the fallen house and dead trees, and the other positive, represented by the live tree. She perhaps now worried that she would lose the nurturance of the therapeutic space and re-enact having negative experiences following disclosure. Lauren refused offers of help, endangering herself to remain independent. For example, when unable to reach a paint pot on the top shelf, Lauren pushed herself to obtain it alone, demonstrating her inability to rely on others. Instead, danger outweighed her safety as she engaged in independent and risky behaviours where she showed little regard and awareness towards her own well-being.

Figure 6.8 Managing risk

The tray shown in Figure 6.8 highlighted Lauren's early development of internal defences in the sessions, symbolized by the emergency vehicles (Daly 1984). The sexualized doll remained hidden beneath the sand. There is a sense of her beginning to manage risk rather than to ignore danger: both emergency vehicles and a tiger are present. There is also the repeated symbolism of Lauren's instinctual-self (the tiger) and her angelic self (the princess).

Young victims of sexual abuse tend not to know that what has been done to them was wrong and normalization leads them to behaving similarly towards others (Ringrose *et al.* 2012), but Lauren was beginning to demonstrate change in her behaviours.

Figure 6.9 Overpowered

When Lauren knew there were no secrets between the carer and the therapist and that the therapeutic space was safe, disclosures regarding sexual violation by her father were made in session 24. In this session, the symbolism in her sandplay suggested that Lauren was 'revealing her abusers'. Beneath the protective shell was Lauren's true essence (the pearl) hiding. The centipede resembled a physical abuser and the snake, a sexual abuser (Daly 1984), with the mother dragon as witness.

The large, imposing spider gives a reflection of Lauren being smothered or suffocating, overwhelmed by her circumstances. As discussed, Lauren's allegation against her carer was likely to be an act of defence to avoid the pain of being rejected by her carer first. However, this led to a double punishment – Lauren not only felt rejected by one she cared for, but also guilty about hurting her when the allegation was made. Although her therapeutic journey was disrupted, there was emerging evidence that Lauren was becoming more protective of herself (the shell). Around this time she was able to tell a young boy in the playground what he could *not* do to her. If we as therapists can help children to do nothing more than protect themselves from future violation, we are happy.

Conclusions

Being the empathic witness

Being an empathetic witness to highly distressed children can be very demanding on the therapist, especially when there appears to be little change in the therapy. I have found Stendhal's words very containing at such times:

> A very small degree of hope is sufficient to cause the birth of love. (2002, p.16)

It is important not to underestimate the responsibility of a therapist's role in a child's life and his responsibility for protecting the child from further mental, emotional and physical harm. Nowhere is this more crucial than for the sexualized child. Lauren experienced a loss of *essence* – her innate qualities had been suppressed. At the start of therapy, she did not have a clear idea of who she was. Lauren switched between contrasting personas and her process of unfolding was evident. Over time, Lauren found much more of her *self* that had been hiding (from herself as well as others).

In this case, an integrative approach was the most effective I felt, and so, while I represent here her story through images, the work was not limited to this approach only. A diversity and flexibility in approach enhances the opportunity for progress for each individual child. At the heart of the work with often multiply abused young children is my role as an empathic witness, as Alice Miller describes (2008). In this sense I can say that no matter what 'approaches' I might use, there is a single primary therapeutic task.

Children, and therefore child therapy, do not exist in isolation

Part of Lauren's story, partially represented here in the images, was one of repeating trauma and patterns. The past does not disappear even for those encountering trauma very early. It manifests both in ways that can be understood and represented as archetypes in the sand tray, and therefore has some 'universal' nature, but of course also in the very individual re-working of these by the individual child. For therapists, while we must be present for and attend to the individual child we must also remember that he does not exist in isolation. We need to balance our focus with the inclusion of family wherever possible. For me, the key is managing to hold onto some compassion for the parents; understanding the inter-generational nature of sexual abuse in particular helps. It is through this capacity that I believe I stand the best chance of halting the continuation of such abuse.

The importance of consistency and boundaries

The impact of uncertainty in Lauren's external life as presented in the sand tray highlighted how consistency must be extremely high on the priority list of professionals helping such unsettled children. The child is more likely to begin to trust the therapeutic process if the therapist can maintain a space that is consistent. Disrupting this stability leads to the re-experiencing of familiar patterns of abuse and neglect (NICE 2010):

> There will always be reason and circumstance to move and change rules. Yet to give in may seem easy. It is more beneficial to stand your ground. If you continue to give in then stability and structure will not be contained and therefore the learning cannot always be absorbed as it evaporates in the constant change. (Anon, n.d.)

The session when Lauren refused to be helped illustrated the benefits of a consistent space. When she was aware that she would have to move placement – perhaps out of this country – she was at least familiar enough with her therapeutic space to try to take control of that environment. It is because it was a familiar space and she already knew where everything was that she could literally *help herself*. This was a powerful reflection of her being let down by adults, but importantly a reflection which could be worked through in the play. Equally, that stability allowed Lauren to maintain the rules regarding time in the space, and toys staying in the room. The implementation of boundaries is what created that safe space for her.

Be prepared for the wretchedness of rejection

It is fairly commonplace that children in care will pre-empt a perceived inevitable rejection in their placements by actions designed to end the placements themselves. Many will also 'trash' the therapist on ending – sometimes ending abruptly to avoid the pain of letting go (see Chapter 8). Particularly in working with the sexualized child, this is something that therapists should be better prepared to deal with. It is not a personal rejection, but rather another means of the child coping with saying goodbye to something that he treasured – like the innocence that a sexualized child would have lost.

In her final session, Lauren gave her therapist a doll to hold and protect saying,'Take care of the baby.' Lauren displayed once again how fragile her own ability was to hold and protect the child that she was at this time of trauma, loss and separation, but also I felt that she had managed to experience the therapy and the therapist as a safe place to some degree.

Lauren's journey

Lauren's experiences left her feeling helpless and dependent on others hearing and understanding her emotional reality. However, due to betrayals and deception, Lauren – like the character Charlotte – was eventually caught and confined within a web that encouraged a cycle of enmeshment, entrapment, infringement and enticement. From Lauren's symbolic language, in which she also verbalized being fed ants in our sessions, one can hypothesize that she had felt terrors of being eaten alive, having no escape and being open to complete violation. Like Charlotte, Lauren would await nothing but a sure death with her own internal world and fragmented sense of self-identity.

While no therapy is 'curative' she was able through our therapeutic relationship and the work through 'play' to externalize helpfully what had previously been experienced as internal chaos and to move towards, as I have described, some re-integration of a self that was previously fragmented, obscured and often punitive. I was able to witness her progress towards a healthier potential for relationships, and this was powerful and special for me.

Chapter 7

'Can I Go Home?'

Art Psychotherapy with Foster Children Returning to Their Birth Family

ELEANOR HAVSTEEN-FRANKLIN

Introduction

Research consistently shows that children in care are more vulnerable, with high levels of arrested physical and psychological development (Roth and Fonagy 2004), and are more likely to develop mental health problems (Golding 2003; McCann *et al.* 1996; Rodrigues 2004 cited in Baron 2012). Consequently, many of these children require psychotherapy to address their emotional needs.

It is essential for the therapist to recognize and acknowledge the child's love for her parents. Her loyalty towards her parents is expressed in many ways. The family in which she has grown up will usually have been her 'lived experience' of family life, including the abuse and neglect (Cooper 2011). Over the years her powerful feelings of anger towards her parents are often defended against and repressed as a means of survival as well as an unconscious recognition that her parent/s cannot manage such feelings. For different reasons, the child often holds a conscious or unconscious belief that it is their fault that she went into care. This may be for a number of reasons; possibly the parent's feelings have been projected onto the child, or due to inadequate parenting the child may be parentified. Often also the child may have made the disclosure leading to social care involvement. It may also be that the child has omnipotent feelings linked to her stage of development (see also Chapter 5).

For a child in care to begin to recognize different complex feelings of anger, rage, abandonment, rejection and often also guilt and confusion, it can be a slow, non-linear therapeutic process. Art psychotherapy facilitates image making and play and is particularly suitable for those clients who struggle with verbalizing thoughts and feelings (Case and Dalley 2014). This chapter presents two case studies on children in care returning home: one focuses on the presenting relational and attachment dynamics and the other on the role of the art psychotherapy. Therapeutic alliances (Stern 1998) had been established as they had both been receiving weekly art psychotherapy for a year before returning home, using a wide range of art materials, dolls house, toys and sand tray.

Alica and James and their siblings were referred to the specialist mental health team (SMHT) before the court judgements for them to be returned to their mother's care were made. Through their work on self-esteem and assertiveness, both mothers had ended abusive relationships with their husbands. Both children experienced a change of social worker and foster placement and separation from their siblings. Consequently, the relationship with their therapist provided a connection between birth family and the different foster care relationships.

Returning home: establishing a therapeutic alliance with the birth family

The loss that both the foster family and the child may experience needs to be thought about when a child returns home. Furthermore, the birth family may feel threatened by this attachment, which can leave the child having to manage complicated loyalty issues. There may be active or residual feelings of suspicion from both sides, with agencies carrying the 'blame' for the children going into care and parents feeling angry, misjudged, criticized and wary of relationships with different services. There is potential for complicated interpersonal dynamics and splitting on several levels between birth family, foster carers and professional agencies, and it is beneficial to have regular multi-professional meetings to prevent this (see Chapter 11).

There are many practical and psychological issues to consider once a court decides to return a child home to the parent's or parents' care. This decision often creates a shift for the therapist in terms of counterbalancing feelings of protectiveness and the need to develop a collaborative alliance with the parent/s. To maintain the therapeutic alliance, it is important that the child's love for her parent, despite the abuse and neglect, is recognized in the transition home. A therapeutic alliance also needs to be established with the family. The two case studies will consider the different emotional and relational aspects and the role of art psychotherapy.

CASE STUDY: ALICA

Alica was six years old when she was taken into care along with three younger siblings aged five, three and under one year. She had a different father to her younger siblings. Her mother and stepfather had arrived in the UK when Alica was four months old. Mother spoke fairly good English, but had no family support and a limited social network. Alica had taken on a caring role with her younger siblings, doing significant tasks such as feeding and nappy changing. Once she was placed in foster care with her three-year-old sister Beth, foster carers found Alica's complex emotional needs difficult to manage and two placements broke down in quick succession. The second foster carers struggled particularly to manage the difficult dynamics between the sisters, and Alica was placed alone with older, experienced foster carers where she settled well. These multiple placement breakdowns within her first year in care mirrored early life experiences of rejection and failure.

Described as a 'very disturbed child' by professionals and carers, Alica was referred to the SMHT after nine months in care due to her aggressive, defiant and impulsive behaviour, mood swings and difficulty with forming relationships with caregivers and other children.

The wish to return home was a recurrent theme throughout her therapy. Alica's siblings returned home over a four-month period, with Alica returning last. She experienced this as another rejection from her mother and reacted very badly. On returning home after being in foster care for 22 months, Alica's individual sessions evolved to include her mother. As well as being an ongoing wish from Alica, the provision of this therapeutic space enabled reconnecting, repairing and positive development of the mother/child relationship by thinking about and reinforcing positive parental role-modelling to the mother and increasing her confidence in her parenting.

Alica's art psychotherapy: theory into practice

Bowlby (1982, cited in Western 1991) stated that disturbed attachments in the first three to four years of a child's life shape the internal working model of relational patterns and disrupt the formation of a ***secure emotional base***. The early relational trauma that Alica had experienced became evident in her poor affect regulation and her stress-coping mechanisms principally being fight or flight responses. Affect regulation is fundamental for the infant's evolving sense of self: 'The baby's social-emotional relatedness of the early environment is the setting in which the infant's inner world is constructed' (Case and Dalley 2008, p.3).

Alica's first year in therapy was dominated by alternating and extreme challenging behaviours. A strong maternal transference developed early in the therapeutic relationship, expressing both Alica's need to be mothered and negative hostile feelings. There was also a strong pattern in her role plays. She was often a baby sucking on her thumb or wanting to be fed with a baby bottle followed by a tragic turning of events that reflected feelings of abandonment and grief. At other times the therapist would have to be the child and Alica would be the scolding parent: 'Why have you got all the wrong things? You are a bad, bad girl...this is why you have to go... No, you can't live here anymore... You have to go to prison now!' Projecting her frustrations, Alica would spit, hit out and throw objects shouting: 'You are rubbish! I hate you! Nobody loves you!' with the therapist's words or (re)actions often experienced as a rejection and confirmation of her being 'rubbish'. Thus, Alica communicated her acute sense of feeling unloved and her fear that the therapist would also reject her.

The engagement with the art materials in art therapy has often been compared to pre-verbal exploration (Dalley 1984; Rubin 1999). For Alica this engagement was sometimes cathartic, but could become regressive and chaotic. It seemed to be indicative of her functioning at an earlier developmental stage and a 'retreat from relating' (O'Brien 2008). As O'Brien (2008) describes, 'Constructing an image is difficult to even conceive of – the only process available at this stage is the bodily felt chaos of dissociated feelings in the making of sloppy mixtures or disconnected marks' (p.41).

Alica explored sensory elements: touching clay, sand and paints and mixing the different art materials. She had a very short attention span and her mark making and imagery was that of a much younger child.

Figure 7.1 Alicia

Alica's work showed how difficult it was for her to think symbolically, and instead the image seemed to be focused on bodily experiences. Alica made painterly prints with her hands, gestural marks with crayons and pens and constantly listed her family members, as if her identity was dependent on her existence in relation to them. Over time the therapist's name was included in the list as a concrete reference point that supported Alica's own sense of self, reflecting the supportive function of the therapeutic alliance. Alica's feelings of deprivation and boundary testing were expressed in how she was never satisfied; she never had 'enough' of the paints, glitter or length of session – never had enough of what she wanted or needed. The therapist in turn felt overwhelmed by Alica's unrelenting demands and remaining calm was a challenge. When Alica was physically out of control, hitting out and throwing things around, the therapist would return to the basic boundaries of keeping each other safe – a few times ending the session early and sitting in the waiting room for the rest of the session. Alica struggled to make sense of her actions and the work often entailed trying to help her to articulate her feelings, without being overwhelmed by them.

Alica's emotional development was clearly delayed and there had not been a healthy resolution of the first individuation process, which is usually completed at the end of the child's third year (Blos 1967). She seemed to easily regress to the toddler phase with constant testing of boundaries and irrational behaviour mirroring the toddler's frustration with dependence and a wish for control (Case and Dalley 2008). Over the course of the next eight months Alica's extreme behaviour lessened. She settled into her foster placement, and in therapy began to internalize a caring parental figure that could contain the angry and destructive projections. She became more able to listen and respond to the therapist's reflections, her behaviour became less defensive and an increasing ability to self-regulate was evident, i.e. noticing herself if she was becoming 'high' with emotions. It was also evident in the narrative of the role plays where the events and endings became less violent and destructive.

Joint sessions: 'making pictures with Mum'

Stern notes 'Affect attunement, then, is the performance of behaviours that express the quality of feeling of a shared affect state without imitating the exact behavioural expression of the inner state' (Stern 1985, p.142). Winnicott (1971) describes such 'imitation' as *mirroring*. He saw it as an essential part of the baby's ego development, where the mother responds accordingly to the baby's expressions, enabling the baby to feel understood and loved by the mother. Kohut (1971) further developed these ideas looking at the failure of sufficient levels of empathy from the caregiver. This may result in an inability to tolerate momentary lack of gratification and generating tremendous swings between over evaluation and devaluation of self and others, sense of entitlement and lack of identity integration (Western 1991). After several months of joint sessions, her mother was consistently very thoughtful and sensitive to Alica in her responses.

Alica needed to feel her mother's love throughout each session in both a physical and emotional sense. The use of art materials was an important part of helping her mother to provide containment and establishing sensitive boundaries with Alica through play and art making together. In Alica's art making with her mother she was able to express her need for mirroring and compensating for what she had missed out on in her early childhood. At first Alica was very anxious about her mother mirroring her, wanting her mother to use the exact same colour, paint the same shape and so on. If her mother did something different to Alica, she found this very hard, getting upset and sometimes reacting by refusing to continue the activity. She seemed to experience this as an annihilation of her 'self' and a further rejection by her mother. Her mother was able to respond to these moments in a caring and attuned manner. In the sessions, the triggered feelings of rejection and the importance of her feeling loved by her mother would gently be thought and talked about. Alica often struggled with direct communication about painful issues, but found the conversation between the adults more manageable. This model of reflecting offers the child a possibility of listening and thinking about the conversation (Ewers and Havsteen-Franklin 2012).

The reparative process

Alica's decreasing need to control the environment paralleled an increasing trust in her mother (and the therapist) to care for her, as well as getting on better with her siblings and being able to form and maintain friendships at school. Alica also moved from being very protective of her mother, evident in several ways such as making sure she was winning in games, protecting her mother from her angry feelings and depositing her projections containing the negative feelings of the 'bad neglectful mother' and 'absent and hostile fathers' on her therapist. It was as if unconsciously Alica was not sure her mother could tolerate these hostile feelings and feared the consequence of yet another rejection.

During the course of their joint therapy these behaviours decreased, indicating that Alica was slowly establishing a stronger sense of self with less splitting in her behaviour towards her mother and her therapist. This shift was also seen two years into her therapy when, outside the 'make believe' role play, she called her therapist 'a kind lady'.

A more secure attachment to her mother formed, where she was able to express to her mother how she truly felt. These changes were also noticed in Alica's imagery, which became more mature and symbolic. She created the image of the two of them together, which was a powerful experience for them, both returning to this image over several sessions.

Later, she added a little dog called 'Cutie' to the picture. Through Cutie Alica began to talk about her difficult feelings towards her mother, saying, 'Cutie really didn't like you mummy when you didn't let her in. You need to say sorry to Cutie because it was really cold outside.' This signified her ability to begin to explore the relational dynamic through metaphor.

Figure 7.2 Alicia, Mum and Cutie

After this, Alica was able to think and talk about her own anger, and begin the slow process of refuting her unconscious fantasy that she went into care because she was 'a bad child', but rather when she went into care, her mother '...was in a very sad place'. Her mother was able to reflect on her inability to care for Alica at the time, and expressed her feelings of guilt. Alica moved from blaming the local authority for removing her to understanding her mother's 'sad' story. However, it is likely that these early experiences of neglect and foster care will be revisited and questioned many times around the significant life stages, particularly if Alica herself becomes a mother.

CASE STUDY: JAMES

James was nine years old when he was referred to the SMHT. He was taken into care with his three siblings, two older sisters and a younger sister, because of domestic violence from the father towards the mother and children, as well as emotional abuse. His mother was very isolated and her only practical and emotional support was from an elderly maternal aunt. Initially James and his siblings were placed together with elderly paternal relatives but this was unsuitable as a long-term placement. They were subsequently placed together in a foster placement, which broke down after six months.

The siblings were then split between three foster placements: James was placed on his own and although he struggled with 'losing' his siblings he settled fairly well. He remained at this placement for nine months until his return home. James was referred to the SMHT because of severe night terrors and his aggressive and destructive behaviour, which seriously affected his relationships and education, leading to school exclusion. He was referred to art psychotherapy five months after going into foster care. When asked about why he was in care he answered, 'because my dad attacked me'. Typically, James would speak of his father and the violence in the family home in this matter of fact way.

Art psychotherapy with James

In his first session James created a scenario in the sand tray of being caught in a war, with five children – almost buried – trying to hide in the sand between two fighting armies saying: 'The children are camouflaging themselves so they don't get seen. I don't know why they are fighting.'

Figure 7.3 Battlefield

The theme of violence continued repeatedly, externalizing his feelings of traumatic past events and fear of rejection by the therapist, because of his violent and aggressive imagery. This perhaps mirrored father's volatile behaviour in the family home and his own aggressive behaviour. James revised this theme by hiding baby animals in the sand session after session. He seemed to be both expressing how he had managed in the family home by dissociating/burying difficult feelings but also showing his need to be protected and 'held in mind' between the sessions.

James began to think about how he could manage his own anger. He first started exploring his fascination with 'The Incredible Hulk' and painting his hands green, talking about his own anger getting out of hand: 'Just like Hulk...he sometimes gets out of control...but Betty helps him to manage it.'

Over time he expressed his worry about how difficult it was to manage his anger saying, 'I wish it could just go away.' With this recognition, James began the process of exploring how he hadn't felt protected and safe in his family. He added, 'I wish I had been safe at home.'

James began to think about identity and belonging. He initially idealized and spoke with respect for his father, but through the imagery he began to talk about the painful and frightening side of father, which scared him. His confusion around the violence was expressed in a series in the sand tray where he created different scenarios with animals. He asked the therapist, 'Who would you save?' adding, 'I would save the chicken rather than the baby...', as if wondering whether the therapist cared enough about the baby/him to save the baby/him. This was James's way of expressing his insecurities about whether adults can, and do, protect children and his experience that adults can't be trusted.

James enjoyed the individual attention and space and was always reluctant to end the session. In the early sessions he expressed his worry about whether the therapist could be trusted in several ways: he created lots of gingerbread men and expressed his fear of being tricked and eaten. He tested the therapist by questioning several times about other children coming to the clinic. This interest in other children led to thinking about his relationships with his siblings and their dynamics. He felt lonely away from his siblings, but he had experienced a different way of family life through foster care, which he liked. Furthermore, he was no longer troubled by nightmares.

Returning home

James had started his gradual return to full-time mainstream education when the court decided that all of the children should be returned home. James's mother, with the continuing support of her maternal aunt, had ended the violent relationship with their father and he had moved out. There was a phased return home over the period of one month. Over the following four months the family was supported by daily visits from a home support team.

James continued with individual sessions and his mother engaged well with the SMHT, coming in for review meetings and also communicating regularly via telephone. They all received family therapy with a colleague, as well as family meetings with both therapists. James was very excited about returning home, saying, 'I think it will be better...mum has got better at managing us.'

However, James was also very anxious; his internal conflicts around his parents reuniting intensified as he feared that his mother would not be able to manage them without his father. This anxiety was communicated in several ways; for example, during one session he suddenly emptied the whole sand tray out on the floor, a behaviour that was very unlike him in the sessions. It was also made very visible in the form of what he described as 'dangerous erupting volcanoes'.

The use of clay to embody anger in art psychotherapy

James made many volcanoes in clay over the next months, repeatedly reworking, hitting and moulding it. Dalley (2008) reflects on the use of clay: 'The sense of clay having "a body" that can survive punishment is useful as the pliability of the clay encourages aggression to be overtly expressed. Giving shape to pent up feelings develops a sense of mastery, potency and self-esteem' (p.77).

James was eventually able to give words to his fears, saying, 'They are erupting and exploding volcanoes, which are dangerous if you go near them... Yes, you never know when it is going to happen.'

Figure 7.4 Exploding volcanoes

He was able to connect this to his own behaviour. When asked if it sometimes felt as if he might get so angry that he would erupt, James answered in a relieved way, 'Yes'. Later in his therapy he was able to link this also to his father's volatile behaviour. Paint was added over several sessions saying, 'The paint is like the lava, it keeps spilling out...'

The volcanoes seemed to express the fascination, unpredictability and potential danger of his father as well as his own sense of repressed anger. Through the models of the volcanoes, James talked about a whole spectrum of emotions: feelings of powerlessness and of fury, saying, 'I am cross with dad, and cross with the judge', and his genuine feeling of loss and confusion about his father, saying, 'I miss my dad 100 per cent.' James agreed with the reflection that he wanted to forget how his dad hurt him and the family, but also wanted his therapist to know how much he still loved his dad. The volcano models enabled James to become conscious of, and work through, ambivalent feelings towards his father and himself.

Metaphor in art psychotherapy

Although he was pleased to be home, James struggled with his mother becoming more confident and assertive in her parenting and this led to more challenging behaviour as he adjusted to the many changes.

Over time, James was expressive in creating layers in various containers from different materials, such as paint and sand. He would return to these objects, uncovering and discovering the different textures and colours, describing them as volcanic rock and earth surfaces. He thought of himself as an archaeologist discovering prehistoric truths. This unfolding discovery also seemed to mirror the ability to create his own personal narrative where he was able to think about why he had gone into care, his feelings about this, his ambivalence towards both his parents and acceptance of his father no longer living in the home. He created a personal hero figure that he described as 'good fighting over evil', saying, 'He has different sides to him but he has chosen to be good and help people.' Likewise 'Hulk' emerged again, with James painting his hands and saying, 'I am Bruce and more calm...it is time for Hulk to go into himself...'

The volcanoes and 'archaeological containers' became metaphors, as they were not just cathartic experiences and concrete representations but they enabled James to stand back and reflect on how the volcano represented his anger. The metaphor represented a relational condition, occurring only when he could begin to mentalize his own and others experiences (Fonagy, Gergely and Jurist 2003). As he felt cared for, this mentalization process was essential in helping him to empathize so that he could become aware of and understand others, enabling him to have more constructive relationships with his family and peers. This helped the process of repairing and nurturing the relationship with his mother, who was now his sole carer.

Images as a vehicle for communication

Through the imagery James could begin to communicate his difficult feelings to his mother, particularly around his angry feelings about not being protected from the violence and the feelings of abandonment and the loss of the father in the family home. It was very important for James to bring to his mother's awareness that he still cared for his father. His mother joined a review session and through the conversations around the images it helped to facilitate his mother's understanding and acceptance that James still loved his father despite everything that had happened. His father was able to sustain limited supervised contact with his children. At the review, his mother expressed her opinion that 'A child belongs in the family home with their mother.' This was important for James to hear and part of the process of strengthening his trust in his mother. As Western discusses (1991): 'The extent to which a child can make use of others to self-soothe and to provide a home base for security from which to explore is seen as a crucial individual difference variable with life span implications' (p.431).

James's experience of family life after his return home was completely different. His mother also understood his needs better and tried to help him to feel more loved and safe at home. However, as he grows into adolescence, his ambivalent relationship to his father is likely to impact on one of the key tasks of adolescence, which is separation. He will be looking to loosen his ties with his primary attachments, which will be complicated by early life experiences of domestic violence.

Conclusion

This chapter discussed Alica and James's journeys back home to their mothers' care. Alica had a strong sense of being 'unlovable' due to early neglect that was intensified by going into care and the repeated placement breakdowns. James experienced domestic violence that manifested itself in his volatile and aggressive behaviour towards family members and others. There were marked differences in the behaviour and capacity for relating as can be seen through their images, as well as their relationships both inside and outside the therapeutic space.

For James, the sense of a good enough mother (Winnicott 1971) was much more evident in the positive transference material, where the therapist was viewed as a companion to explore the world around him. He was able to use the space to express himself through art and play materials but was also able to talk about his experiences. This contrasted greatly with Alica's interactions where the therapist often had the experience that Alica expected the therapist to fail her and fall apart, usually in a humiliating way. The therapist's countertransference was commonly that of feeling worthless and useless, reflecting a harsh judgemental quality in relation to Alica's experience of feeling very fragile. The pace of change was slow but Alica could eventually experience good enough care and was able to enjoy and sustain positive relationships. When she returned to her mother's care, this process continued and was strengthened by dyadic art psychotherapy sessions.

Creating a trusting therapeutic alliance with the mothers took time, as there were issues around fear and distrust of authority. Any residual or unresolved issues impact on the process of engagement and the ability to engage with therapy. These could be issues that are transgenerational, leading to the transmission of dysfunctional attachment patterns and/or poor internalized parenting model, where the parent is seeking to be parented themselves and is unable to consider the emotional needs of her children. In Alica and James' case the child/parent bond ultimately became stronger and healthier.

Through the art and play, painful and difficult feelings were communicated and understood with the help of the therapist. Their mothers were both able to accept her child's ambivalent feelings, engage in the reparation process and develop their ability to attune, reflect and respond appropriately to their children's emotional needs.

Chapter 8

'The Anarchy and the Ecstasy'

The Therapeutic Journey with Children in Care

JEUNE GUISHARD-PINE AND HANNAH BARON

> Anarchy: 'A theory that proposes the cooperative and voluntary association of individuals and groups as the principal mode of organized society.'[1]

Introduction: the limitations of attachment-based psychotherapy with the children in care

Attachment relationships are seen to play an important role in the aetiology of mental health difficulties (Bowlby 1969, 1973). Bowlby (1988) developed his original theory to suggest that an attachment to the therapist provides a significant springboard for recovery to psychological health. Child mental health clinics across the UK receive a steady flow of referrals of children in care, most of whom are described as having *conduct disorder* or an *emotional disorder* (Dimigen, Del Priore and Butler 1999; Meltzer *et al.* 2003). However, despite the ongoing controversies of the diagnosis and of attachment theory itself[2] many children in care are described as having an *attachment disorder* or *attachment difficulties*[3] (Minnis *et al.* 2006). There is a paucity of research into which interventions are effective with children in care (Blower *et al.* 2004; Cocker and Scott 2006). More specifically, there is no known definitive or effective therapy to treat attachment disorders

---

1 www.thefreedictionary.com/anarchy

2 For example, to see the debate, refer to Badulf, J. (2005) *Can We Use Attachment Theory as a Basis for this 'Attachment Disorder?* Rochester Institute of Technology and Wood M. (2005) *Reactive Attachment Disorder: A Disorder of Attachment or of Temperament?* Rochester Institute of Technology. Available at www.personalityresearch.org/papers/wood.html

3 The NICE scoping exercise highlighted data to suggest that only 10 per cent of children in care had a secure attachment to their parents. In contrast, an estimated 80 per cent of children who suffer maltreatment are classified as having disorganized attachment (NICE 2013).

in children in care (Aslam 2012; British Association of Adoption and Fostering 2006; O'Connor and Zeanah 2003; Puckering *et al.* 2011; Ratnayake, Bowlay-Williams and Vostannis 2014).

While attachment difficulties are not an inevitable consequence for children in care, many are likely to have greater exposure to weak or broken attachments characterized by rejection (Howe and Fearnley 2003). It is believed that many children in care may experience issues with attachment relationships to some degree. Regrettably, once in care, some children experience a variety of placements and professional input, resulting in further disruption to their attachment relationships.

Attachment-focused interventions typically emphasize the importance of establishing secure relationships. Howe and Fearnley (2003) proposed that children in care take different pathways to relationships, which are dependent on the type of early experiences they have endured. They suggested that many children in care will have developed strategies such as control and avoidance when forming new relationships, resulting in them aiming to control and not engage with people (Howe and Fearnley 2003). Golding and Hughes (2012) propose that the role of the therapist is to adopt an attitude of playfulness, acceptance, curiosity and empathy. While there is some evidence to support the positive effects of dyadic developmental psychotherapy (DDP) (Hughes 2005), it is not intended as direct psychotherapy with children in care.

The therapeutic relationship with children in care

There is some evidence to suggest that children in care want permission to be a legitimate co-worker in the interventions offered to treat them (Bowman and SCIE 2007; Department for Education and Department of Health 2015; Furnivall *et al.* 2012). The Cocker review (2004) highlighted that specialist child mental health services for children in care were mostly provided by social workers and clinical psychologists who indicated that the most common types of therapy they used were 'non-specific therapeutic techniques'. However, the review did not clearly define the term 'non-specific therapeutic techniques' nor did it explore the views and wishes of children in care as to whether or not this approach to therapy was useful and positive.

Taking on board the idea of the 'voice of the child', this chapter heralds the somewhat anarchic (cooperative, voluntary and organized) aspects of practising eclectic psychotherapy as an approach to individual psychotherapy with children in care. Eclectic psychotherapy will suggest that different people have different needs and consequently they will require different approaches at different times. While the idea of therapy being anarchic is intended to be 'playful' (Golding and Hughes 2012), the idea of co-creating the therapeutic relationship is serious: 'Co-creative processes produce unique forms of being together, not only in the mother–infant relationship, but in all relationships. Co-creation emphasizes dynamic and unpredictable changes of relationships that underlie their uniqueness' (Tronick 2007, p.476).

Anarchic therapy highlights that each individual has changing needs across the duration of therapy and the therapist's focus needs to be on maintaining a viable and valid relationship with the children in care. Thus anarchic therapy highlights the benefits of focusing on the therapeutic relationship rather than techniques. Moran (2010) noted that 'the relationship between the therapist and the child was the vehicle for the therapy' (p.47). Her research supported the notion of the importance of a focus on the quality of the therapeutic relationship – the 'emotional feel' – for children with attachment difficulties. This is largely supported by James (1994).

The importance of the therapeutic relationship is a well established feature of successful therapeutic work. Hence, the work should 'focus on therapist's "being" qualities rather than "doing" skills' (Spinelli 2005, p.173). This is consistent with literature suggesting therapeutic orientation might be secondary to other factors in distinguishing effective therapies (Stiles, Shapiro and Elliot 1986). In the main, practitioners of eclectic psychotherapy are described as pragmatic (Norcross and Prochaska 1988). Such practitioners are primarily concerned with what works, delivering a bespoke package to address individual need.

This chapter also draws on recent qualitative research on how children in care experience and evaluate the therapeutic journey. The research focuses more specifically on the ending of the therapeutic relationship. It looks at the inferences that can be drawn about the quality and benefits of the active therapeutic relationship based on 'being' rather than 'doing'. Thus, contrary to somewhat contemporary approaches to measuring *outcomes* as simplistic scores on numerous rating scales, anarchic therapy explicitly considers recovery as a journey rather than a destination.

Theoretical underpinnings that complement an anarchic approach

Far from being about disarray and chaos, anarchic therapy is organized around the thinking of humanistic and existential psychology. This is seen as focusing on the accumulation of experiences that contribute to the personal growth of an individual and places a corresponding emphasis on psychological constructs such as feelings of intimacy, loss, security, belonging and self-love. It embraces the existential assumption of the essential uniqueness of human experience and the need to be authentic: there will only ever be one you. Thus, no matter how hard you try to be like someone else or how much someone else tries to be like you the incontrovertible fact is you are the only person who will score 100 per cent for being you. Regardless of one's stance on the relevance of the theoretical model to the work of the therapist, the unavoidable paradox in any therapeutic relationship is that someone who is not you can assist and support an individual in deepening his understanding of himself, that is, the essential 'you'. This then reinforces the reality that one size can never fit all when it comes to psychotherapy: we are all individuals. Tronik (2007) had this to say:

> Other than lip-service reiteration of an overly general and featureless belief that 'of course relationships are unique', little thought has been devoted to questions related to the uniqueness of relationships: How do relationships come to be unique? What are some of the features of their uniqueness? It is a striking oversight because in our work with patients we always work with the unique. (p.474)

The 'fourth force' in psychotherapy is that, increasingly, practitioners will be expected to be prepared to flexibly meet the needs of patients who not only present with multiple issues at one time, but who also come from a range of ethnic and family cultures. Therefore, approaches should be multi-theoretical and move towards integrative psychotherapy (Brooks-Harris 2008; Crittenden 1997; Jones-Smith 2012).

In her study of the experiences of children in care of ending therapy, the second author was able to access qualitative data on the rich experiences of therapeutic relationships of children in care. Other researchers have attempted to examine the differential effects of attachment to therapist and the experience of therapy (Lilliengren

2011; Lilliengren *et al.* 2014: both cited in Liliengren *et al.* 2015). Rather than being an attempt to investigate the complex matrix of variables that potentially influence the outcomes of therapy, Baron's study, which sampled narratives with children in care who had concluded their therapeutic journey, revealed that irrespective of the theoretical model, all of the children in care felt the therapeutic relationship was a significant factor in the therapy experience. Her study revealed ways in which therapists may work with children in care to maximize gains of therapy which are guided by the young people themselves.

A study into the therapeutic journey of children in care

The development of the therapeutic relationship is common practice among many treatment models, and empirical research supports how it benefits the process, particularly with individuals who experience trauma in their lives (Paley and Lawton 2001). In support of this view, Mann (2005) conducted an in-depth qualitative study using interpretative phenomenological analysis (IPA) methodology to explore how children in care experience mental health services. Among a broad range of findings, this study revealed that children in care reflect on the uniqueness of the therapeutic relationship, which seemed to offer a degree of consistency often lacking in other areas of their lives. Mann's study explored the views of children in care and demonstrated the importance of the therapist relationship with them but did not examine the process of therapy itself.

The findings from Baron's study confirmed the value of focusing on the therapeutic relationship. Her study was prompted by her direct experience. She was struck by the range of responses that clients expressed, both verbally and in their behaviour when she came to the end of her placement as a trainee clinical psychologist and consequently had to end their therapy. In short, she became crucially aware of the existential given that each client had a unique experience of the therapeutic relationship and demonstrated this in their diverse responses. Baron had this to say:

> Although the young people described that ending therapy was not on a same level as other experiences in their lives, most significantly,

> the experience of coming into care, the feelings created by the end of therapy served to highlight the significant impact that the ending of the therapeutic relationship can have on a young person. The comparison to them leaving their parents and coming into care, for me, demonstrates the significance of the therapy relationship and how this is valued in their lives. (2012, p.66)

Her study adds to the growing body of research demonstrating the importance of supporting young people through the transition to end the therapeutic relationship.

The therapeutic relationship as a model of cooperation

Inherent in the concept of anarchy is the cooperative and voluntary association of individuals – it emphasizes collaboration rather than forced participation or instruction. This is particularly pertinent for children in care, many of whom have a negative experience of being dominated or controlled.

The relationship between control and children in care is evident in the literature (Solomon, George and De Jong 1995). Research has suggested that many children in care are likely to have experienced unpredictable and complicated early lives, resulting in them developing a controlling strategy as a desperate attempt to predict a volatile world (Solomon *et al.* 1995). Beneath a controlling presentation their minds can be filled with dangerous and frightening thoughts and impressions that the world is unsafe and unpredictable (Hodges *et al.* 2003). For these reasons, a sense of cooperation is the keystone of the therapeutic relationship with children in care. The finding in Baron's study that young people experience a sense of unpreparedness together with feeling out of control is consistent with research which highlights the importance of using a collaborative approach in order to facilitate a positive experience of therapy (Baum 2005).

It is important to point out here that the concept of cooperation may engender some concern that this overall message leads to some confusion about the therapist's role and responsibilities: that somehow a cooperative relationship cannot sufficiently give the child the boundaries and limits that it needs in order to grow emotionally and socially. However, there is the competing view that cooperation is the *only* way to model safety in relationships (Gianino and Tronick 1988). Cooperation involves people working together towards the same goals. In the case of therapy, it is working towards psychological health in an ethical way.

The therapeutic relationship as co-created

Humanistic psychotherapy has as its central concept the idea that the client and the therapist must work together to create the conditions to maximize personal growth (Rogers 1961). Existential psychotherapy starts with the belief that people feel conflicted about the fact that we are essentially alone in the world because we long to be connected to others (Yalom 1980). Hence we struggle to be free from the anxiety and frustration that we feel because we cannot always have the quality (and quantity) of the meaningful relationships that we want. The individual therefore must be facilitated to accept that ultimately who he is and who he wants to be is always generated from within him, and therefore he always has a free choice about how he reacts to his experiences, including how he reacts to what the therapist does or says. Therefore, it is like a 'dance' (Gianino and Tronick 1988).

Thus, the child in care that is 'acting-out', furious and intolerable can, in the course of therapy, find that the therapist can tolerate his justifiable fury. It is that tolerance that makes him feel safe. The child gains confidence that the therapist will support him on a journey through the fire until he can begin to make a choice about how and when to express his rage and fury and, more importantly, to understand and accept his anger about what has happened to him (his fury possibly about not having a family life that was safe and nurturing).

In Baron's (2012) study children in care valued having some control and preparedness over the duration of their therapy. She found that the young people experienced ambivalence and uncertainty when the therapeutic relationship was coming to an end based on their underlying cognitions of a need for a world that is controlled and predictable. A further indication of this strong need for control was the young people's attempts to take charge of the ending phase of therapy. This provides an important insight in to what young people may experience when ending therapy, which may be entering an unsafe world.

The therapeutic relationship as a continuing bond

A large proportion of the therapeutic work with children in care is about establishing a therapeutic relationship and fostering new relationships. This reinforces the position that people can learn new ways of relating, reflecting a limitation of focusing exclusively on the early attachment experiences. It is of interest, therefore, how their life experiences and constructions impact on their experience of the duration of the therapeutic relationship.

With his specific experiences of multiple losses of significant relationships, it is intriguing to consider how a child in care comes to experience the therapeutic relationship and, after the process of developing such a relationship, how he then experiences the ending of that relationship.

Baron (2012) found that many of the young people maintained a connection with their therapist post therapy, which is consistent with the experience coined as a 'continuing bond' (Klass, Silverman and Nickman 1996). The connection described by the children in care was in some ways a psychological connection, which seemed to be helpful for most of the participants. This challenges the need for 'letting go', which is seen in earlier literature as essential for overcoming grief (Klass *et al.* 1996). Furthermore, this finding is inconsistent with Bowlby's (1973) original three-stage model for separation and loss, which describes a stage of detachment as essential for healthy development. The trend for 'continuing bonds' is a recent trend in grief literature, which purports that people maintain a link and continue the relationship over time (Klass *et al.* 1996). The maintenance of the connection with their therapist was experienced as comforting, upsetting and also facilitating for the young people in her study. Perhaps such a connection, as experienced by these young people, could be viewed as continuing bonds, consistent with experience of loss.

The therapeutic relationship as a template for future relationships

It is acknowledged that their experience of multiple losses may mean that the ability of children in care to not only initiate, but to also sustain friendships may be impeded (NICE 2010). On a more positive note, their participation in community contexts has been linked to them establishing secure and enduring relationships which have in turn impacted positively on their personal identity and also their need to belong (Hicks *et al.* 2012).

In addition to relational needs of children in care with carers, birth family and professionals, their wider social needs are also recognized within the literature (O'Neill, Holland and Rees 2013). Research into the relational needs of children in care has shown the importance of *being loved* within the provision of a nurturing environment: specifically, that this is associated with high self-esteem and emotional well-being (Dickson, Sutcliffe and Gough 2009). Sinclair (2008) asserts that 'children's happiness and well-being goes up or down with their relationship with the people currently looking after them' (p.5). So what is it that therapists can do to promote 'children's happiness'? How can the therapeutic relationship lead to ecstasy? There is growing evidence that the successful therapeutic relationship can form a blueprint for future relationships.

The evidence from research and from practice is that the saying 'it's not where you start it's where you finish' is a truism. There is one children's board game that exemplifies the journey that children in care can make in the course of a successful therapeutic relationship and that is Snakes and Ladders.[4] In work with children in care, however, Snakes and Ladders is merely an allegory for the ups and downs of life that we all have to accept as inevitable, eternal and infinite. It was not surprising therefore when in Baron's study the children in care who described a positive therapeutic relationship often described the ending phase of therapy as both a positive and negative experience. The study therefore demonstrated the potential for both loss and gain to be experienced during the ending phase of therapy, a finding acknowledged by other researchers (Knox *et al.* 2011).

4 Snakes and Ladders originated in India as a game based on morality called Vaikuntapaali or ParamapadaSopanam (the ladder to salvation). The moral of the game was that a person can attain salvation performing good deeds whereas by doing evil one takes rebirth in lower forms of life. The English counterpart contained the same amount of snakes and ladders on the board. This concept of equality signifies the cultural ideal that for every sin one commits, there exists another chance at redemption.

Therapy as a journey rather than a destination

My caring reflected Erikson's (1963) Trust versus Mistrust stage of infancy, where maternal care, especially through touch, enables basic confidence and trust in the world (Lawrence-Mahrra 2014).

The concept of the therapeutic alliance has developed great emphasis in recent years as the important ingredient in the therapeutic process of psychotherapy for different patient populations (Paley and Lawton 2001). Many treatment models for children in care, such as DDP, focus heavily on developing a strong therapeutic relationship with clients to facilitate change. This is also the aspect of therapy valued by children in care themselves (Mann 2005). This finding begs the question: 'How is therapy, based on developing strong therapeutic relationships, negotiated for this population?'

Baron's study produced evidence that despite their profound multiple experiences of loss, children in care can maintain a potential to form new therapeutic relationships, demonstrating strength and resilience in daring to try again. This positive finding challenges beliefs that children who are deprived, often tragically, reject the help they so badly need, a phenomenon which has been described as 'double deprivation' (Williams 1974). That children in care were able to form these relationships at all signifies the importance of the therapeutic relationship and quest for focusing on the impact of making these connections – and of co-creating.

In their review of the views pertinent to children in care regarding mental health services, Davies and Wright (2008) concluded that despite NICE guidelines focusing on intervention type, other aspects of staff interactions may in fact be more important to children in care. This may be of particular relevance as it demonstrates the potential challenge of adopting prescriptive treatment plans and offering the same approach for all children in care. Therefore, Baron's study and existing literature illuminated the importance of being responsive to the young people's needs and that it is the therapists' attunement with the young person that is significant in the experience of therapy.

The anarchy and the ecstasy? The therapeutic relationship and outcomes for children in care

Consulting relevant literature revealed that little was known about how children in care experience therapy generally (Murphy and Fonagy 2012). In their study of adults, Lilliengren *et al.* (2015) gave us much to think about to challenge an exclusive focus on attachment-based therapies as the intervention/s of choice for children in care. They point out the potential of the therapist's own attachment status being a prerequisite for the child to form a secure attachment to the therapist, which has been questioned in other adult studies (Petrowski *et al.* 2013; Wiseman and Tishby 2014). This is highly controversial, as in order to robustly assess the quality of the child-therapist attachment, it would not only mean that all registered child mental health therapists would need to undergo an assessment of their attachment status, but in order for it to have validity and reliability, studies will have to be done to investigate the differential outcomes using therapists with a range of attachment styles and children in care with a range of attachment styles and diagnoses. Also, their research looks at long-term interventions with adults, whereas in the UK there is a distinct movement towards shorter-term interventions with most children regardless of their needs (Jackson 2012). In addition to this, there is a view that more use should be made of social media and technology due to 'high levels of unmet need' (Murphy and Fonagy 2012, p.9) that would totally circumvent the co-creation of the therapeutic relationship.

The combined ideas presented here suggest that perhaps more research needs to look at the therapeutic relationship and outcomes for children in care as although it formed part of the research, it was not the main focus of Baron's study. However, her study was able to pull together a number of relevant points regarding the significance of the therapeutic relationship in meeting the mental health needs of children in care: the idea of putting the child at the heart of the intervention and the idea of co-creation.

Aligned to the concept of loss, the finding of inevitability of ending the therapeutic relationship and the link to the experience of life itself was an unanticipated finding from Baron's (2012) study. By interviewing adolescents who were looked after about their experiences of ending therapy, this unique outcome emerged. She continued that:

> This is something that I had not come across in the literature review. A key finding from this research was that the young people seemed to approach therapy and subsequently ending therapy, based on a discourse of 'inevitability to end'. (p.91)

This finding may be a reflection of the acceptance of children in care of the 'ups and downs' in life: the agony and the ecstasy. The therapeutic relationship with children in care therefore may be analogous to Tronick and Beeghly's (2011) idea of dyadic synchrony: 'Our dancing is hardly perfect; there are missteps, apologies, tries, retries, match ups, and missteps again.'

It should be borne in mind in our work with children in care that the therapeutic journey is a unique and highly personal process of transition for the children in care. Ultimately, being mindful of this may contribute to better outcomes for their mental health and for building resilience.

Chapter 9

Professionalizing Foster Carers

JEUNE GUISHARD-PINE, SHERI MOSURO
AND DEVINIA MALCOLM

> There is a need for more research on this (Children in care) population, especially in the following areas:
>
> - the value of early intervention and outcomes of different treatments and therapeutic approaches
> - what protects some looked after children from developing mental health problems.
>
> (Mental Health Foundation 2002, p.5)

The mental health needs of children in care

Research conducted in the UK shows that foster carers reported higher scores on child and adolescent mental health problems for their foster children, in comparison to normative data (Maguire 2005). This finding is consistent with results from earlier studies conducted on the foster child population (Bonnet and Welbury 2004; Kelly *et al.* 2003; McCann *et al.* 1996; McCarthy, Janeway and Geddes 2003). Mental health difficulties, it is estimated, are experienced by one in five looked after children (Sempik, Ward and Darker 2008). In addition to this, many children in care are excluded from school, which adds to their vulnerabilities to poor psychological health (Social Exclusion Unit 1998).

Due to the decline in residential care, foster carers are looking after children with ever more complex needs. The *Care Matters: Placement Working Group Report* (Laming 2011) made an impactful case that:

> Foster care gives children the opportunity of living in a family environment, and of experiencing positive role models. With the right support, it offers an effective means of meeting children's needs

> and at the same time recognizes that these young people are likely one day to have their own families. (p.11)

This recommendation has led to a situation where some 48,530 children, or 74 per cent, of the children in care in England, are in a foster placement; a figure that is 4 per cent higher than in 2010 and 15 per cent than in 2007 (House of Commons Education Committee 2013). Overall the limited use of adoption and residential care as options for children in care over the last 20 years has led to increased use of the foster care placement (Harber and Oakley 2012). Consequently, fostering families are more likely to be involved in facilitating the provision of care to children who are experiencing emotional and behavioural difficulties (Department for Children, Schools and Families 2008; Ruegger and Rayfield 1999), placing greater demands and expectations on foster carers to have the knowledge, expertise and skills to care for such children. Young Minds has found that foster carers are consistently people who foster children will trust to share their worries with (Young Minds 2012). This range of factors indicates that the professionalization of foster carers – through training – is an inevitable development across the foster care system.

Foster carer training

The term 'foster carer training' refers to the training or educational process designed to provide foster carers with the skills or information needed for their role. Pasztor and Evans (1992) observed that although parental training dates back as far as the 1800s, foster carer training is a recent development. Group training programmes that were broadly aimed at meeting the needs of foster carers looking after children of all ages have been developed both by the state and private fostering agencies since the late 1960s (Zukoski 1999). Foster carer training developed along two broad lines, the first being skills focused and relating to the developmental needs of children, and the second focusing on helping foster carers develop an understanding of the responsibilities of their role, taking into consideration some of the issues that may arise (Hampson 1985).

The fostering task is potentially easier when the foster carer has good insight into children's emotionality (Howe, Feast and Coster

2002). The work of a specialist CAMHS team for children in care recognizes that the mechanism for reducing the risk of placement breakdown pivots around improving the fit between the foster carer's threshold of tolerance and her understanding and respect for the child's communication of her turmoil. Annexed to this is the hugely important point that the key to foster carers increasing their understanding of children will be accomplished through the parallel process of increasing their self-understanding of why the child evokes a range of feelings in them (Guishard-Pine *et al.* 2007).

Richardson and Lelliott (2003) highlighted the need for training in understanding the mental health needs of children in care. There is some concern that those undertaking the foster care task may not have all the skills and capacities necessary to care for the special needs of children in care, particularly those with challenging behaviour. Therefore, it is essential to gain a deeper insight into what carers themselves own by way of personal background, experience and perception about their role.

Although training programmes have proliferated, there has been minimal evaluative research to determine whether they are effective (Piescher 2013). Some of this research is based on responses to vignettes. There is some limited evidence to suggest differences in the results derived from 'real-life' situations compared with hypothetical situations (Jorm 2000) indicating the need for more 'action' or 'practice-based' research.

This chapter describes the background and research that examined the impact of a counselling skills course on mental health awareness and on foster carers' confidence and competence in responding to the difficult feelings expressed by their foster children. It was found that enhancing their ability to communicate by teaching them counselling skills would enable carers to give more assistance to the children in their care because they would be better equipped to handle emotional conversations with these children (Mosuro, Malcolm and Guishard-Pine 2014).

The need for research into the impact of foster carer training

The White Paper, *Care Matters: Transforming the Lives of Young People* (Department for Children, Schools and Families 2006) stated that 'carer stress and the need to respond to difficult behaviour account for a high proportion of placement breakdowns' (paras 3.28ff). It is now more commonly believed that one of the important factors for successful outcomes of foster carer placement is foster carer training. Research has repeatedly identified the need for training for foster carers to increase their responsiveness to troubled children. Although foster carers generally appreciate training, so far there has been no research to demonstrate a link between the level of training and placement success (Sinclair, Gibbs and Wilson 2004). In contrast, a lack of training was associated with failed placements (Runyan and Fullerton 1981).

Training interventions focused on a variety of areas including discipline (Chamberlain *et al.* 2008), challenging behaviour (Macdonald and Turner 2005), attachment (Sprang 2009) and co-parenting (Linares *et al.* 2006). Described as a 'dearth' of evaluation of mental health training (Burton 2012), there is limited evidence of the effectiveness of foster carer training programmes in the longer term (Davies, Webber and Briskman 2015).

There have been three reviews relevant to foster carer training:

- A Cochrane Review by Turner, Macdonald and Dennis (2007) focused on cognitive behavioural training programmes for foster carers managing difficult behaviour but found little supporting evidence and recommended further research.
- Dorsey *et al.* (2008) was a USA study that reviewed one type of foster carer training and found little evidence to support it. However, their findings were not of more general application.
- A very much wider systematic review of any type of intervention on foster and kinship care by Kinsey and Schlösser (2013) covered 30 studies relating to 20 interventions, most of which were with children.

The evidence presented suggests that counselling skills could be helpful in the development of mental health awareness by enhancing the communication skills of foster carers. It also suggests that counselling skills could develop an individual's ability to cope through enhancing communication skills. Although this is not the first research into the impact of training on the well-being of foster children (e.g. Boyd and Remy 1978; Gibbs, Sinclair and Wilson 2004; Hampson, Schulte and Ricks 1983; Lee and Holland 1991; Simon and Simon 1982), it is the first that examines the impact of a formally accredited child mental health course (Fostering Network 2012; Skills for Care 2012).

The professionalization of foster carers

There is a current drive for all professionals working with children in care to access specialist training so that they make adequate responses to the complex needs of this vulnerable group of young people (Department for Education and Department of Health 2015; NICE 2010). In the *Care Matters* paper (Department for Children, Schools and Families 2006) the UK government of the day made the call for foster carers to become more professional, with more training and support. The paper further acknowledged that carers cannot simply be expected to rely on 'normal' parenting skills when caring for children whose responses are complicated by a history of ill treatment, neglect or challenging behaviour. Accordingly, these changing demands denote a level of professionalization that should be acknowledged. On the face of it, full professionalization seems a neat and plausible solution to some of the problems faced by foster carers. Research has shown recurrent issues of recruitment and retention of foster carers, with social services departments losing as many as 30 per cent annually (Colton, Roberts and Williams 2008). As the assessment process takes up to one year, this wastes resources and, more importantly, can intensify children's mental health needs due to recurrent losses from moves. Recognizing foster care as a profession, with a commensurate salary, might well attract more people into opening their homes, so helping ease the chronic shortfall across the UK.

Increased training will enable foster carers to be better equipped to support children in care in their path to recovery. The House of Commons Children, Schools and Families Committee report (2009) on children in care suggested that a national register should be set up which would improve the take-up of training and cement the status of foster carers in the teams of professionals caring for a child (para 94). Educating foster carers about the adverse effects of untreated mental health problems in children in care may also be of benefit.

However, there is a potential collision between the goal of the government to 'professionalize' foster carers and the lack of higher education among carers (Maguire 2005). The establishment of an accredited course in child and adolescent mental health was seen as a way of forming a bridge between these two facts.

The need for mental health awareness among foster carers

Mental health awareness as an aspect of mental health literacy can prevent deterioration in mental health and promote post-abuse recovery. The lack of research on mental health awareness in foster carers means there is little understanding regarding the association between mental health awareness and the emotional and mental health needs of children in care.

Since foster carers are more likely to be caring for children who have been abused or neglected, there is a particular need for them to be well equipped in the recognition and understanding of the psychological needs of children in care in general (Guishard-Pine *et al.* 2007).

It is an important aptitude for foster carers to accomplish as a large proportion of children in care have suffered previous abuse, which is associated with mental health disorders (Richardson and Lelliott 2003). Despite the importance of mental health literacy for foster carers, there is little research on this in the foster carer population (Bonfield *et al.* 2010; Lauber *et al.* 2003).

Earlier research found that 49 per cent of the foster children who scored in the *abnormal* range of a well-established measure of psychological well-being were not receiving a service from the CAMHS (Bonfield *et al.* 2010). O'Neill *et al.* (2013) speculated that this was indicative of a shortage in CAMHS provision which in turn prohibited social workers and carers from making referrals. If this were typical across the country, this means that half of the foster children with mental health needs were not having their mental health needs adequately met. In any case, this suggests that the needs of children in care are not being met by appropriate services.

Why would foster carers benefit from counselling skills?

Foster carers are central to the lives of children in care, many of whom experience trauma as a result of multiple instances of abuse and neglect, including sexual abuse. Many of these children over the time of their placement disclose layer on layer of detail of their experiences of abuse. Some may be calm during their disclosures, but some may be very anguished. Is it possible that counselling skills as an enhanced form of communication are likely to increase the foster carer's ability to manage emotional conversations so that the child becomes less distressed?

Burnard (1997) simply states that 'at the heart of the counselling process is communication' (p.106). Sanders (2007) defines counselling skills as 'interpersonal communication skills derived from the study of therapeutic change in human beings' (p.19). Aldridge and Rigby (2001) identify four key components:

- attention giving – the effective use of non-verbal communication such as gestures, posture and facial expression to convey to the speaker the feeling that she is being listened to
- observing – the ability to understand verbal and non-verbal cues sensitively and to respond at an emotional level as well as at a surface level
- listening – listening carefully to the content of what a speaker is saying and how the speaker is saying things
- responding – questioning appropriately, paraphrasing, summarizing and reflecting.

All of these components are often referred to as active listening, which allows the speaker to know that she is being listened to.

Counselling skills are associated with good communication skills (Aldridge and Rigby 2001) and it has been long established that good communication is linked to increased help-seeking behaviour (Schonert-Reichl and Muller 1996; Seiffge-Krenke 1989), a key feature in mental health awareness. There is also an established relationship between good communication and coping skills (Walsh-Burke 1992).

The House of Commons Committee (2009) emphasized the importance of placing foster carers in a system that allows them to build relationships with children. The report also found that foster carers find that their personal relationship with the child is undervalued. They conclude that how happy children are in care is just as important as other child-focused outcomes such as educational attainment. In order to redress this focus, we need to do more to assess quality of placements and quality of relationships.

Child and adolescent mental health services in the UK are likely to be the main source of specialist support (Wolpert and Wilson 2003) to address the emotional well-being of these children. Mental health services for this population have been underused, with studies in this area reporting significantly lower rates of use than would be expected (Bonnet and Welbury 2004; Butler and Vostanis 1998; Garland *et al.* 1996; Indyk 2015; Kataoka, Zhang and Wells 2002; Kerker and Dore 2006; Maguire 2005; Minnis *et al.* 2001; Meltzer *et al.* 2003; Pecora *et al.* 2009; Pecora 2010; Phillips 1997), suggesting that the mental health needs of children in care are not being met by specialist services. This could be due to very limited resources as well as long waiting list (Phillips 1997). Services may also be reluctant to take on complex cases (Richardson and Joughin 2000). While there are often delays due to the demand of this group of children outstripping supply, equipping foster carers with counselling skills may be very supportive to children with mental health issues or in distress while they wait for a mental health service.

How did training in counselling skills help?

Twenty-two foster carers in total have now completed a 30-hour nationally accredited 'Introduction to Counselling Skills' course. It was modified and entitled: 'Counselling Skills for Foster Carers' (McCall and Guishard-Pine 2011) and delivered six five-hour sessions on various dates over a period of three months (Skills for Care 2012). Didactic teaching was followed by role-play sessions between foster carers. The course was facilitated by a psychologist and a psychotherapist who were also qualified counsellors. The foster carers completed assessed tasks to receive a certificate. Transcripts of audio conversations with a child or other foster carer were analysed for assessment. These were marked against set criteria. In addition to this, the assessment included two time-limited papers to assess their knowledge of the taught curriculum. These were devised as a multiple-choice paper and a paper using cloze procedure. An external examiner ratified marks on their assessed tasks.

The course was skills based, therefore it was important for the course facilitators to create a warm, confidential and welcoming environment in order to develop counselling skills. The size of the group also allowed the foster carers to feel safer to share her worries about being formally assessed, as some of them had not followed a formal course of study for as long as 46 years.

The findings from this research suggested that improved communication had a positive role to play in the child's reparative process. The carers who attended the training course all felt that they had improved their mental health awareness and were altogether more confident and competent in supporting some of the emotional needs that the children in their placement presented.

Conclusion

The framework of professionalizing carers is incomplete without the provision of good quality training to underpin it and develop the effectiveness of carers. Research demonstrates there are links between the following three factors: foster carers feeling well supported, attendance at training events and the retention of carers (Fostering Network 2004). There is, nonetheless, a prevailing myth that many foster carers are involved in fostering because of the allowance that is paid to them (Doyle 2007; Duncan and Argys 2007; Meadowcroft and Trout 1990). Kirton (2001) confirmed that for the majority of carers the financial allowances are not enough to motivate them to remain positive about the fostering system.

Information collected during a study of global trends in foster care contributed to an international comparative analysis of the main issues facing foster carers. Three key themes emerged from the study: motivation and capacity to foster; professionalism versus altruism; and criteria for kinship and unrelated carers (Colton *et al.* 2008). An international perspective is useful because it enables careful crafting of a constellation of mental health services to enhance the experience of being in care (Vostanis 2010).

It is accepted therefore, that training foster carers is by no means a panacea for the number of issues that potentially improve the mental health of children in care. Former research has found limited impact on the management of behaviour (Minnis and Devine 2001; Pithouse, Hill-Tout and Lowe 2002; Robson and Briant 2009; Wilson *et al.* 2004); however, training of foster carers can be seen as an affirmation of their commitment and competence (Allen and Vostanis 2002; Golding 2003; Hill-Tout, Pithouse and Lowe 2003).

There can be a mismatch between the goals and ambitions of foster carers and the professionalization agenda because many foster carers still see themselves as having more of a parenting role than a professional role with children in care (Swain 2007). The benefits of this counselling skills training is that it went beyond a managerial focus on the professionalization of foster carers that brings attention to the financial aspects of the professionalization agenda (Kirton, Beecham and Ogilvie 2007; Wilson and Evetts 2006). Rather, it describes how formal, accredited training can be an additional motivator for foster carers to enhance their parenting and communication skills. Although limited in its scope, this research goes some way to emphasize both the direct and indirect benefits of specific training on child mental health needs as an approach to increasing the professionalism of foster carers.

Chapter 10

'Pass the Parcel'

Keeping Therapeutic Relationships Accessible for Very Traumatized Young People in Care

SUZANNE MCCALL

Beginnings

I cannot think of one theoretical orientation in the 'therapeutic world' that does not, to one extent or another, argue for the primacy of relationships generally, and the therapeutic relationship particularly, in understanding how a human being is to be understood and supported. As a very basic statement then, as Oatley (1984, p.3) remarks, '...if we discover ourselves primarily in relationships then it is within the relationships, not the individual, that transformation is to be sought'.

Thus it is hardly a new idea that it is 'the relationship that heals' and yet it is the subject of this chapter to explore how this simple truth still sadly seems to escape being embedded into professional and therapeutic practice with children in care. Doubtless much of this can be attributed perhaps to often unhelpful 'systems' – organizations and funding structures – that seem obstinately to refuse to acknowledge the longer-term needs of this vulnerable group. In a care system where children can be left feeling like an unwanted parcel that is passed from person to person and place to place, as therapists we need persistently to highlight the centrality of consistent relationships in emotional well-being and argue for our therapeutic relationships to endure where appropriate. However, after ten years of social work practice and 12 years of specialist practice with child mental health services engaging 'hard to reach' adolescents who have primarily been children in care, I suspect the explanations for continued and consistent avoidance of their needs and the consequent poor outcomes for them in their lifetimes lie closer to home.

This chapter also briefly explores the idea of impaired contact, and how working with this has been useful with those children in care who are most alienated from relationships of any kind, but most vehemently those of the 'professional' type. They are the ones for whom relationships feel dangerous and immensely painful and for whom I have frequently observed there is a simple equation in terms of providing therapy:

High psychosocial need = low capacity to engage

Throughout I hold in mind five children in care I have worked with who I would regard as representative of the issues presented here. While one cannot say – ever – that they are 'typical', they are certainly not *untypical.* They have all experienced changes in social workers, previous specialist mental health team (SMHT) interventions – and most also disruptions in education – but certainly they have all experienced multiple placements throughout their time in care. I worked with them from mid-adolescence to at least the age of 17 years.

Identities

When I think about my own experiences of emerging identities as a child and adolescent and those of my own children, I am conscious of the powerful role others play in the sense of continuity and cohesiveness of the community of selves. For sure, peers are important in this process and increasingly so throughout adolescence, but the founding building blocks remain in the arena of the family. At its best, the family provides a robust but flexible and pervious container for emerging identities. As I am sure the reader will be aware, the literature on the subject of identity is vast and will not be discussed here. However, the depth of the fragmentation of identities for children in care needs revisiting.

LEE'S STORY

I am sitting in a looked after child review for a seven-year-old. I am not the therapist for the child since he is too young for me to work with, but I am consulting to the 'system' – the adults and professionals around the child. Quite unusually the previous *and* current foster carer are present as the child has recently had a placement breakdown and we are in a transitional phase where the child has just moved. I am listening to the description of the young boy (I shall call him Lee) and becoming increasingly confused. I shuffle through my notes and flash a questioning look at the previous foster carer with whom I have been working. The look is meant to portray my feeling that I am sitting in the wrong review. Who is this child? He bears no resemblance to the child I have been thinking about with the carer and professionals over the past few months. He has changed physically, apparently, he no longer has asthma or hearing issues, he loves vegetables especially broccoli (which he detested). He also displays none of the behavioural difficulties that have plagued the previous placement. I am very familiar with the 'honeymoon syndrome', but this is simply bizarre. I ask myself; where has 'Lee' gone?

As I reflect on Lee and his recreation of himself into the image of what he thinks is acceptable I am profoundly sad. It is energy that he will only be able to sustain for a while, hence the phrase 'honeymoon', but it is also a terrible indictment of what children in care endure in a constant struggle to find a place where they fit; where they feel liked (if not loved) and where, for a while, they are part of something. While it has its irritating moments, being with old friends, as with family, provides us all with something intensely important – a history, a place from where we have come and, maybe, to where we are going; an identity or a cohesiveness of identities. To be without this reference point, to be passed from professional to professional and carer to carer, leads to a fundamental fragmentation of self.

The 'Do you remember'/'I remember' game

The adolescents I have referred to above taught me, as clients often do, what they have valued in the relationship that we have called 'counselling'. Towards the ending phase, which may take six months, I noticed that they began to introduce the 'do you remember' game. Working with them during the years in which they transitioned from children to adults I was not infrequently the longest single professional relationship they had that spanned these years. They frequently asked these questions:

- 'Do you remember where I was when we first met?'
- 'Do you remember how I used to come in and I wouldn't speak?'

- 'Do you remember when I lived...' (insert various placements/ carers)
- ...and so on.

It was not unusual in our long road to an ending for sessions to be taken up largely by reminiscing. Recently I heard the phrase to 'knit a novel' as part of the creative writing process, and it has felt sometimes as if the ending phase of therapy was about gathering up all the threads of a young person and helping him to knit a whole person. If around at all, parents were unable to do this for him for a number of reasons, notably a complete fragmentation of their own images of themselves and others and thus the inability to reflect anything whole back to the adolescent. Stern (1977) gives very detailed accounts of how very early a healthy carer/infant relationship – a complex 'dance' – provides the earliest building blocks for self-image.

As is often my experience, while I seem concerned to know complex theoretical things, my clients point me to the importance of the very simple and fundamental things they need from me. Sitting with these young people as a consistent figure over their development through adolescence, I find they direct me to understanding that it is my continual presence physically and psychologically that they have found most useful – what I have *been*, rather than said; as Rogers (1980) notes, 'a way of being'. I find myself in absolute agreement with Margaret Hunter (Hunter 2001, p.26) when she says: 'Therapists of children in care have extra responsibility for gathering up and integrating the child's experiences. For some children this aspect of therapy alone is a valuable therapeutic experience; being remembered, being known, being important.'

I have reflected back the adolescents' 'do you remember' game with my own 'I remember' game and they have always loved to hear my stories about them.

That's not therapy!

The theory of 'therapy' and most particularly so with more complex young people, is naturally abound with words such as 'containment', 'boundaries', the 'clinical space'. The domain of 'safe therapy' is also very much understood within these parameters. I believe also the majority of therapists themselves enjoy the rhythm of 'same place, same time, same person'. I have no issues with this at all; or that is to say only *one* significant issue which is that, early in trying to engage chaotic, fragmented, relationship-averse older adolescents, it *didn't appear to work very often.*

When I first commenced work in the SMHT it was common not to offer therapy to children in care who were not settled in a secure longer-term placement. As Hunter notes:

> There has been in fact a reluctance among psychotherapists to work with such children – generally seen as being poorly motivated, lacking self-observation, prone to acting out and suffering 'external' difficulties in their lives beyond the reach of psychotherapy. (2001, p.viii)

But, if the young person had no consistent place to be and he would not attend the clinic due to his previous bad recollections of going there, it was very hard to have a consistent place for therapy. I do also believe that in my years of going to meet *them* rather than them coming to me, there was some important symbolism for the young people. It felt with those who moved a lot as if this demonstration alone connected the world up for them a little. They were visibly pleased that, once again, in a world that could so easily miss their existence, or lose them entirely, *I had found them.* For balance, lest I should make myself seem perfect, I have also met weary eyes that have communicated 'not *you* again'!

While it is now documented that the lack of a secure placement should not be considered a contraindication for therapy (Department of Children, Schools and Families and Department of Health 2009) I still hear these judgements being made. Back then, as a therapist undertaking what might be termed 'assertive therapeutic outreach', it felt as if I might be doing something wrong; there were times when I felt alone and this was a powerful countertransference. The support of a strong team who understood my motivations and ethics was critical.

While it is still hard to write since it remains a difficult feeling, I think it is important to describe one example of such work.

DAVID'S STORY

'David' who was 17 had moved, yet again, this time into supported lodgings. David could never tolerate the clinic, it simply terrified him, so I had always visited him and found the best space I could in which to work. I had negotiated with the woman offering the supported lodgings (the 'landlady' as David called her) that we could use her front room for an hour a week. I arrived at the house and rang the bell to be greeted by a very tense-looking David. 'You can't come in, I'm sorry.' Naturally I was concerned that I had somehow upset him during our previous session. However, as it turned out his landlady had said that she didn't want me coming round any more and that he was not to allow me in.

That session was conducted on her front garden wall. David was hugely upset. This event had encapsulated terribly his sense of having nowhere to be, no power or rights; he was deeply ashamed at having to refuse me entry. I did not tell him, perhaps I should have done, but he wasn't the only one feeling shame. In my whole professional life I have never encountered such an overwhelming sense of humiliation. It occurred to me later that I should really thank the woman for giving me such a powerful insight into the world of some children in care. There is a well-worn person-centred term 'to meet the client where they are'. Quite literally and metaphorically I found myself very uncomfortably there.

A colleague once commented when I was discussing my work, 'That's not therapy!'. 'Proper' therapy happened weekly at least, in a consistent space (a carefully controlled environment within the clinic) and the promise at least of permanence in the external world. Whatever one's conviction about the client group you work with, being without a comforting set of rules is deeply challenging. As Val Wosket notes: '...I shared with my supervisor my disquiet over the suspicion that I was becoming a theoretical and procedural outcast from every respected and recognized school of counselling...' (1999, p.ix).

This thing called 'therapy'

I have had to think hard about what therapy actually is, and if it is something that a significant proportion of the most damaged adolescents in care cannot engage in, then of what use is it? At the heart of therapy has always been the building of a relationship that is therapeutic. Like all therapists I have my own favourite definition of this thing called therapy, which is 'therapy is a relationship which might make a difference, which might allow one to know oneself and the other' (Oatley 1984, p.7). The key word here in my mind is 'might', for it is focusing on the idea of possibilities with young people that is central.

But as I have noted above, there are significant hurdles to these young people receiving direct therapy (see Bazalgette *et al.* 2015 for a full exploration). Among the hurdles are two particular presentations that I shall think about further here. Highly generalized, of course, but I present them as 'fight and flight'.

Those adolescents in the 'fight' category often present with a range of externalizing behaviours; they tend not to wish to come to any clinic, but especially not one with the title 'mental health' in it. They are typically very hard to engage since they have chaotic internal and external lives, are highly distrustful of adults generally and professionals in particular. In what might be seen as a 'transference', since many of their previous relationships have been perceived on a spectrum from abusive to just plain unhelpful, they expect and encounter nothing new when meeting a therapist: that is to say, they perceive what they have previously experienced. They often do not receive a service because they simply will not engage with services offered in a traditional therapeutic model.

MANDY'S STORY

Mandy actually ***has*** come into the clinic. She wants me to know how much she doesn't need another referral to a SMHT for therapy. 'You don't care about me at all, you just do this because you are paid to, you're just like all the other f***ing professionals; you're all the f***ing same.' She storms out impressively, stopping only to switch off every plug point along the hallway: 'Don't you f***ing people care about the planet?' I follow her at a distance as she exits, wondering what on earth it is that I might be able to help with and how, if at all, I can open up with her the possibility of a relationship.

Those in the 'flight' group present very differently. They employ defensive manoeuvres to keep themselves safe, retreating so far into a psychological protective state that the experience of meeting with them is that they are *not there.* They are often considered unsuitable for therapy since it is felt that their ego state is too weak, and it is also very hard to determine if one has permission to work with them. They walk into the clinic like lambs to the slaughter, making no protests. Protest is beyond them.

JENNY'S STORY

Jenny is 14 when we start weekly sessions, and on her way to 18 when we finish. She is delivered by taxi from school, seems to have no particular feelings about being here and just accepts that this is what happens each week. For the first six months she does not speak at all, has no curiosity about the process or me. She smiles politely on meeting, a smiley face that slowly slides away in the clinic room, where she initially occupies herself with no reference to me at all. And then she curls up into a little ball and falls asleep. She sleeps all session, and I wake her five minutes before she is due to be collected again by taxi to go to her foster home. The 'sleeping phase', lasting a few months with some exceptions, is in my mind a need to totally withdraw from any contact at all (there are of course many other interpretations that could be made). It is followed by several weeks during which she sits and methodically snaps the leaves of my favourite plant. Since it is a succulent it has a pleasing 'snap' to it as it breaks. After this, I endure some months of her indulging in a soft ball game which mainly entails her throwing them at me, or more importantly, threatening non-verbally to throw them. She teases and taunts me. During these latter two phases I am concerned to reflect back in a very simple way what she is doing, and after some time, how I *feel* about what she is doing. I am concerned not to interpret but to 'notice'. After about a year we begin the long process of encouraging her to join in verbalizing the feelings. Her placements change frequently.

Impairment of contact and 'one-minute moments'

While I am now an integrative counsellor, my roots are in person-centred practice and it is to these roots I have often returned when dealing with some of the more traumatized young people. Person centeredness demands the fierce acknowledgement of the relationship as the work that allows change, rather than the relationship as the mechanism by which the real work is *then* done. There is a very important difference in these approaches; this difference becomes critical in working with such young people.

This is particularly so when thinking about two of Roger's Core Conditions that are often ignored:

- two persons are in psychological *contact* and
- that client is able to perceive the core conditions.

With both the 'flight' and 'fight' adolescents I have worked with the issue of establishing psychological contact is, in itself, problematic. What others may call transference can be understood as basic perceptual neurobiology. As Sutton notes:

> Deprived, abused and neglected children are aware of a depriving, abusing, neglectful world...it makes sense, given what we know about perception, that this is how they will experience relationships in general, even when something different is on offer. They simply will not see it that way... (2014, p.15)

In this sense, they do not see me, and may be unable to see me as offering anything helpful for some time; our ability to connect psychologically is sometimes severely impaired.

Working with Jenny it was very clear that she needed to severely curtail her psychological contact with me. Not unlike the 'dance' described by Stern in young infants: 'The infant is a virtuoso performer in his attempts to regulate both the level of stimulation from the caregiver and the internal level of stimulation in himself' (Stern 1977, p.121).

For other adolescents they have been adept at distracting and diverting attention from what has wounded them. They talk about 'stuff'.

Even now, especially when there is a lot of pressure from other professionals to make what they see as progress with the *issues* (behaviour/trauma/past abuse), it feels as if I am making no progress. I feel some degree of panic even. At these times I have learned to remind myself of three things. First, to go back to the basics of what I believe in. With these young people the therapeutic task is very distilled; it may not be to work on the past abuse, and very often not to 'change cognitions', but to continually refocus on the relationship. For some children in care, to be able to risk a relationship is work enough.

Second, to wait for the 'one minute'. As some relationship is built, no matter what the nature of the impairments of contact is, there is one minute in most therapy sessions when it feels to me the young person risks reaching out for something; it is as if he peeks out from behind a wall of defences to see what I will do. I work hard on noticing this opportunity and using it *just enough* but not too much.

Third, as Perry and Szalavitz (2006, p.91) simply note 'people are not interchangeable'. This succinct thought has given me the courage sometimes not to pass on a young person when I have been struggling, unless of course it is in his best interests for whatever reason that I do so.

Don't pass the parcel

As Sutton notes:

> The problem is how to build news ways of relating when the very process of relating itself is often frightening... The task of the therapist, like that of a new mother, is to offer a world into which the child can be truly taken, with all his or her impulses and forces of feeling – paradoxically including the child's fear of being taken in by the therapist. (2014, p.15)

Without vigilance, children in care face a form of discrimination. The profound wounding they have encountered has often 'disbarred' them from psychotherapeutic help. There is a marked and rather odd irony here since, surely, if therapy claims any expertise at all it is within the realms of understanding the primacy of, and establishing, relationships.

As therapists we can too easily join the game of pass the parcel; we cannot help, they do not fit our service, they are unsuitable for our therapy – and all too often, if they are given therapy then this sadly aims to abate a behavioural symptom of deep emotional trauma and once they *stop behaving badly* we close their file. It would of course be bizarre to suggest that every child in care referred should be seen endlessly, and this is not my point. But I would argue that a key decision in closing therapeutic work with them should be to carefully reflect on the place of the therapeutic *relationship* in *each* child's particular world. As my colleague in Chapter 12 has described, work with such young people can be rather tough on one's ego, and in the absence of a professional system that understands how such work may not fit a format of 'open case/fix problem/close case', feelings of uselessness can mount. These feelings must be carefully sorted through: am I 'useless' to the young person or do I just feel that way?

At the beginning of this chapter I suggested that it may not just be just the practicalities of service provision that so often lead to him not receiving therapy or for the therapist to rather swiftly dispatch a looked after child. It is certainly difficult work at times; he can frustrate and deskill us, filling our minds and bodies with helplessness and uselessness. He throws back in our faces our very best attempts to help; we offer out a hand and he bites it. I can certainly confess to being filled with sheer dread at the thought of an impending session – the 'punishment' I knew I would encounter and that, once again, I would be left wondering if I was of any use at all as a therapist. I think in return we may sometimes unconsciously punish him with theories that suggest he is unsuitable for therapy – beyond the pale. Almost seamlessly we slip and slide into mirroring his parents; it is the young person who is to blame and who must be dismissed.

But more than this, in attempting to prioritize the needs of children in care for therapy I *feel* (an important word since it is what I have received rather than what was intended) what I have encountered on occasions is irritation from some colleagues. It is as if they want me to shut up. And maybe there is some truth here. It would be so much easier just to forget them and move on to clients who make us feel good and our statistical outcome measures impressive. With children in care that may take some time – until, that is, we have as Sutton notes, helped them to experience 'the music of emotional connection' (Sutton 2014, p.17). Unlike the music during pass the parcel, this music means the parcel has found some safe hands to rest in awhile.

Chapter 11

The Illusion of Individual Psychotherapy for Children in Care

Integrated Working as a 'Kaleidoscope'

JEUNE GUISHARD-PINE AND EMILY WILKENS

> Kaleidoscope: 'A constantly changing pattern or sequence of elements.' (Oxford Dictionary)

Introduction

The theme of a keynote speech at a conference on supporting children with severe emotional and behavioural needs was 'Eternal Verities' – the idea of seeking irrefutable concepts, undisputed truths. One by one, the audience failed to come up with any idea that was robust enough to reach the criterion of being an eternal verity. As a psychologist who has worked in health, education and social services, I have seen agencies erect barriers and develop cultures of blame for the failure of a range of interventions to support very damaged children. Hence my eternal verity is simply 'You can't do it alone'. Thus agencies need to find a way to synthesize their perspectives to keep the child the centre of their focus. This is the spirit of true integrated working. This chapter highlights the challenges of integrated work, and a model of child mental health service delivery to counteract these challenges by illuminating and resolving difficulties in interagency communication. It specifically pinpoints research Cooper (2011) has undertaken on how child mental health services can bridge the support that the foster carer offers in order to aid the recovery process of the child in care.

Integrated working as central to child welfare

Although interagency collaboration has been a central driver for child protection and child welfare work in the UK for a number of years

– namely: Audit Commission (1998); *Quality Protects* (Department of Health 1998); the Care Standards Act (Department for Education 2000); the Children (Leaving Care) Act (2000); Every Child Matters (Department for Education and Skills 2003); The Social Exclusion Unit report on the Education of Children in Care (Social Exclusion Unit 2003); the Children Act (2004) – there remains some cynicism about the 'rhetoric' of interagency working (Atkinson *et al.* 2002; Hammill and Boyd 2001; Horwath and Morrison 2007; National Working Group on Sexually Exploited Young People 2008; Morrison 1996; Webb and Vulliamy 2001).

Every Child Matters (2003) tells us that: 'Integrated working focuses on enabling and encouraging professionals to work together and to adopt common processes to deliver front line services, coordinated and built around the needs of children and young people.'[1] While on an international perspective, UNICEF (2000) suggests that integrated working supports a child-centred approach by focusing a range of professionals on working together to provide the effective support needed to improve child outcomes.

Although integrated working is the preferred concept, some authors have highlighted the confusion created by the multitude of labels to describe the same phenomenon (Warmington *et al.* 2004).[2] Others have raised concerns about the real evidence of integrated

1 http://webarchive.nationalarchives.gov.uk/20100422120431/http://dcsf.gov.uk/everychildmatters/strategy/deliveringservices1/iw

2 Present policy enthusiasm for developing 'joined-up solutions to joined-up problems' has generated a plethora of terminology to describe the collaborative approaches required: 'interagency', 'multi-agency', 'inter-professional', 'inter-sectoral' and 'partnership' being prevalent (Lloyd, Stead and Kendrick 2001). Moreover, portmanteau terms such as 'interagency' and 'multi-agency' may be used to imply a range of structures, approaches and rationales. The literature reviewed herein is derived from studies of diverse models of 'interagency' or 'multi-agency' working. For this reason, the review is not concerned with prescribing an exhaustive definition of the term 'interagency working'. However, Lloyd *et al.* (2001) offer useful, albeit tentative, definitions that loosely encompass most of the structures and practices described in current literature. These working definitions include: Interagency working: more than one agency working together in a planned and formal way, rather than simply through informal networking (although the latter may support and develop the former). This can be at strategic or operational level. Multi-agency working: more than one agency working with a client but not necessarily jointly. Multi-agency working may be prompted by joint planning or simply be a form of replication, resulting from a lack of proper interagency coordination. As with interagency operation, it may be concurrent or sequential. In actuality, the terms 'interagency' and 'multi-agency' (in its planned sense) are often used interchangeably. Joined-up working, policy or thinking refers to deliberately conceptualized and coordinated planning, which takes account of multiple policies and varying agency practices. This has become a totem in current UK social policy.

work, and the robustness of these various policy documents as effective accountability frameworks. They question their ability to ensure that successful interagency partnerships can be formed and sustained (Frye and Webb 2002; Harker *et al.* 2004b; Peck, Trowell and Gulliver 2001; Tomlinson 2003). No more are the barriers tested than in relation to meeting the needs of children in care.

Possible barriers to effective integrated working

There are multiple reasons why the ideal of effective integrated working evades childcare practitioners: some are related to the organizational culture (ethos) and some are related to the processes and protocols (systemic) while some are related to individual attitudes (see Table 11.1).

Table 11.1 Potential barriers to effective integrated working to support children in care

Ethos	Systemic	Individual
Non-acceptance of the child-centred approach as *the* professional way of working	Lack of clarity about parental consent and parental responsibility	Risk-averse approaches to dealing with risk
Conflicting priorities of different agencies	Jargon and language	Non-commitment to ensuring a child-centred approach
Disrespect for the autonomy and competence of other agencies	Time for all parties to meet	Lack of understanding of one's own role and responsibilities
Lack of understanding the role of other professionals	Lack of sharing information	Approaches to assessment
Conflict resolution across the 'team around the child' not established	No overview within each agency	Level of knowledge and skills
How joint decisions get acted upon	How joint assessments are implemented	How recommendations are responded to

Essentially, the barriers that exist, or are actively created, manifest as differing perspectives on what the child needs versus what the agency 'does'. The eternal verity that 'you cannot do it alone' crystallizes the idea that the child needs and has a right to expect that the agents empowered to make a difference to her life place her central to the intervention instead of being a pawn in the middle of interagency rivalries and systemic flaws (Furnivall *et al.* 2012; Granville and Langton 2002; Wigley *et al.* 2012). Lewis (2011) eloquently underlines this point:

> The stories one hears about what happens after a child is placed in foster care can be, paradoxically, more upsetting than the ones leading to the foster care placement. Foster care is a system created to protect children from an unsafe home environment, yet multiple foster home placements, conflicted or non-existent relationships between foster parents and birth parents, long, drawn out court battles, and the reality of living in an on-going state of not knowing when or if they will be going home are just some of the challenges many children in care are expected to manage. Many of these children wind up in therapists' offices during some point of their foster care stay, sent by well-intentioned caseworkers who are hopeful that therapy will minimize problematic behaviour. The therapists, told to 'fix' the problem, often have minimal information about the emotional and litigious process of foster care and the crazy-making paradoxes that are inherent to the system's structure. Without a guide, frustration and resignation are often accompanying feelings for therapists, as symptom reduction is hard to come by and the work feels more inert than transformational. (p.437)

Individual therapy for the child is but one of many aspects within her recovery process. The epistemology of a successful specialist child mental health team for children in care must include the notion that working collaboratively with agencies and both birth and fostering families is a necessity and as such is non-negotiable. This way of working is found to increase permanency of placements, and to meet the unmet emotional and mental health needs of referred children and their carers in order to disrupt a downward spiral. However, what specialist mental health work with children in care has illustrated is that when the agencies collaborated and communicated well, the outcome(s) were generally more beneficial to all concerned (Guishard-Pine 2013). This is a crucial indicator of successful *integrated working* (see Figure 11.1).

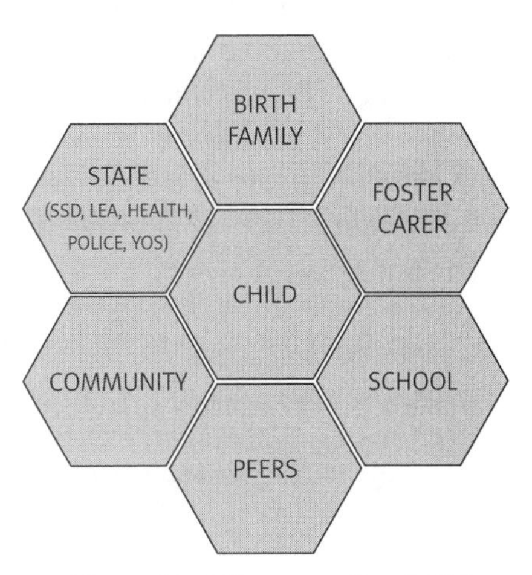

Figure 11.1 The protective shield
(from Guishard-Pine, Hamilton and McCall 2007)

Hence true integrated working provides a 'protective shield' against a deterioration of the child in care's mental health (Guishard-Pine *et al.* 2007; Mosuro *et al.* 2014) and placement stability (Hunt 2011). Changing the culture and ethos of service delivery may be one way in which this is achieved (see also Chapter 13). Reflection and transparency must be promoted and modelled by all members of the professional network. Although the members may change, and consequently the lenses change, the constituent bits and the centre do not: the child must always remain at the centre, hence the protective shield as a *kaleidoscope.*

What the professional network does to limit or sabotage integrated working

Many practitioners who see themselves as 'reasonable' or 'competent' sometimes deliberately and sometimes inadvertently disrupt the trajectory of recovery for children in care who are receiving individual therapy. For example a professional may want to be seen as the 'good' or preferred or trusted one, so will carry messages inappropriately to make other people in the network seem less worthy. Similarly, issues within a child's life that relate to an individual professional's past can trigger instinctual drives that propel such behaviour (Lawrence-Mahrra 2014).

Over the years a strong theme has manifest in a diverse range of ways, yet all equally impactful in inhibiting the progress of therapeutic recovery – and sometimes on the placements themselves. The benefit of the protective shield is that it provides an *accountability framework* for the work to keep the child's recovery as a central focus.

The kind of behaviours that potentially limit or sabotage therapeutic recovery manifest as follows:

- disrupting therapy by refusing to bring the child to the clinic
- refusing to make a private space available for the therapy
- raising the issue of halting therapy because the child is 'off-curriculum'
- refusing to adapt the system/routines to accommodate the therapy
- refusing to attend professionals' meetings
- refusing to attend school-related meetings
- poor or non-communication of key changes, for example cancellation or non-arrangement of transport, non-attendance due to competing priorities
- discussing other adults in disparaging terms in front of the child or to each other
- making unreasonable demands on the therapist, for example to transport the child
- enquiring about the nature of the therapeutic session in front of the child
- direct reprimands to the child for not improving her behaviour quickly enough once therapy has started
- refusing to be flexible about the time of therapy/being inflexible about therapy
- prejudged opinions/attitudes about the utility of therapy

- presuming that the therapy is not helpful if their relationship with the child has not changed
- defining how the child is 'better' according to their own frame of reference
- rigidly maintaining a unilateral view of the child
- refusing to see that changes (or rigidity) in the system can be inhibiting to progress for the child
- expressing strong opinions about what should be happening in therapy, for example 'she's just playing', 'she doesn't talk to the therapist'.

Ultimately achieving an understanding of their role in the child's protective shield is the best antidote to subverting the course of therapy. Rather than disengage as a professional or from other professionals, the key is in fact to carve out a role for oneself that is tolerable and doable (Wakelyn 2008).

Multiple perspectives – shared understandings

The questions of whether or not it is in any way appropriate to view placement stability as a proxy measure of therapeutic recovery, and whether or not there is always a mutual relationship between placement stability and mental health have been asked before (Biehal *et al.* 2009; Perez-del-Aguila 2003; Selwyn, Frazer and Quinton 2006; Sinclair 2005; Vanderfaeillie, Van Holen and Coussens 2008). The evidence is that foster carers' concerns about the behavioural difficulties of the children in their placement consistently remain the main cause of placement disruption (Bazalgette *et al.* 2015; Oosterman *et al.* 2007; Rock *et al.* 2013; Strijker, van Oijen and Knot-Dickscheit 2011) and the main reason for a referral to child mental health services to be made (Arcelus *et al.* 1999; Meltzer *et al.* 2003). Such research indicates that there is a striking absence of foster carers being present during the subsequent therapy sessions (Barth *et al.* 2005; Caw and Sebba 2014). For children in care referred to child mental health services there has been limited research exploring which therapeutic interventions are most efficacious. Although literature exists (e.g. Clausen *et al.* 2013), there is also a noticeable lack of studies that have specifically explored the foster carer-child relationship, particularly in terms of how their individual perspectives might be negotiated within their interpersonal relationship as a psychological intervention.

Due to the potential cumulative effect of past experiences, children in care may be less likely to view the world as safe enough to seek nurturing and support from others. These insecurities may present as anger, aggression or controlling behaviour within the fostering family (Golding 2003). There may even be differences in the way in which children in care and their foster carers view a typical family (Ellingsen, Shemmings and Storksen 2011). The result of this can place severe strain on those foster families in which children are placed, which may further render placements more susceptible to breakdown (Farmer, Lipscombe and Moyers 2005; Stanley, Riordan and Alaszewski 2005). Gaining multiple perspectives could therefore be considered an important avenue to pursue.

Cooper (2011) sought an alternative explanation as to why children in care have so many unstable placements. She explored the unique and personal perspectives of an individual foster carer and her foster child using a personal construct psychology (PCP) approach. Personal construct psychology originated from the writings of George Kelly (1955) and is based on the notion that:

> A person's view of reality is formed by his/her perceptions of what s/he sees, hears, thinks, feels and anticipates in his/her world. These perceptions are his/her personal constructs which are unique and real to him/her and actively guide his/her thoughts and actions. (Giles 2003, p.18)

What they said was analysed using thematic analysis (Daly, Kellehear and Gliksman 1997) and PCP concepts were used to analyze the interactional processes between the children in care and their carers.

She found that a sense of a *fragmentation of the self* was a major theme highlighted across the interviews (Table 11.2). Similar themes have also been evidenced in previous studies (Dance and Rushton 2005; Rostill-Brookes *et al.* 2011).

Table 11.2 Main themes emerging from the thematic analysis

Overarching theme	Superordinate themes	Subordinate themes
View of young person	Experience of a fragmented sense of self	Dichotomous view of self
		Playing a role
	Visibility and invisibility	Difference from others
		Concealed identity
View of foster carer	Living a provisional existence	Shifting sense of identity
		Experiencing an inauthentic self
View of family	Ambivalence	Sense of belonging to foster family
		Connection to birth family
	A pervasive sense of difference	The impact of family beliefs
		Negotiating difference

(from Cooper 2011)

It may well be that for children in care, the experience of abuse or neglect could shatter core assumptions concerning parental responsibilities regarding care (Janoff-Bulman 1992). By fragmenting herself, this may allow the young person to preserve beliefs concerning the 'goodness' of her parents.

Comments raised by the young people in Cooper's research highlighted their ongoing struggles to make sense of belonging to two separate family entities. The term *ambiguous loss* (Boss 1999) may help to understand why some children in care do not settle into their placement as well as one might expect. It could therefore be that these young people, particularly those who have experienced multiple placement moves, perceive their relationship with carers to be in transition and not permanent (Lee and Whiting 2007). Hence this is reciprocated in the foster carer's perception of being transitory, which creates a train of living 'a provisional existence' (Ironside 2004).

The shared experience of the fragmentation of self that emerged from the perspectives of both the child in care and the foster carer has been demonstrated in other studies (e.g. Rostill-Brookes *et al.* 2011). Both perceived themselves as never quite being fully authentic to their true selves. The potential enduring strain of living such a partial existence could certainly have a considerable impact, not only on the foster carer-child relationship, but also on relationships with other family members, and on both of their overall physical health and emotional well-being.

Although several studies have indicated the importance of exploring the interaction between foster carer and child characteristics (Sinclair and Wilson 2003), Doelling and Johnson (1990) emphasized that the *quality* of the relationship between foster carer and young person, in addition to the 'goodness of fit' between their characteristics and expectations of the placement, will affect the overall success of the placement.

It could be argued that the experience of abuse and/or neglect, in addition to separation from the birth family, multiple placement moves and the subsequent requirement to establish multiple relationships within foster care, are likely to have a profound effect on the looked-after child. As such, it is probable that children in care might experience a lack of trust in others, in addition to difficulties in developing enduring interpersonal relationships. There is a reciprocal effect on carers who may find it difficult to develop trust in one who cannot trust them, an unrequited 'love' if you will. The inference is that this relationship can be 'treated' through a therapeutic intervention like any other (Robson 2014; Rocco-Briggs 2008).

The illusion of direct mental health services for individual children

There are two principle illusions in the delivery of mental health services to children in care:

1. that individual psychotherapy can be the sole means to assist with the recovery of mental health for children in care
2. that although many professionals and carers see themselves as a helper, they often separate their 'self' from the solution.

For many cases, work has to be done simultaneously with the adult network because the issues described within the referral are often not only about the child's behaviour but often also about the behaviour of the adults in the professional network. As such, what follows is a discussion of the phenomenon that, despite it being an individual child's name on the referral, there is often an essential need for multi-generational and multi-agency (integrated) approaches to the therapy. Therefore interventions are usually required not just for the identified patient (IP) but also for her birth family and the fostering family, and from time to time for the schools and social care agency.

There is no role that anyone in the professional network can do that is too small if the aim is to be a part of the solution rather than part of the problem. By adopting a transparent and consistent interagency model, it has been argued that this will provide a 'protective shield' against mental ill health (Guishard-Pine *et al.* 2007) and subsequently promote confidence in the young person that her carers and professionals are reliably working together. This assurance is likely to empower her to develop her full potential.

Lessons to be learnt from the research: integrated working as a psychological intervention

Kelly described a concept called the 'sociality corollary' which asserts to 'the extent that one person construes the construction processes of another, he may play a role in a social process involving the other person' (Kelly 1955, p.95). This notion implies that for individuals to interact effectively, they are required not to see things similarly, but to understand and accept how the other might see things differently from them (Kelly 1955). Therefore we have '...a proposal to explore the implications of a new viewpoint, even to the extent of experimenting with it actively. Now, let me see if I can shake the kaleidoscope for you. Watch closely. See what happens' (Kelly 1966, cited in Fransella *et al.* 2005, p.77).

It is stressful for children in care to maintain connection with their birth families while also having to negotiate integration into a new and unfamiliar foster family. The paradox, therefore, is that for the foster carer-child relationship to be validated they have to *accept difference,* or in the alternative be inauthentic, which is a risk to their emotional well-being.

From a PCP perspective, the concepts of validation and invalidation may magnify these unsettled feelings. Validation can be described as an anticipation that turns out the way we expected, or a perceived acknowledgement from others confirming the view we have of ourselves (Butler and Green 2007). Invalidation occurs when our viewpoints and expectations are discredited. It might therefore be that a foster child's behaviour can be explained in terms of her feeling that their way of being is validated or invalidated by her current foster family. The foster carer being perceived as insubstantial compared with the birth family also leaves her feeling invalidated. Consequently, both the foster carer and the foster child have to play a role – to be inauthentic – in order to live together. This is unhealthy because there is a risk that it becomes cyclical, as disturbed relationships have been shown to generate much higher levels of invalidation (Neimeyer and Hudson 1985). In light of this research, evidence overwhelmingly suggests that validation remains paramount in the criteria by which children in care assess their security within the fostering family. This validation is essentially a facet of care and love (Anyan and Pryor 2002; Becker-Weidman and Hughes 2008).

The role of the carer as part of a therapeutic intervention

The interaction between children in care and their foster carers is unique and affects the young person's behaviour and emotional well-being and subsequently affects placement stability. This highlights a challenge for clinicians as interventions advocated for these difficulties might have increased effectiveness when foster carers are also involved. There has been a wide range of therapeutic interventions proposed and developed to promote placement stability, but there is relatively limited evidence regarding their specificity and clinical effectiveness (Everson-Hock *et al.* 2009; Kelly *et al.* 2003). It is evident that the research base largely assumes an individualized focus as studies have evaluated either coordinated interventions targeted predominantly at the foster carer as the main agent of therapeutic change (Minnis and Del Priore 2001) or individual therapeutic work with the young person aimed at reducing her presenting problematic behaviour.

Cooper (2011) highlighted the difficulties experienced by children in care and their foster carers in maintaining a coherent sense of self, how their personal and family constructs might impact on this and strategies which might be employed to protect themselves emotionally. Although the findings from studies such as this, which utilize small samples, should not be generalized without caution, they do seem to reflect previous findings, in addition to providing new and illuminating insights into the way in which children in care and their foster carers might perceive themselves. It therefore raised a number of important recommendations for clinical practice. It suggests that by surfacing the multiple perspectives, integrated working can be a psychological intervention aimed at reaching a shared understanding albeit of difference.

One simple way to achieve this is to have two therapists allocated to work with each case: one to work with the individual child and one to work with the network. The benefit of having at least two therapists allocated to the therapeutic work with the individual child becomes apparent when one considers these very real issues for the children in care who are not only dependent on the adults around them to make decisions on their behalf but are assuming that the decisions are being made with their best interests at heart (UNICEF 1989).

Summary

It is often important for children in care to have an individual therapist to work through their feelings, which may include negative feelings about the birth family, social worker, foster carer/s etc. They most benefit from this work if they feel assured that this is confidential. However, this is not work that should happen in isolation. It is evident that the research base largely assumes an individualized focus as studies have evaluated *either* interventions targeted predominantly at the foster carer/s as the main agent of therapeutic change *or* individual therapeutic work with the young person.

In this chapter we hope to have presented ideas and research highlighting that an attempt to suggest we can 'do it alone' misses vital opportunities to develop shared understandings, even if this is an understanding of difference. This is simple to achieve; allocating two therapists to each case – one to work with the child and the other to work with the network – not only opens up new possibilities to include all stakeholders but importantly also avoids the mirroring of fragmentation evident in the research, and that which we know exists for the child in care as part of past narratives.

Chapter 12

On Becoming a Mental Health Specialist Working with Children in Care

A Polemic

ZOË LANDER

'Elite specialist services working with the hardest to reach young people.' That was my perception of mental health services for children in care. Legislative guidance has also raised the profile of the services to this group of youngsters (Department of Health and Department of Education 2015). However, what I have come to learn is that because these young people can be highly complex and challenging, some professionals seem to feel intimidated with this client group. Feeling generally confident working with young people and enjoying a challenge, I found that this appealed to me. I wanted to know how one became an effective practitioner, as quickly as possible, with this client group.

In England, there is an official acknowledgement that the skills and competences of mental health practitioners working with children in care and their carers 'must have the right knowledge, skills, attitudes and values…at specialist, named and designated level' (Royal College of Paediatrics and Child Health 2015, p.7). It continues that 'such post holders require specific knowledge and skills that are distinct from individuals whose primary focus may be centred on child protection and safeguarding' (p.7).

These specific requirements may not be relevant to other countries. Other countries – whether the rate of children in care is higher or lower than England's – may expect healthcare professionals to learn how to work with this client group using a *sitting by Nellie* approach: '…the process of learning by observation is referred to as "sitting by

Nellie"...the phrase now has general use to refer to in-service training' (Partridge 1992, p.274).

However, who did Nellie sit next to? The main focus of this chapter is a personal discussion of the costs and dividends of learning to provide a mental health service to this highly complex group of children without any additional training or experience: in short, learning 'on the job'.

Early days

When I joined the service, my new colleagues had high hopes of my role. Their expectations included that a clinical psychologist should be able to alleviate the distress of all of the young people and 'therapize' them into well-being. My first lesson was that expectations can be difficult to manage: there was a perceived pressure on me as a conscientious practitioner to take on any work to meet the expectations of other staff, rather than be more measured in my responses, or be encouraged to empower others.

I had almost accepted that a sense of inadequacy was integral to any new postholder of a mental health specialist role for children in care. There was no quick way to get knowledge and competence in this area. Reading books and going on courses are fine – but there are not masses of texts that have been published aimed at this specialism and even then, most of these are mainly theory based and thus do not highlight practical issues for a clinician new to this area to consider. I kept asking my supervisor for any useful courses and texts, hence my contribution to this book.

There isn't an explicit therapy that can be used in a rigid way (see Chapter 8). In fact, most research shows that it is the therapeutic relationship that is key to the effectiveness of therapy (Norcross 2011). Creativity, empathy, gentleness, nurture, patience and sensitivity seem to be the most powerful tools. Although I do these things and am very creative, this is not a list of my strengths. I am stronger at building trust and a sense of safety in the therapeutic relationship. I'm more buoyant and optimistic when I am building trust with a young person – I use a lot of humour and reframing. I have also been able to use these strengths to build relationships with young people to enable them to tolerate receiving a less positive response from the many others who are displeased with their conduct. I build relationships so that they might eventually prefer and receive nurture through the authentic relationship that we have.

Later

Frustratingly, experience in this field has taken time. It happened as I did my job, using what I already knew, and learning what I didn't as I went along. My feelings of competence or inadequacy have been almost totally unreliable as measures of how effective I am as a practitioner. Being a clinical psychologist in this specialist role is not all what I expected. It is far more about being what people need (which may not be part of my job description) rather than being a particular kind of professional.

For example, I had not really appreciated before how much distress and trauma carers experience by living alongside and caring for young people who are in such painful and difficult circumstances. I have found it very powerful to give compassion and facilitate reflective practice (I will define this a little later) when carers struggle with the experience of being alongside the raw pain and distress of a young person in care. I could have easily wept with a carer who described the pain of a young person who she had brought back into the care home after he had run to his mum because he was distraught at being told he was being taken away from her. Perhaps it would have been more validating of her feelings and provided more effective support had I been less typically professional and just wept with her?

I tried to reduce distress by responding quickly to referrals from carers and offering early appointments for direct therapy to young people in crisis. I was surprised that these sessions were mostly turned down by the young people. I learned that it can be the carers who are struggling more and are more in need of support to contain their own anguish.

Many of the young people wanted help from the carers who they knew and trusted. It was from the carers that they sought comfort, nurture and care to soothe some of their distress. By the time the young people were due to see me, they had already got what they wanted. In the interim it was the carers who were left carrying the worry and emotions. It was the carers who were in need of reassurance and help to contain their own feelings of distress and their fears of being overwhelmed by the emotions integral to their role.

Learning from experienced colleagues has been priceless, as has been working within a supportive, honest and caring team, learning and coping with difficult experiences, like the first time a young person absconds from your session. I also learned that sometimes there isn't a right thing to say. It is discouraging, but also ironic to be offering empathy and care and then to be attacked by a young person with comments like: 'What do you mean I've done really well under difficult circumstances?' 'I'm no different to anyone else!' 'Don't tell me what I think because you don't understand what I've been through because you can't even imagine it!' I learned that this is a common dilemma for children in care – not wanting to be different yet feeling different from everyone else.

Foster carers can share the similar dilemma of being different yet wanting to be like an ordinary family. A foster carer may ask for guidance but then reject it, explaining why it doesn't apply to his foster child. As disempowering as it feels to not give professional advice, there really is no point in giving the *right* answers and sounding knowledgeable if it isn't the response that is wanted at that moment. Helping the carer to find his own answers and supporting him emotionally is often more palatable and helpful to the carer.

I should add that being able to laugh at oneself is an essential part of learning and surviving in this area of work!

Recently

Reflective practice has been essential to everything I have learned. Reflective practice is the skill of learning from one's own experiences and actions by stepping back from one's own situation to think about how an experience is viewed from other perspectives, how it makes you feel and think. What action did you take, and why did you respond to it as you did? As part of this process one automatically applies the knowledge we have to help us understand, appraise and learn from the lived experience (Hargreaves and Page 2013; Johns 2013; Schön 1984). We constantly evaluate and re-evaluate, thinking about what else we might have done, how else we might have reacted and what alternative outcomes might there have been.

Reflective practice has helped heighten my sense of self-awareness, understanding of the local culture and greater sensitivity to the young people, especially what they are trying to communicate (often at odds with their exact words) and how they are affected by their environment and by me (some of this is touched on in Chapter 1 of this book). Their feedback has been my main educator: they have taught me more, and refined my practice, so that I can respond more effectively and this has been wholly unanticipated. Perhaps they are the best judges.

I have learned about the importance of being part of a 'safe' team. Experienced practitioners around me have provided me with the necessary guidance and reassurance to keep me moving forward in my learning. Those people are still the people I go to if I have a tricky situation, because I value their honesty and judgement. As my judgement is becoming more akin to the people I recognize as being experienced, I am feeling more validated as a practitioner and I think that this is possibly a measure or signal that I am becoming an experienced practitioner. I am noticing indicators that others are also judging me as experienced and people are increasingly coming to me for my experience, and not merely because of my profession. I had not expected that it was a process that creeps up on you at the pace it has. I had also not expected that it would mainly be people outside the team who make the judgement rather than the people within the team.

More recently I have come to ponder on the questions: what unites professionals and children in care and what do professionals bring to the support network for children in care? A wise person suggested to me that I look at our young people and consider how our experiences mirror those of our service users. That is a powerful insight into the people for whom we care (see Chapter 11). They find it difficult to be heard – so do we; our service can be marginalized just as our client group can be. We are both viewed as special cases and as different and not part of mainstream groups. We are members of a small group – young people in care and their workers. The service and young people's need for time and resources is high and the understanding of why so much is needed for such slow improvement, or sometimes deterioration of circumstances, is not always grasped by some in the local professional community.

Then there is the defensiveness, blame and shame that are felt by carers and young people. The staff usually seem to feel less trained, less confident and less equipped than they feel they should be and are not getting the outcomes or feedback that make them feel they have done a good job. Similarly, our young people share these feelings about their own lives and behaviour. I have not found my needs for non-judgemental acceptance and encouragement any different from the needs of my clients or colleagues. As humans, we all seem to need the same kind of environment in which to develop and flourish. We can model care and acceptance. We also model resilience and tolerating feelings of inadequacy, as we stand with our young people and we are touched by their ongoing distress and their overwhelming feelings. We all need our diverse experiences and feelings to be validated. That includes validating the fear that some staff have of truly being inadequate to meet the needs of young people who have been through so much. We also need to celebrate what we do achieve and not minimize success, nor measure it against other services and young people who do not face the same challenges.

Now

Professionals who seek consultation with me still have some unrealistic expectations and think I have skills that approximate magic. Others have become disillusioned that I cannot 'fix' a child rapidly or immediately, or at all. On the whole, I find that I am able to make valuable contributions to the teamwork around the child. This process of working alongside colleagues enables us to share understanding about what we do, and why, and dispel many myths. Unhelpful perceptions (for example, that these youngsters are broken people) seem to exist and working together is the best way to reduce the misunderstandings of everyone involved. There is a growing understanding among some colleagues that these young people might be 'normal' children who react in a normal way to abnormal circumstances. Therefore their defensiveness/aggressiveness and desire to protect their inner selves are understandable and they are good at it (Kenrick 2000; O'Neil 2004; Stovall and Dozier 1998).

I have never seen so many professionals working with the same young people as I have for many of our clients. This was conceptualized initially as a 'protective shield' (Guishard-Pine *et al.* 2007) but has been enshrined in legislative guidance now as the 'team around the child'. Different professionals have raised my awareness that my part of this teamwork is small. The perspectives of colleagues can both provide insight into the young people and hinder progress. Professionals may use the same language, but our professional training refines the meaning, which can be very specific and easily misunderstood. Our priorities are often different and the politics of service rivalries can be disheartening. When everyone's own personal and cultural understanding of what parenting should look like is added, this can make very complex interactions (see also Chapter 13). It can also make professional meetings really long! This in turn is mirrored by the young people, in the same way that the network can often mirror the flaws in the young person's family of origin. The young people experience the same misunderstandings and differing goals, and they encounter each of us individually, which is far more time consuming.

The future

There is jargon in this field that is shared by all professions, but it tends to refer to young people that professionals have encountered along their career. When you are new to a specialist mental health team for children in care, it takes longer to learn this kind of jargon and become part of the history of the service. It can also make a new employee in the service feel very inadequate and unable to contribute to some conversations. It makes a conversation quite exclusive and you have to be part of the child's network to have a true understanding of some conversations.

However, just as the stories of these young people's lives can be convoluted and complex, so too is the journey that a new postholder has to take towards becoming a specialist in working with children in care. No single method of training or learning is sufficient: it is not just about going on a structured course, or reading a single article or book, or having access to experienced practitioners or even being in a good team – it is a combination of all of those things. Add to this the wealth of knowledge that is gained from becoming a part of these young people's lives, both past and present. Once again, experience and an appetite to learn together lead to building and acquiring knowledge. These are key to developing expertise.

Chapter 13

Culturally Competent Practice for Children in Care

GAIL COLEMAN-OLUWABUSOLA

Introduction

The concept of a potentially shared culture for children in care has to be recognized if we are ever to think about becoming culturally competent practitioners. This chapter begins by naming issues often associated with abused or neglected children in care, largely by summarizing a review of the evidence and with a significant focus on the voice of the child. The chapter then briefly begins to explore specific processes related to the emotional world of the child, the emotional world of professionals and professional systems. It is proposed that both the issues and the processes outlined in this chapter contribute to a concept of a shared culture for children in care.

Whose culture is it anyway?

Culture in the broadest sense is shared understanding of meaning. Some definitions include:

> Culture consists of the derivatives of experience, more or less organized, learned or created by the individuals of a population, including those images or encodements and their interpretations (meanings) transmitted from past generations, from contemporaries, or formed by individuals themselves. (Schwartz, White and Lutz 1992, cited in Spencer-Oatey 2008, p.2)

> Culture is a fuzzy set of basic assumptions and values, orientations to life, beliefs, policies, procedures and behavioural conventions that are shared by a group of people, and that influence (but do not

determine) each member's behaviour and his/her interpretations of the 'meaning' of other people's behaviour. (Spencer-Oatey 2008, cited in Spencer-Oatey 2012, p.2)

Interestingly the idea that *culture is transmitted* from one generation to the next is arguably evidenced when an adult who was in care as a child has his own child taken into care. Recognizing the often but not always subtle influence of culture on ourselves and others is arguably the substance of what is commonly defined as 'cultural awareness'.

Is there a shared culture, spoken and unspoken, visible and invisible that we can associate with abused or neglected children in care and those who work with them? To consider this question we can look at outcomes for children in care, such as employment, education and so on, which are generally poorer (Department for Education 2014c). However, we can also consider the voices of children and young people. Dickson *et al.* (2009) conducted a comprehensive review of studies (N=38). Thirty-five studies included the views of children in care. These views were from studies between 1995 and 2007. Nine major themes emerged. These include: 1) love, 2) a sense of belonging, 3) being supported, 4) having someone to talk to, 5) contact with birth parents, 6) stigma and prejudice, 7) children and young people in care and education, 8) professionals and 9) preparation and support for leaving care. However, for the sake of this chapter, it can be useful to consider the nine themes in three categories (see Figure 13.1):

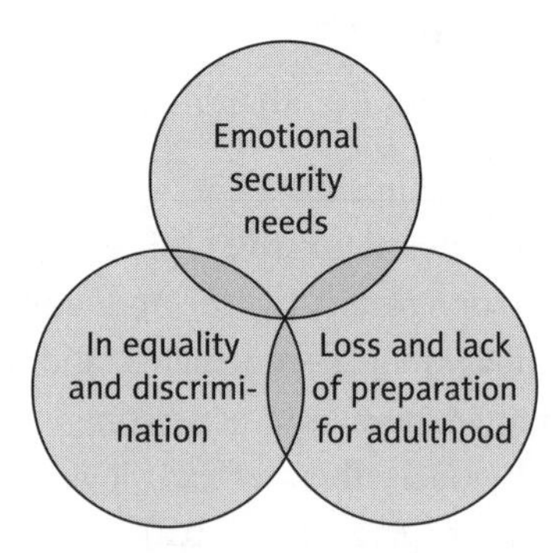

Figure 13.1 Significant issues contributing towards the culture of abused and neglected children in care

Emotional security needs

This was represented prominently in themes 1) love, 2) a sense of belonging and 3) being supported. The need to feel loved and to give love was prominent, with this being related to becoming a parent and giving a child what she herself had lacked. This is supported by Harlow and Frost (2007) who noted that 'Young women leaving care aged between 16 and 19 are more likely to be young mothers than other young women of that age group' (Stein 2002, p.61). In terms of the need to genuinely feel loved, the concept of having paid professional carers felt at odds with this. Hence with regards to shared culture there were narratives about trusting the love that is offered along with a felt urgent need to give love to others.

In terms of a sense of belonging, one quote highlighted the need for children in care to feel 'at home' rather than in 'a placement' (Dickson *et al.* 2009, p.26) and this was often in relation to feeling as loved as the birth children of the foster carers. Other barriers to belonging included the sense of impermanence, feeling like a 'parcel' (see Chapter 10); conflict for some around being part of two families and related concerns about being disloyal to their birth family. This was particularly emphasized when those families belonged to different ethnic groups. The Dickson *et al.* review concluded that social services needed to be proactive in sustaining some form of family contact. For example, the following quote is cited:

> I feel that, from being brought up in care when I was really young, I lost out... I didn't really have an identity, cultural or any, I mean one of the places I was put into they changed my name and everything so a lot of my identity was taken away and it was white folk I was living with, so it was like there weren't no positive black role models or nothing. So I did have identity problems if it weren't for going to live with like a few of my family members. I think it was that that brought me closely in touch with my cultural roots, and from then it's like I know who I am now, I like the black side to me. Obviously I'm mixed race so I've got white and black, but I identify with my black roots. (participant data – Barn *et al.* 2005, cited in Dickson *et al.* 2009, p.28)

Hence unsurprisingly, the need to belong appears to be further emphasized for children in care who have multiple identities associated with experiencing inequalities and discrimination. Although not emphasized in the Dickson review, this would likely also apply to children with disabilities and transgender, gay, lesbian or bisexual young people who feel isolated with their experiences. For example, studies have found that young disabled people leaving care may experience abrupt or delayed transitions from care due to restricted housing and employment options and inadequate support (Stein 2002, cited in Harlow and Frost 2007).

With regards to the third theme of being supported, in the Dickson review there is reference to having at least 'one person' who is there for them emotionally and who encourages them to progress. The 'one person' described in the review included foster carers, mentors, older peers in care and birth family members coming back into their lives at times of crisis, such as homelessness or imprisonment. This particular aspect of the culture of children in care is in line with the concept of a secure emotional base as discussed in attachment theory (see Schofield and Beek 2009).

Inequality and discrimination

A culture of inequality and discrimination is perhaps best highlighted in the Dickson review by themes 4) having someone to talk to, 6) stigma and prejudice and 7) education. Having someone to talk to in confidence was particularly important and Dickson *et al.* (2009) distinguish this theme in the following way:

> In addition the issue of confidentiality was the crux of this theme. It separated the theme from simply 'knowing' someone is there for you to feeling that someone will act in a particular way, and on your behalf, based on the concerns and issues you have raised and will maintain your privacy in that process. (p.34)

The need for confidentiality for children in care was described as pervasive across the studies reviewed and this appeared to be related to two things: additional exposure of personal information which can be recorded in very public ways, e.g. files for all to see, and fear of causing trouble due to the need for professionals to act. Hence despite a strong desire to speak to someone, the experiences of children in care can often remain silenced. Reinforcing a sense of powerlessness can unfortunately promote inequality in accessing support.

Experiences of stigma and prejudice included name calling in school, 'annoying' experiences of people being curious or expressing pity and a strong desire to feel 'normal' rather than different. As I read this in the review, the parallel I could draw was in my own early childhood wanting to wash off my dark brown skin in response to racism and as way to feel 'normal'. However, the relative invisibility of this prejudice for children in care is best summarized in the following quote:

> Unlike other forms of prejudice, such as race or sexual orientation, which are discussed at length in the media, the public is mainly unaware of the discrimination faced by looked after children. (author analysis – Martin and Jackson 2002, cited in Dickson *et al.* 2009, p.44)

Strategies to address this included making support, for example in schools, less conspicuous. This is supported by recent NICE guidance on attachment difficulties for children in care, adopted or at risk of going in care, which states:

> When providing support for interventions in schools and education settings, staff should: be aware of the possibility of stigma, bullying and labelling as a result of any absences from school; [and] take into account the child or young person's preferences for the setting of the intervention. (NICE 2015, p.12)

With regards to inequality in education, children expressed a desire to be encouraged to achieve and to have emotional support to achieve. Without emotional support many children in care reported feeling overwhelmed by the impact of their earlier experiences of sexual, physical or emotional abuse or neglect and found it difficult to continue with an education. While there were some good examples of such support, there was unfortunately evidence of barriers to progressing in education due to low expectations from teachers.

Further practical barriers included financial support, for example to pursue university education, and in addition to this, problems with accommodation, for example during university holidays. Practical and emotional support for education was also felt to be less available in residential than in foster care. The potential for schools to provide continuity in the midst of placement moves was also highlighted in addition to the insensitive way in which schools can be changed with placement moves without prior consideration of the impact on the child or adolescent in care.

Loss and lack of preparation for adulthood

A culture of loss and being pushed into adulthood prematurely seemed a prevalent and at times unspoken culture for children in care. This emerged in themes 5) contact with birth families, 8) professionals and 9) leaving care. Professionals were often viewed as barriers to contact with birth families. This resulted in some children in care secretly meeting with their family. Some children and young people either expressed quite clearly that they did not desire contact with parents (or birth family) or were ambivalent and confused about contact. It is important to note that in all three scenarios the issue of loss is still relevant. Across the studies reviewed, many of the children coped by distancing themselves from their families or by constructing idealized images of family members.

The lack of control children in care experience with regards to where they live and whether or not they are separated from siblings, is evidenced by recent initiatives to ensure that children aged ten years and over can express their views to judges about what they would like to happen to them in cases where they face being taken into care (Ministry of Justice 2015). The real impact of such initiatives is yet to be seen. In practice, however, this lack of control associated with loss is often evident when children in care go to great lengths to ensure control of social situations and are subsequently labelled as antisocial.

In terms of systems repeating experiences, the 'loss' of professionals in the Dickson review was linked to the emotional impact of having to repeatedly retell their story (due to high staff turnover) when feeling vulnerable and scared. Hence, children in care did not feel heard in meetings because their new social worker did not know them. Conversely, children and young people in care took pride in having a sense that the professional genuinely cared for them, that they were listened to and that the professional was accessible and reliably there for them and did what was promised. The theme here appears to be a culture of potentially being forgotten by professionals, just as memories and stories of birth families can be forgotten. The important role professionals have here is to remember and genuinely keep in mind the children and young people we work with. Recognizing the impact of loss, recent NICE guidance states that in order to ensure stability, children in care, adopted or at risk of going into care should have '...the same key worker, social worker or personal adviser or key person in school throughout the period the child or young person is in the care system or on the edge of care' (NICE 2015, p.3).

With regards to the ninth theme to emerge from the review, there was a focus on the lack of practical and emotional preparation and support for leaving care, for example cooking and budgeting, and this happening too late. For some, the role of the foster carer in this capacity was highlighted as a place where care leavers received continued support. There was concern about a lack of information about entitlement and about some leaving care teams paying 'lip service'. Financial support was also viewed as inadequate and was linked to homelessness. There were concerns about sub-standard housing, housing for young mothers, being accommodated in the equivalent of a halfway house and being exposed to and vulnerable to criminal activity. The review also notes concern about 16-year-olds being expected to live independently. Hence the theme of inequality and discrimination continues for care leavers, and the *corporate parent* appears to be found wanting.

Related to this point, commenting on the work of the SCRIPT Team,[1] Guishard-Pine states:

> In our first or second year of operation, we quickly realized that children in care do not have any rites of passage or official recognition of becoming an adult. Jews have a Barmitzvah and many of the African and Asian cultures also have some sort of rite of passage. We found that children in care have their own personal story of the transition to adulthood pivoting around being 16 and what that means for different children in care, i.e. going back home, going to find siblings or other birth family, being able to leave school and choose whatever college they want to choose rather than the one the social worker or foster carer finds most convenient, getting a job and fend for themselves, go into a hostel. (personal communication, 27 December 2015)

1 The Service to Children Requiring Intensive Psychological Therapies (SCRIPT) was a multi-award-winning child mental health team in Luton set up to provide community psychotherapy for children in care and consultation and support to foster carers, schools and social workers (Guishard-Pine 2013).

Impact of the emotional world when working with traumatized and neglected children in care

The impact of emotional processes of the traumatized child and the impact of the emotional world of individual professionals and organizations, when working with children in care, has been acknowledged in the literature for a number of decades (e.g. Carr 1989; Conway 2009; Emanuel 2002). Due to the interaction of emotional worlds, professionals can find themselves paralyzed, overwhelmed with feelings of powerlessness, confused and scared in their work with children in care and with the professional networks around them.

Practitioners and carers are familiar with the scenario of children in care 'pushing boundaries' to see whether this particular adult is going to stay around. This includes at times communicating their emotional needs and struggles in distressing ways, including oppositional behaviour, isolation and withdrawal, self-harm, suicide attempts and attempts to seriously physically assault others. For example, although offending rates are falling, they are still higher for children in care than for all children (Department for Education 2014d). Unfortunately, young people communicating in this way may be viewed as 'manipulative' and 'behavioural' – that is in complete conscious control of the choices they are seen to make about their behaviour. Hence without space to reflect on such communication and resources to support the work, individuals working with the child and with systems around the child can find themselves and the organizations they represent emotionally depleted. This can include a lack of empathy for the child. This can mean that organizations present with institutional defences as a way to manage the emotional impact of work with children who have physically survived emotional, sexual and physical abuse or neglect, but for who psychologically the concept of 'survival' and indeed recovery is something that is perhaps in progress and may never be fully realized without continual redefinition. Hence as Roberts (2003) states:

> the nature of the work in various settings across the helping services affects the worker, giving rise to collective and institutional defences, which in turn determine organizational structures and practices. (p.110)

One example of an institutional defence is an organisation viewing itself as a 'superior alternative' to other organisations. As such I propose that the culturally competent practitioner for abused and neglected children in care has to beware of the potential impact of the emotional world of the child, her own emotional world and how these may combine into institutional defences (see Figure 13.2). Taken together, these processes subsequently impact on the collective capacity for multi-agency working. Importantly, however, we also have to be attuned to potential institutional offences – that is specifically when a child's coping strategies are triggered by the way in which an organization and professionals within it interact with her, due to what is happening in the organization as whole.

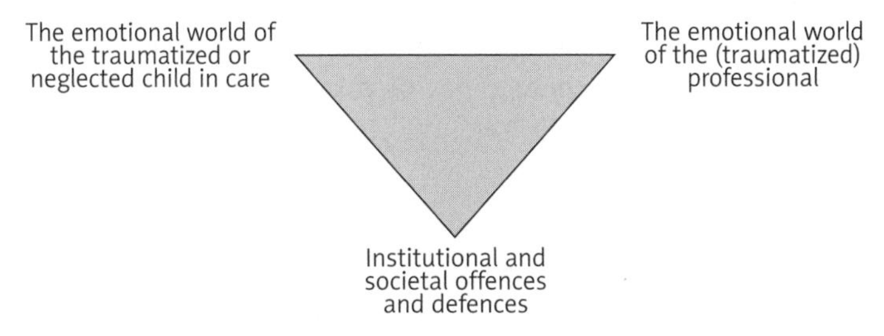

Figure 13.2 Significant processes involved in the culture of abused and neglected children in care

With regards to an organization often subconsciously – but at times more obviously – viewing itself as a superior alternative, this can result in a split between professionals representing these organizations, despite best efforts to work together and maintain communication, as advocated by the Working Together policy (Department for Education 2015). Conway (2009) maintains that we need to have a better understanding about how traumatized young people communicate their distress in order to put into practice well-intentioned policy around placement stability and education. Specifically she refers to the use of psychoanalytic concepts of splitting and projection as a way to reflect on multi-agency working for children in care.

With regards to the first concept of splitting, this is in response to feeling overwhelmed by a mix of distressing emotions and the mind essentially placing all the 'good' in one person or place and all the 'bad' in an alternative person or place as a way to organize the distress. This is also based on historical experiences of not being able to trust the 'good' that has been offered in the past. Hence the 'good' can quickly turn 'bad'. In such situations, professionals can find themselves invited to play the omnipotent (all-knowing) rescuer, or at other times are demonized and blamed entirely for the failings of the collective system: in other words, the victim. The important response here is for individual professionals to have space to observe the roles they are being invited to play and think about what this may be telling them about the child's emotional needs and the organizational defences. Ideally this will be followed by the professionals coming together to observe and discuss what is being generated in the system. Communication in this way is key as a way to manage the dynamics of the 'all-good' rescuing organization and the 'all-bad' destructive organization. However, this appears to be something that is not consistently practised across services. Additionally, systems are often not set up to withstand these types of discussions in an emotionally safe way. Carr (1989) advocates employing an external professional to facilitate such discussions.

I have also found the 'all-good' position to be just as burdensome as the 'all-bad'. With the former position professionals are faced with the 'self-assigned impossible task' of saving the day (Roberts 2003)! With the latter there can also be complex situations in which the system appears to want to deny the level of emotional vulnerability the child presents with, viewing the child as 'naughty' or 'a normal adolescent' and a worker may be left feeling as the bad person who wants to disrupt this collective denial by pointing out how much the child is attempting to communicate her distress.

Much of the evidence in this area of work is case-study based. With regards to projection of the child's emotional world onto the system around her, Emmanuel (2002) provides some useful clinical examples of how the emotional world of the child and foster carers can be re-enacted in the system. For example, in reflecting on an invitation to 'fight' over the child, Emmanuel states:

> In the same way as children may convey a preference for their foster placement over their birth home, which can result in the disruption of the placement, a similar dynamic may have been operating between me and the team managers, resulting in similar disruption. (2002, p.173)

For additional case examples, please refer to Briggs (2012). The process of using projection to think about meeting the needs of the child can be simple and complex at the same time. In simple terms this can mean professionals asking themselves, what do I feel when I sit with this child or young person? Do I feel incompetent, angry, abusive, as if I want to rescue her? Do I feel rejecting? And a really difficult question – do I feel as if I like this child? The last question is a particularly difficult one to reflect on but allowing ourselves to think in this way ultimately allows for more effective practice, in that we are open to think about what is happening for the child. For example, in practice when I have found it difficult to stay in a room with a child, this often represents a child who has faced significant rejection or loss and mistrusts the ability of adults to stay. When I am invited not to like the child, for example she has presented as physically or verbally abusive within the system, I have found this to be related to strong need in the child for self-preservation. I would argue that the culturally competent professional for children in care has to have the capacity to withstand discussions on the impact of the emotional and frequently unconscious world of the child on the professional system and relationships within that system. Furthermore, what we also have to do in this process is think about what these interactions tell us about our own emotional needs.

For example, Roberts states:

> To the extent that people are drawn to work in a particular setting because if offers opportunities to work through their own unresolved issues, these settings may well attract staff with similar internal needs and a similar propensity to fit with certain kinds of defences. (2003, p.112)

In practice I have seen this evident when professionals identify with a young person. It is only in individual discussions with these professionals that links to their own lives become apparent and the ability to disentangle this from their work is explored. Again, the need for safe space to explore such links is paramount but unfortunately can be lacking when clinical supervisors or line managers have not become routinely accustomed to facilitating such discussions but instead act out certain roles themselves, such as the preoccupied or abusive parent. When professionals sense that their supervisors or line managers lack self-awareness, the result is often that they remain silenced and at times paranoid about their own emotional world.

Conclusion

In this chapter I have proposed that it is essential for the culturally competent practitioner for children in care to be aware of some of the issues and emotional processes that enable us to begin to think about shared assumptions, meanings (spoken and unspoken) and experiences for children in care – that is a shared culture. The chapter has not explored specific 'sub-cultures' at this stage, such as unaccompanied asylum seekers. The chapter largely focused on issues; however, the emotional processes involved are as important as this has implications at all levels. For example, despite continued policy, the current political focus on austerity measures in the UK requires a degree of emotional detachment which denies the reality of the level of needs, such as managing emotional processes of emotionally, physically and sexually abused or neglected children and young people in care and the professionals and organizations that work with them.

Chapter 14

'Safe Therapy'

Involving Children in Care in Developing Child Mental Health Services

SIDRA ASLAM

Introduction

Although the feeling of safety is a key concept to the effectiveness of most psychological therapies, there is very little formal research that has been done on this area (Gilbert *et al.* 2008; Lynch 2012; Weiss 1993) and an associated dearth of literature on this subject. Rather, there is a current trend towards examining what aspects of psychological therapies are harmful and may make a client feel worse (Boseley 2014; Jackson 2015). The concept of safety in psychotherapy appears to be linked to attachment theory and its concept of security (Bowlby 1969, 1988). Fonagy (2001) argues that attunement is the building block to how one learns to be connected to others, build relationships, and feel safe in the world. One could argue that as corporate parents, all professionals working with children in care should aim to display emotional attunement through having an understanding of attachment theory. However, a more contemporary view is that feeling safe is about feeling confident (Greenspan 2002; Guishard-Pine *et al.* 2007), which introduces the notion of maximizing the use of one's internal resources (such as resilience) and connections to people in one's social environment as tools towards self-recovery. Oaklander had this to say:

> What is healing is Jimmy's expression of what he needed to express in his scene understood by him perhaps on a very deep intuitive level, the feeling of safety in my office, the easy relationship that we have developed, the acceptance and respect he feels from me, the knowledge that there are limits and boundaries that I set and take

> responsibility for (as, for example, time), and his feeling of control and power within those limits to do what he needed to do without interruption. (1997, p.308)

For children in care, one of those tools is likely to be a therapist within a child mental health service. However, global research has indicated that these children underutilize mental health services and/or do not engage. This may also be due to the fact that self-referral is uncommon (Improving Acess to Psychological Therapies 2012) and therefore children rely on adults to refer them to mental health services for help with their mental health problems (see Chapter 1 for a review). For children in care, their vision of self-recovery may be quite different from their social workers and carers. Thus it is important to facilitate children and young people in care as service users to express their views about what they need from health services – the essential concept of 'no decision about me without me' (Department of Health 2012).

User involvement

Choice is an inherent part of user-led services. This is consistent with the NHS White Paper *Equity and Excellence: Liberating the NHS* (Department of Health 2010), which emphasizes the need to place the voices of those who use services at the heart of commissioning and delivery. User involvement as a concept has had an international focus since the World Health Organization (WHO) proposed that governments should encourage involving their residents in innovative service development. This was formalized by the World Bank (2000) and taken forward by many countries across Europe. Despite this, it has been argued that this amounts to rhetoric (Tritter and McCallum 2006). The available resources often have an impact on the seriousness with which the idea of user involvement is approached (Beecham 2006). Watson (2010) notes that the economic conditions of any country can lead to 'patchy implementation' of user involvement as a government agenda (p.147). Consequently, a true client focus is sidelined. Others still have argued that in such circumstances user involvement is applied least to the marginalized and the vulnerable groups and communities (Begum 2006; Cowden and Singh 2007; Stewart 2008).

Over the last two decades, research incorporating children's views on mental health services such as child mental health services has been a growing area (Claveirole 2004; Day 2008; Day, Carey and Surgenor 2006; Street 2004; The NHS Confederation 2011). There are a few small-scale studies focusing on such views but very little 'effectiveness' research in this area incorporates a user perspective. In one UK sample of care leavers 31 per cent had been referred to mental health services and most of them had been dissatisfied with the services they had received, describing them as 'crap', 'stupid', 'a waste of time', and complaining that they had been 'treated like a child' by mental health professionals (Saunders and Broad 1997). Similarly, service users in another study referred to mental health services as 'mad' and 'mental' (Young Minds 2012). One study with 12–19-year-olds reported that service users particularly appreciated the informal approach of mental health services offered by the voluntary sector. They also welcomed being given a choice in whether or not they participated in counselling or therapy, or another service (Stanley and Manthorpe 2002).

Child mental health services and children in care

In Britain, the National Service Framework for children (Department of Health 2004) and Every Child Matters (Department for Education and Skills 2003) acknowledge that children in care are a group who are particularly vulnerable to psychological difficulties. Despite this, earliest research has shown that they are often denied access to services. This combination of facts inspired the development of dedicated mental health teams for children in care. The alternative and more accessible models for children in care have manifest through designated time offered by existing specialist mental health staff, the development of jointly commissioned posts, and designated teams. Designated posts integrated within a specialist child mental health service may be appropriate for smaller districts and rural/semi-urban areas, whereas designated teams may be more effective in inner-city areas. Teams similar to the SCRIPT team[1] have been set up around the country and offer direct access and treatment to children in care, and consultation and training to carers and staff (foster carers, social workers, residential care staff) (Callaghan *et al.* 2004; Golding 2010).

1 The Service to Children Requiring Intensive Psychological Therapies (SCRIPT) was a multi-award-winning child mental health team in Luton set up to provide community psychotherapy for children in care and consultation and support to foster carers, schools and social workers (Guishard-Pine 2013).

Young Minds, in partnership with the National Child and Adolescent Mental Health Support Service (Young Minds 2007), has published descriptions of designated mental health services for children in care. Table 14.1 summarizes the key characteristics of a successful mental health service for children in care based on the examples.

Table 14.1 Ten characteristics of a successful mental health service for children in care

1) Flexibility	Many children in care have complex needs and do not readily access traditional child mental health services.
2) Joint commissioning	Mental health services for children in care are at the interface of health, education and social care. Each party needs to understand the systems, timescales and expectations of the others, and have a commitment to working in new ways.
3) Strong leadership	Individuals with vision and a passion for providing relevant, accessible services to help turn around children's lives.
4) Engagement	Taking time to engage with children and young people whose past experiences have often caused them to mistrust all adults and to battle through life alone.
5) Long-term work	The ability to offer long-term support, where appropriate, sometimes at an intensive level and at other times in a low-key way, is important.
6) Holistic	Support for the whole child, not just mental health needs.
7) Systemic thinking	Using systemic thinking to engage all those in contact with the child and family.
8) Participative	It is important to listen to the young people about what they want from a service, develop formal and informal mechanisms for consulting with young people.
9) Evidence-based	The importance of evidence-based practice. Evaluation, to ensure that service developments produce effective outcomes, is fundamental.
10) Reflective and responsive	Building in processes of reflection and review and responding to feedback from all stakeholders is implicit in their successful development.

(adapted from Young Minds 2007, p.11)

The reality is that there is significant variation in designated child mental health teams for children in care at a national level, making it challenging to determine what configuration of services and approaches are most appropriate to meet the needs of children in care.

The need for more and diverse research on mental health services to children in care

The voices of children in care are no longer viewed as peripheral to the process of health service development (Department of Health 2009). The views of children in care's access to and experiences of mental health services were obtained by Beck (2006) using a postal questionnaire. The results highlighted that relatively few children in care were able to suggest what sort of services might help them with their problems and a number of those who responded to this question simply said that they wanted something different. A key limitation of this study was the use of a postal questionnaire to explore the experiences of children in care. Rather, using a qualitative method may have supported one to further delve into the themes, for example, exploring what 'wanting something different' would look like through a dialogue.

The Mental Health Foundation document *The Mental Health of Children in Care. Bright Futures: Working with Vulnerable Young People* (2002) recognized the need for more research on the looked after population. The research summarized here suggests that more evidence on the impact of therapeutic interventions for children in care is required. Research using qualitative methods to obtain rich data from children in care receiving therapy to identify what aspects of a therapeutic intervention they valued is essential (Davies and Wright 2008). The paucity of qualitative research within the existing literature gives grounds for employing a qualitative approach to the present study. This research used a number of service users as accessing multiple perspectives has a distinct advantage over a single viewpoint: the evidence is often considered to be more compelling, making an overall study more robust (Herriott and Firestone 1983). The full study detailed accounts of children in care's experiences of accessing child mental health services, and paid particular attention to evaluating the therapeutic intervention they received (Aslam 2012). Thus, this chapter summarizes children in care's experiences of child mental health services and discusses how their experiences can shape future child mental health provision to meet the mental health needs of children in care.

The voices of service users

The experiences of marginalized and vulnerable individuals are of vital importance to understanding factors that may contribute to poor outcomes (Atkin and Rollins 1993; Baxter and Jack 2008; Begum 2006; Watson 2010). Therefore, in order to obtain an insight into children in care's experiences of attending child mental health services, four service users were interviewed. The contribution of these young people was analysed using a specific qualitative method called *cross case synthesis* (Yin 2009) as this type of analysis looks at the information collected as a whole rather than the individual contribution of each service user.

Originally used in a school setting, Wearmouth's (2004) '*talking stones*' technique was employed to facilitate the interviews because of its reputation for promoting 'self-advocacy...for disaffected students' (2004, p.7). The novel technique involves presenting a child/young person with a selection of stones and shells which are different colours, textures and sizes and asking him to choose stones and shells to represent his emotions and experiences. This tool was used as a non-directive way of facilitating children in care to tell their story about their experience of child mental health services and would be useful to enable them to reflect on their experiences. This method is also sensitive to the process of expressing potentially difficult feelings about the traumatic experiences from their past (Davies *et al.* 2009).

The service users in this study

These service users were all young people in care aged over 16 years. The length of each young person's therapeutic intervention varied, with the shortest intervention lasting six months and the longest intervention lasting one year and eight months. A therapeutic intervention consisted of direct, one-to-one intervention of a psychologist, family therapist, or primary mental health worker (MacKay and Greig 2007). Table 14.2 provides further details about the service users.

Table 14.2 Summary of the service users participating in this study

	Ali	David	Tina	Sarah
Sex	Male	Male	Female	Female
Ethnicity	South Asian	South Asian and African Caribbean	White	White
Age	17 years old	16 years old	16 years old	17 years old
Time in care	12 years	13 years	11 years	5 years
Current care placement	Foster care	Foster care	Foster care	Foster care
Placement stability	5 foster placements	7 foster placements	10 foster placements and 2 residential placements	3 foster placements
Length of child mental health service involvement	1 year 10 months	1 year 4 months	9 months	1 year 6 months
Length of therapeutic intervention	1 year 8 months	1 year 2 months	6 months	1 year 1 month
Child mental health service professional delivering therapeutic intervention	Clinical psychologist	Family therapist	Primary mental health worker	Clinical psychologist

What the service users said about their experience of therapy

The overarching themes related to this question are presented in Figure 14.1.

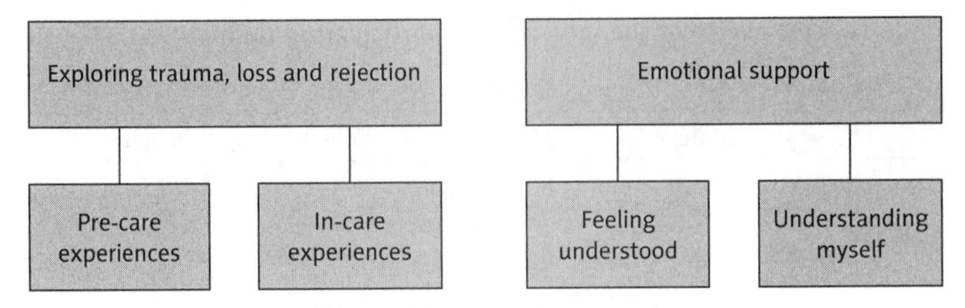

Figure 14.1 The themes arising from the children in care's therapy within the child mental health service

Exploring trauma, loss and rejection

The overarching theme of '*Exploring trauma, loss and rejection*' highlighted that their individual therapy supported the service users to process and resolve difficult past experiences. Most of these service users spoke of how they had not discussed their feelings towards their birth parents with other professionals or foster carers because it caused them emotional distress to do so. However, they felt that the therapeutic help that they received from their therapist enabled them to feel safe and secure enough to explore difficult feelings.

Pre-care and in-care experiences

Interestingly, although life story work is described as a model for 'facilitating the construction of personal narrative for foster children' (Cook-Cottone and Beck 2007, p.1) the service users in this study said that compared to therapy, life story work did not enable them to explore the trauma, loss and rejection they had faced throughout their life prior to and during care. Bowlby (1988) likens the therapist to a parent 'who provides her child with a secure base from which to explore' (p.140). These service users therefore used their therapist as a secure base from which they explored unhappy and painful aspects of their past and present.

Emotional support

Emotional attunement consists of an adult responding to a foster child's verbal and non-verbal cues in a way that the child feels understood (Fonagy 2001). This attunement is important to a child's ability to learn to regulate his nervous system and deal with distressing events. The service users in the current study were able to feel understood and understand themselves through the emotional attunement offered via the therapeutic relationship with the therapist. They felt that the personal qualities of the therapist were attuned to their emotional needs at the time of the therapeutic intervention. The importance of attending to the way that the therapist related to the young people was particularly significant, given that children in care's responses to professionals can be influenced by previously damaging interactions with adults (Golding *et al.* 2006; Hughes 2004).

Feeling understood

In the sub-theme '*Feeling understood*', the service users highlighted the importance of rapport with the therapist providing the therapeutic intervention. They described their therapists as approachable and able to enter into a genuine helping and trusting relationship with them. Service users highlighted the importance of rapport with the therapist delivering the therapeutic intervention. This relates to the therapist's capacity for emotional attunement – the ability to hear, see, sense, interpret and respond to the looked after young person's verbal and non-verbal cues in a way that the young person felt and understood (Fonagy 2001). They experienced professionals who were approachable and able to enter into a genuine helping trusting relationship with them. They felt that the personal qualities of the therapist were attuned to their emotional needs at the time of the therapeutic intervention. This is consistent with literature suggesting therapeutic orientation can be secondary to other factors in distinguishing effective therapies (Davies and Wright 2008; Davies *et al.* 2009; Stiles *et al.* 1986).

Understanding myself

The service users recognized how their internal emotional states changed once they had attended the therapeutic intervention. These were made explicit through elaboration of constructs during the interview:

> ...like we did this flipchart exercise where I wrote down the things I did, and the things I was feeling and thinking. I had one paper with how I felt about going into care. One paper with how my parents and

sisters and brothers would have felt. And then how I felt now. That exercise was amazing. That's when I began to understand myself. (Ali)

In Tina's case, denial was a defence mechanism used to protect herself. The therapeutic intervention attended to defence mechanisms for the service user to feel understood and understand themselves.

Facilitators and barriers to attending child mental health services

A key facilitator in promoting attendance at child mental health service was that the therapist was the adult that was most available and who could be trusted. In fact, this aspect emerged as another of the main themes from the research, as illustrated in Figure 14.2.

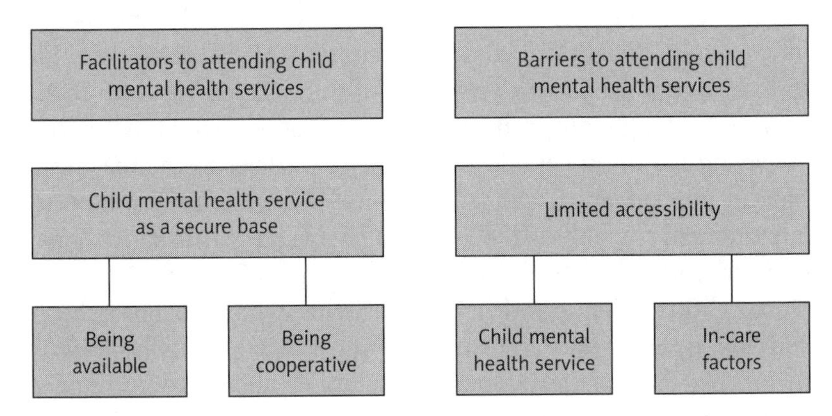

Figure 14.2 The themes related to the factors that helped or hindered attendance for their therapy within the child mental health service

Being available

As well as child mental health service professionals, the service users were in regular contact with their social workers, foster carers, teachers and contact supervisors. Service users spoke of how other professionals were not always 'available' for them, therefore they didn't feel safe:

Seeing Aubrey every week helped me to feel safe, because before that I was always seeing new people and my social worker had changed six times in one year. So it was nice that I was seeing Aubrey for over a year. (Sarah)

I felt safe because no one apart from Inez knew me at the child mental health service so I would just wait in waiting area and she would come get me. She would always ask me first where I wanted to sit. (Tina)

I knew that the child mental health service was a safe place for me to talk about my past and how I felt about my birth parents with Zeke. I couldn't do that with anyone else because that wasn't their job and I didn't feel like I could really trust them. (Ali)

Being available is a dimension of caregiving identified by Ainsworth, Bell and Stayton (1971) that relates to being able to trust in order to experience emotional well-being and social functioning (Schofield and Beek 2009). The service users' comments highlight that they felt they could trust the therapist and this facilitated their attendance at the child mental health service over a period of time. The message that children in care particularly value relationships with professionals that are stable is highlighted in the Munro Review of Child Protection (Department for Education 2011a).

Being cooperative

These service users reported that their therapist was cooperative, which facilitated them to attend a therapeutic intervention.

I understood why it would be good for me to go and the child mental health service even asked me if I wanted to have family sessions on the first day I went and I said yeah because I felt like that way I am not on my own with it and it didn't feel as uncomfortable and I really felt that the family sessions made a big difference to why I didn't move home again. We didn't used to have that many arguments after the family sessions, like Mrs Nicolai would say things to me differently now that I think about it and it made me less angry. Like instead of saying, 'Come down right now and have your dinner', she would say, 'Would you like to have dinner after you have washed your hands' and it made such a difference. (David)

> She asked me first what I wanted to talk about or if there was anything on my mind. No one else did that with me since I have been in care, it was like they were just ticking boxes and trying to just quickly see me and go leaving me to deal with all my problems on my own. Inez wasn't like that though, she always gave me choices about the sessions and that's why I wanted to come to them. (Tina)

The service users stated that they were given autonomy and choice at the child mental health service – something they did not expect when accessing a mental health service. Their comments suggest that they felt effective and empowered by experiencing a cooperative therapist. These findings contrast with previous findings of care leavers who were dissatisfied with child mental health services and complained that they had been 'treated like a child' by mental health professionals (Saunders and Broad 1997). The service users here spoke of how they rarely experienced cooperative adults and they found that professionals and adults in their life were often either too controlling and intrusive or too passive and ineffective. Consequently, experiencing cooperative adults facilitated their attendance at the child mental health service.

In-care experience

The service users highlighted that the therapeutic intervention made them reflect on the bipolar construct of unloved/loved. Ali and Sarah stated that they felt 'unloved' throughout their experiences of being in care. However, after attending the child mental health service they felt 'loved' and were able to reflect on aspects of care experiences which made them feel 'loved'.

Child mental health services

The data obtained from the current study offers a new perspective in understanding what supports children in care to attend mental health services. Child mental health services can act as a secure base for children in care through being available and cooperative, which supports long-term attendance at child mental health services to meet their mental health needs, but they can also repel young people when the therapist is not attuned to the service user.

Overall the service user's experiences of attending a therapeutic intervention through child mental health services were positive.

They highlighted improvements in managing behaviour problems and improved current relationships to be significant outcomes of the therapeutic interventions they undertook. Furthermore, the young people recognized how their internal emotional states changed once they had attended the therapeutic intervention. These were made explicit through elaboration of constructs during the interview. These findings offer rich and detailed insight into the impact of therapeutic interventions from children in care's perspectives, an area which previously was under represented in relation to measuring child mental health service outcomes for children in care.

Emotional regulation

Although there has been some debate as to the prevalence of attachment disorders among children in care (Howe and Fearnley 2003; Millward *et al.* 2006; NICE 2010), the evidence is that they present mainly with symptoms that are diagnosed as *conduct disorders* when they are aged five to ten years and *emotional disorders* when they are aged 11–15 years (Meltzer *et al.* 2003). For these service users, there was a sense that the ability to manage their anger about what has happened and is happening to them was one of the explicit benefits of therapy. Sarah stated that prior to the therapeutic intervention she had felt 'angry' and that this feeling changed to 'relaxed' after her involvement with the child mental health service. Others shared their journey towards anger management with more detail:

> Yeah, like I brought stuff I had from my mum and dad and we talked about them and the attachment I had with them. At first I didn't understand why we did it. But then I could see that it helped me. Like I used to be really negative and not saying anything good at all about my mum and dad. But Wendy helped me to think about the positive things with my dad and mum. Especially my dad because I didn't like talking about him at all and then I remembered some good things which made me less angry. (David)

> It was somewhere for me to talk...because before that I used to just bottle everything up and just deny that my mum left me and that my dad was hurting me. I used to make excuses for them. But now I understand and accept things...it's like...I am less angry now inside. (Tina)

Developing mental health services

The following ideas for service development arose from this study:

1. The first aim of therapy with the child in care should be to develop a trusting relationship at his pace. The secure base lies at the heart of attachment theory (Bowlby 1969) as it defines close relationships as a means to an important end; trust in the availability of help and support reduces anxiety, which was demonstrated to the therapists by the service users. These findings have implications for all professionals supporting children in care through highlighting a need to provide a secure base by being available and cooperative.

2. Changes of therapist should be avoided, especially if the youngster is engaged in therapy.

3. For children in care to talk openly about personal and often painful problems requires trust in a professional, and a change in professional or a short working relationship can mean the child always having to put his trust in someone new (Department for Education 2011a). This is congruent with findings from Davies *et al.*'s (2009) study in which children with disrupted attachments commented on appreciating the relationship they had with the therapists. This offers insight into how attachment theory informs the relationship between the looked after child/young person and the therapist delivering the therapeutic intervention.

4. The therapist needs to negotiate signposts towards self-development and mental health with the young person, such as understanding himself, feeling less angry about his past, acceptance, and so on. The therapeutic intervention within the child mental health service provided a safe, dependable, empathetic and attuned presence that enabled the service user in the study to do some of the 'growing up' he could not do in the unsafe early environment.

5. The therapist needs to model for the young person that his best resource is himself in order to build resilience to disappointment and unexpected change. Some studies have emphasized the importance of choice and respect for children

in care (Davies and Wright 2008; Stanley *et al.* 2005). Choice and autonomy can lead to feelings of empowerment for children in care (Department for Education 2011b). Rutter's (1990) research emphasizes the benefits of empowerment: children with positive feelings of self-esteem, mastery and control can more easily manage stressful experiences. This is especially pertinent given the nature of the complex mental health needs of children in care.

The reflections of these service users reinforce how professionals working within child mental health services should be aware of meeting the emotional needs of children in care in a way that is underlined by the Young Minds (2012) report. This is also supported by recent research such as Zilberstein and Popper (2016) and NICE/ Social Care Institute for Excellence guidance which recommends a core training module for all mental health professionals providing a service to children in care to develop an understanding and awareness of the emotional needs of this vulnerable group (NICE 2010). However, while separate reports have presented the views that children in care have of their social workers (Oliver 2010), their teachers (Cann 2012; Harker *et al.* 2004a, 2004) and of mental health practitioners (Aslam 2012), the current trend is to recognize and acknowledge that practitioners within education, health and social care all have a critical role in promoting the emotional well-being of children in care (Bazalgette *et al.* 2015; Happer, McCreadie and Aldgate 2006). Hence, lessons for all childcare professionals lie within the voices of young people.

Chapter 15

Kith and Kin

Providing a Therapeutic Space for Kinship Carers

OLATAYO AFUAPE

> Questions regarding the *efficacy* of psychotherapy refer to the benefits derived from it, its potency, its impact on clients, or its ability to make a difference in people's lives. Conventional statistical comparisons between groups tell us very little about the efficacy of psychotherapy. (Jacobson and Truax 1984, p.12)

In Britain there have been no studies conducted on the therapeutic impact of groups on a solely kinship carer population. This is surprising given that kinship care has always been a normal feature of family life. Historically, in England, Wales and Ireland, in the absence of and because of the child welfare systems, children had no alternative but to be taken into extended family networks or placed with relatives when birth parents or primary carers were unable to provide for them. However, they have only been studied formally in the last decade or so in the UK (Aldgate and McIntosh 2006; Broad, Hayes and Rushforth 2001; Broad and Skinner 2005; Farmer and Moyers 2008; Flynn 2002; Hunt 2003; Hunt, Waterhouse and Lutman 2008; Ince 2009; Richards and Tapsfield 2003; Roth and Ashley 2010; Saunders and Selwyn 2008; Selwyn and Saunders 2006; Smallwood and Wilson 2007; Welland and Wheatley 2010).

A review of the literature on studies looking at therapeutic support for kinship carers also focused on other parts of the world where the benefits of kinship placements are more often supported, formalized and valued, such as the USA, Australia, New Zealand, Africa and Europe. Even within this more extensive review, studies which involve working therapeutically featured kinship carers in support groups, focus groups, training groups and parenting programmes (Green and Gray 2013; Kenrick, Lindsey and Tollemache 2006; Strozier 2012; Zlotnick *et al.* 2000) alongside birth parents (Zlotnick *et al.* 2000), child welfare workers and community leaders (Green and Gray 2013) or foster and adoptive carers (Kenrick *et al.* 2006). Today kinship care is an essential feature of extensive family life, worldwide. Most indigenous cultures such as the tribes and cultures in West Africa use kinship care as a way of looking and supporting their elders, socializing their young and imparting traditions and cultural expectations (Chukwudozie 2014; Hegar 1999; Nitter and Onate 2013). The Maori in New Zealand, who use kinship care to perpetuate a sense of community and togetherness, arrange for the eldest child to be placed with an elder aunt, uncle or grandparent who in turn passes on important traditional practices to the next generation (Ernst 1999). This chapter is concerned with the evaluation of therapeutic groupwork with two groups of kinship carers.

Defining kinship care

The Buttle report (Nandy *et al.* 2004) recognized that the term 'kinship care' varies throughout the world. In most parts of the developed world, kin is defined by 'shared blood' but in other parts of the world, godparents, clans and neighbours as members of the community are considered part of the extended family network (see Greef 1999 for review). In fact, Bowie (2004) suggests that in some cultures parents prefer their children to be raised by members of the community who are not blood related.

In the UK, the complexity of deciding what is or is not kinship care is due to the fact that different parts of the UK define 'kin' differently. In Scotland, for example, 'kin' is determined by blood, marriage or civil partnership (with no restriction on closeness) (Scottish Government 2009) or alternatively might be a person who has a pre-existing relationship with the child. She might be a close friend or may be part of the child's network (Aldgate and McIntosh 2006).

Legal differences between kinship and foster care

In the UK, the Children Act 1989 acknowledges kinship care and grants local authorities the power to offer kinship carers financial support under section 17: the child 'in need' category. However, even within this legislation, kinship carers are not afforded the same rights to support and financial assistance as foster carers or given the same legal standing as adoptive parents and special guardians (Wade, Dixon and Richards 2010). On this basis, a discussion paper on *Family and Friends Care* for the Department of Health argued that the eligibility for services should be 'based on the needs of the child, not on the type of placement being considered' (Department of Health 2002, cited in Morris 2003). The paper emphasized that family and friends 'make a significant contribution to providing for the needs of children in a variety of circumstances', in spite of them experiencing greater economic difficulties and having lower economic status than foster carers or adoptive parents (Berrick, Barth and Needell 1994; Hirsch 2008; Social Exclusion Task Force 2008). The Department for Education (2011b) formalized the guidance for kinship provision. Such developments make bring attention to the uniqueness of kinship care and the specific needs of these placements.

The challenges of being a kinship carer

Williams (1974) recognized that severely deprived children were doubly deprived, first by their neglect and second by separation from their birth parent and family (no matter how abusive). This enabled clinicians to understand why a child in a safe environment and stable placement would act out and sabotage relationships with their carers. In addition to the traditional reasons why children come to be cared for by kin, it is important to note that the children who are referred to child mental health services have often left their birth family at the point of family crisis. These children tend to be severely deprived as well as traumatized.

Caring for the traumatized child

The Diagnostic and Statistical Manual of Mental Disorders (DSM-5) defines trauma as an event which involves actual or threatened death, serious injury or a threat to one's physical integrity. In childhood, trauma can include bereavement or separation from a parent. The associated trauma of children who have gone in to care has been identified for several decades. Connolly (2011) suggests that in addition to traditions being handed down through the generations, so too can trauma be handed down. She defines intergenerational trauma as being combined or extreme and cumulative over generations. She advises that therapists working with survivors of these types of trauma need to adapt their analytic technique, focusing less on the 'here and now' of the transference and countertransference and holding in mind the reality of the past trauma.

During the pilot kinship care group, there was a powerful undercurrent of loss which was only implicit in the group's dialogue and its thematic analyses (Aronson 1994; Atkinson and Heritage 1984). The theme of loss was often reflected on by the facilitators during and after group sessions and this was thought about in terms of the facilitators' countertransference connection to the participants' past trauma. This idea receives wider support (Kernberg 1965; McCann and Pearlman 1990; Racker 1957; Ziegler 1996; Ziegler and McEvoy 2000;). McEvoy (1990) states that 'countertransference can be appreciated as a primary source of insight and compassion into the [survivor's] past experience and present reality' (p.1). The impact trauma and deprivation have on relationships with others (especially carers) has been noted by Holmes (2013) citing Bowlby's (1969, 1973, 1977, 1980 and 1988) theory of attachment. He describes how a child who has experienced neglect, rejection, abuse or loss at an early age comes to experience his environment as hostile, unsafe and unpredictable. Attachment theory is best explained by Holmes's 'spatial theory' (p.67) whereby in healthy attachments, closeness to one's loved one determines how happy or sad one feels. In a traumatized attachment the child devises a faulty internal working model of the world based on a repetition of his early experiences. His way of relating to his primary carer is either through avoidance or adherence, which leads to avoidance or ambivalent attachment patterns of behaviour (p.79). This is supported by Schore (1994), who asserted that traumatized attachment relationships impacted on a child's neurological functioning.

Rationale for therapeutic groups and theories on the group process: psycho-educational versus psychoanalytic

Elder *et al.* (2008) state that groups are not just cost effective, they are also more efficient. They cite Byrne and Byrne (1996) who argue that individuals coming together, sharing experiences and learning from others who have been in a similar situation has far more emotional benefits than individual support. They cite Earley (2000) who distinguish between problem-focused groups where specific problems are addressed through information sharing with people in crisis, and general process groups where deeper character change is facilitated by addressing problems as they arise through the interpersonal group process. These processes are often unconscious and it is often the role of the therapist (or other group members) to make them apparent. The function of the psycho-educational group is to reinforce a family's strengths and resilience by informing group members about mental health difficulties, where to obtain resources and support within the community and to problem solve issues pertaining to these difficulties.

Within this web of need, kinship carers may benefit from both a therapeutic space to process feelings and traumatic experiences and a psycho-educational framework which would be the structure for the group. This is consistent with Wheelan (2005), who suggests that in order to understand groups they should be conceptualized as complex, dynamic systems requiring diverse ways of conceptualizing, supporting and responding to their needs.

The kinship care therapeutic group (KCTG)

Although informed by the well-known principles of group psychotherapy described by Yalom (1985) and Yalom and Leszcz (2005), this particular group therapy approach was based on the broader principle of psycho-education practiced within social work and mental health (e.g. Golding and Picken 2004; Middleman and Wood 1990; Montgomery 2002; Trevithick 2005) where theoretical knowledge (concepts and ideas), factual knowledge (research) and practice knowledge (direct experience) are synthesized and applied within the helping process (Trevithick 2008).

Each session lasted two hours, which included a 15-minute teabreak, and was divided into two teaching/discussion slots and two activities slots. The participants were given literature (articles, newspaper cuttings, extract from books, etc.) to read in order to furnish and complement their existing and developing knowledge about the needs of their child/ren. The groups were run over a period of two years. Figure 15.1 shows the programme of topics that were introduced to the group.

KINSHIP CARER THERAPEUTIC GROUP SESSIONS

Initial meeting

Session 1	Introductions and needs of group
Session 2	Role of being carer
Session 3	Impact of separation, introducing attachment
Session 4	Attachment, trauma and behaviour
Session 5	Emotional well-being and behaviour as a means of communication
Session 6	Play as way of connecting, relating and understanding
Session 7	Relationships: the child, the family and the outside world
Session 8	Your child and school and endings

Figure 15.1 The programme of topics that were introduced to the kinship carer therapeutic group

In the KCTG there was an equal proportion of paternal and maternal grandparents looking after their grandchild. In our groups, step-grandparents consisted of 11 per cent of the participants (see Figure 15.2).

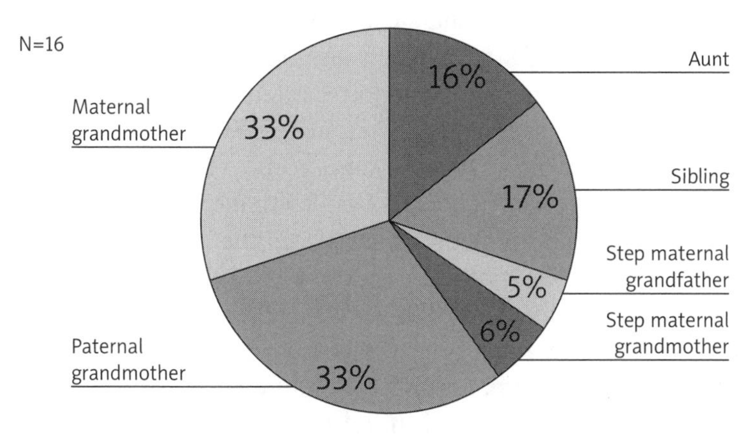

Figure 15.2 The relationship of kinship carers in the KCTG to their children

Although there is a growing body of research in the Antipodes on grandparents as parents (see Backhouse and Graham 2009 for review; Yardley, Mason and Watson 2009), and in the US (see Williams 2011 for review) there is little to no research on the specific impact kinship care has on paternal grandparents as the majority of kinship children are cared for by their maternal grandparents (Harden 1997; Hayslip and Kaminski 2005; Nandy *et al.* 2004). Overall, there is a paucity of research about the differential impact of male and female grandparents as kinship carers on the outcomes for their grandchildren.

The need for research into kinship care

One of the most under-researched areas of child and adolescent mental health clinical practices is the appropriate approach to working with kinship carers. This is reiterated by Waterhouse and Brocklesby (1999). They propose that the lack of research and knowledge about how to best assist kinship carers might profoundly affect any decision-making regarding the families' emotional welfare and mental health concerns. Richards (2001) concurs that the diverse and varying cultural perspectives on kinship depreciate the true prevalence of kinship care and the implications and impact this has on communities and society generally.

Rationale for the research

Many referrals of young people in kinship care placements have common themes such as intergenerational issues, deprivation and trauma. The needs of kinship carers and their children are different and generally more complex than foster carers and adoptive parents. Kinship care can be seen as a vicarious undertaking often because the carer is seen as having divided loyalties to his young relative/s and to the birth parent who the court has determined has either caused the child/ren significant harm or has placed the child/ren at risk of significant harm. The vicarious nature by which the kinship carers often came to care for their child set their needs apart from adoptive parents who would have gone through an arduous matching and selection process. Waterhouse and Brocklesby (1999) concluded that understanding the background, history and circumstance of kinship care would enable the clinical team to better support their needs.

Evaluating the impact of group work with kinship carers

Measurement is widely seen as the lynchpin of evidence-based practice, (Margison *et al.* 2000). Margison *et al.* (2000) argue for a recognition of 'clinically responsive measurement methods' (p.123) that can render psychotherapy as being measurable. This research project was based on an evaluation of the impact of a kinship carer therapeutic group on the emotional well-being of the youngster and also the coping capacity of the carers and comes within the domain of what is known as 'practice-based evidence'. The coping capacity of the carers was evaluated using comparisons between the before and after scores on the Parenting Stress Index (PSI) (Abidin 1992). The children placed with them were given the Strength and Difficulties Questionnaire (SDQ) (Goodman 1997, Goodman *et al.* 2000) and Goal Based Outcome Measure (GBOM) (Law 2013) as pre and post measures. The project had two strands: first to provide evidence of the validity of the group intervention and second to explore the process of change for the members and facilitators using a discourse analysis method (Antaki *et al.* 2002; Attride-Stirling 2001; Stenner 1993; Strauss and Corbin 1998; Taylor and Ussher 2001).

The research questions for the groups were thus:

- What can kinship carers tell us about their experience that informs our clinical practice?
- Can the KCTG reduce the child's degree of challenging behaviour?
- Can the KCTG reduce the carer's stress levels?

Reflecting on the kinship carers therapeutic group

The reflection of the group as a complex dynamic system was informed by many theories. Malinowski (1929) and Mead (1928) enabled us to think about the ethnographic nature of groups and the impact that the facilitators had on the group process as participant observers. Skoll (2012) advocated that certain psychoanalytic techniques complemented ethnographic approaches. He recommended self-analysis, using dream analysis and free association in an attempt to enhance the goal of researching human behaviour as a social phenomenon. Although an intriguing prospect, the intergenerational themes and psycho-educational framework among other things would have a contaminating effect on this approach.

The groups' moment-to-moment experience and their process both during and after sessions were informed by Freud (1922), Wertheimer (1924), Bion (1961), and Obholzer (1994), who suggested that an important part of the group process was to deny unpleasant and painful experiences. In contrast to Freud's (1921) idea that the group can bestow its thinking and decision-making capacities onto the person perceived as leader, thus disabling its own efforts, we experienced a reciprocal exchange of knowledge and information between facilitators and group members. The inextricable link between theory and practice was evident during this process as the facilitators developed their knowledge and first-hand understanding of the experiences and needs of kinship carers.

The majority of children being cared for were between four and seven years and over 35 per cent of those in care had suffered neglect, physical and sexual abuse and had parents who were mentally ill, misusing drugs or both. There was a high propensity of grandparents in groups 1 and 2 (see Figure 15.2). There were equal numbers of paternal and maternal grandparents and significant number of step-grandparents, which had a specific impact on both the groups. Seventy per cent of kinship carers in both groups were aged 56 years and over. Sixty per cent of kinship carers in both groups were retired and 20 per cent of kinship carers had to return to work in order to financially support the kinship child. Seventy-five per cent of kinship carers were looking after a child or children informally, meaning that there was no formal involvement from the local authority; kinship carers did not have or share parental responsibility with the birth parents and received little or no financial support from birth parents or local authority services.

How did the KCTG help the children and the kinship carers?

There was a distinct difference between the quantitative feedback as assessed through outcome measures and the qualitative feedback.

The outcome measures yielded some useful data. The data showed that over 40 per cent of kinship carers in both groups reported that their child's behaviour fell below the level of clinical risk after the intervention (Figures 15.3 and 15.4).

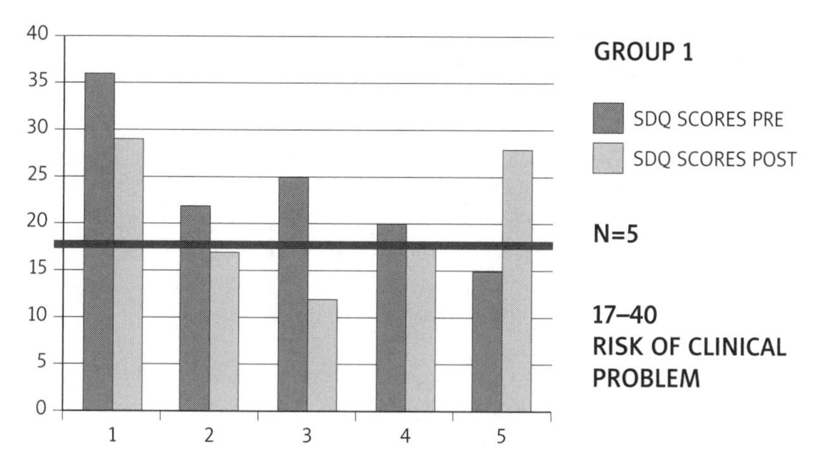

Figure 15.3 Graph to show pre- and post-SDQ scores for Group 1

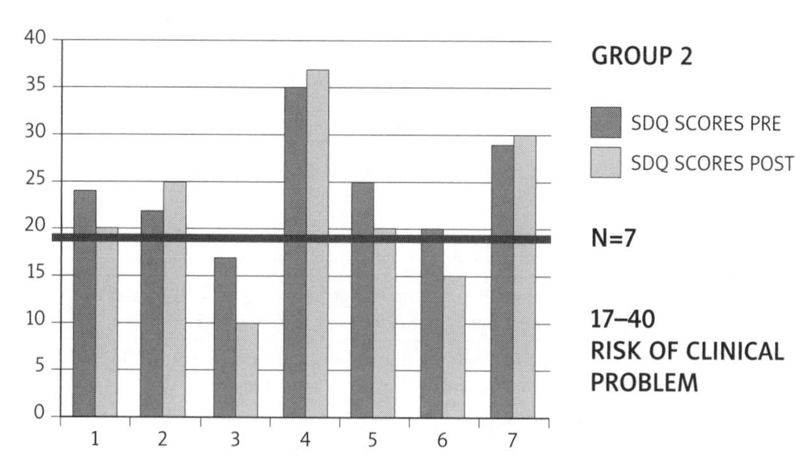

Figure 15.4 Graph to show pre- and post-SDQ scores for Group 2

Positive feedback was also captured by the GBOMS and the thematic analysis, providing some useful information about group members' individual and collective experiences and needs.

The measures used showed that the KCTG reduced the challenging behaviour below the level of clinical risk for just over half of the children (54%). With regard to the PSI, Abidin (1992) stated that the clinical significant range is 90 and above. Although there were clinical decreases in the stress levels of 59 per cent of the carers, they did not fall below 90. The KCTG programmes were rated highly, receiving an average of 90 per cent for all but one goal (see Figures 15.5 and 15.6).

How close are you to your goal?
Key: The nine goals + average score achieved (0 = not at all met; 10 = goals reached)

Goal 1	9.33	To discuss and share the challenges of being a kinship carer and what research highlights about the role of kinship care.
Goal 2	9.33	To discuss and share the impact of separation on your child and the understanding of this in relation to attachment.
Goal 3	9.67	To understand trauma and how this has affected your child, especially in relation to brain development and functioning.
Goal 4	9.67	To discuss and share how disruption and family breakdown may affect your children's behaviour, emotional and general development.
Goal 5	9.33	To discuss and share ways of thinking about and strategies for managing your child's behaviour.
Goal 6	9	To discuss behaviour as a form of communication, using Maslow's Hierarchy of Needs to help you think about children's needs in relation to their behaviour.
Goal 7	9	To discuss and share kinship carers' experience of play and how this impacts on their relationship with their child.
Goal 8	9	To offer support and advice to kinship carers regarding their rights (legal and financial), access to information and support.
Goal 9	9.5	Other.

Figure 15.5 The scoring of the goal-based outcome measure for Group 1

How close are you to your goal?
Key: The nine goals + average score achieved (0 = not at all met; 10 = goals reached)

Goal 1	9.33	To discuss and share the challenges of being a kinship carer and what research highlights about the role of kinship care.
Goal 2	9.33	To discuss and share the impact of separation on your child and the understanding of this in relation to attachment.
Goal 3	9.67	To understand trauma and how this has affected your child, especially in relation to brain development and functioning.
Goal 4	9.67	To discuss and share how disruption and family breakdown may affect your children's behaviour, emotional and general development.
Goal 5	9.33	To discuss and share ways of thinking about and strategies for managing your child's behaviour.
Goal 6	9	To discuss behaviour as a form of communication, using Maslow's Hierarchy of Needs to help you think about children's needs in relation to their behaviour.
Goal 7	9	To discuss and share kinship carers' experience of play and how this impacts on their relationship with their child.
Goal 8	9	To offer support and advice to kinship carers regarding their rights (legal and financial), access to information and support.
Goal 9	9.5	Other.

Figure 15.6 The scoring of the goal-based outcome measure for Group 2

Under the 'additional comments' section, Group 1 indicated the need for more sessions. Both groups felt that the size of the group was adequate and the sessions were full of information that enabled them to learn more about their children. One kinship carer suggested that kinship carers should go on a KCTG before taking on a child so that they would know what to expect.

Thematic analysis

The groups' experiences, preoccupations and concerns were captured through a thematic analysis (Aronson 1994). The emerging themes are presented in a pictorial form (see Figures 15.7 and 15.8). For Group 1 the thematic analysis highlighted the competing forces of holding on and letting go of their child. The additional competing forces were the loss and anger experienced by the kinship carer and the child.

Figure 15.8 shows the global theme for Group 2, which was *breaking the cycle* with organizing themes focusing on *strategies, generative roles, support and unconditional love.*

Despite the KCTG's common programme themes, the processes of Group 1 and Group 2 as highlighted by the thematic analyses were quite different. Group 1 seemed very in touch with their internal and external conflicts but overwhelmed by the needs of their child and their role as primary carers. Group 2, like Group 1, seemed overwhelmed by their responsibilities as kinship carers but seemed to demonstrate more hopefulness and resilience as indicated by their strategies theme and themes around unconditional love. They seemed less connected with (or willing to discuss) their internal conflicts, which included their intergenerational narratives.

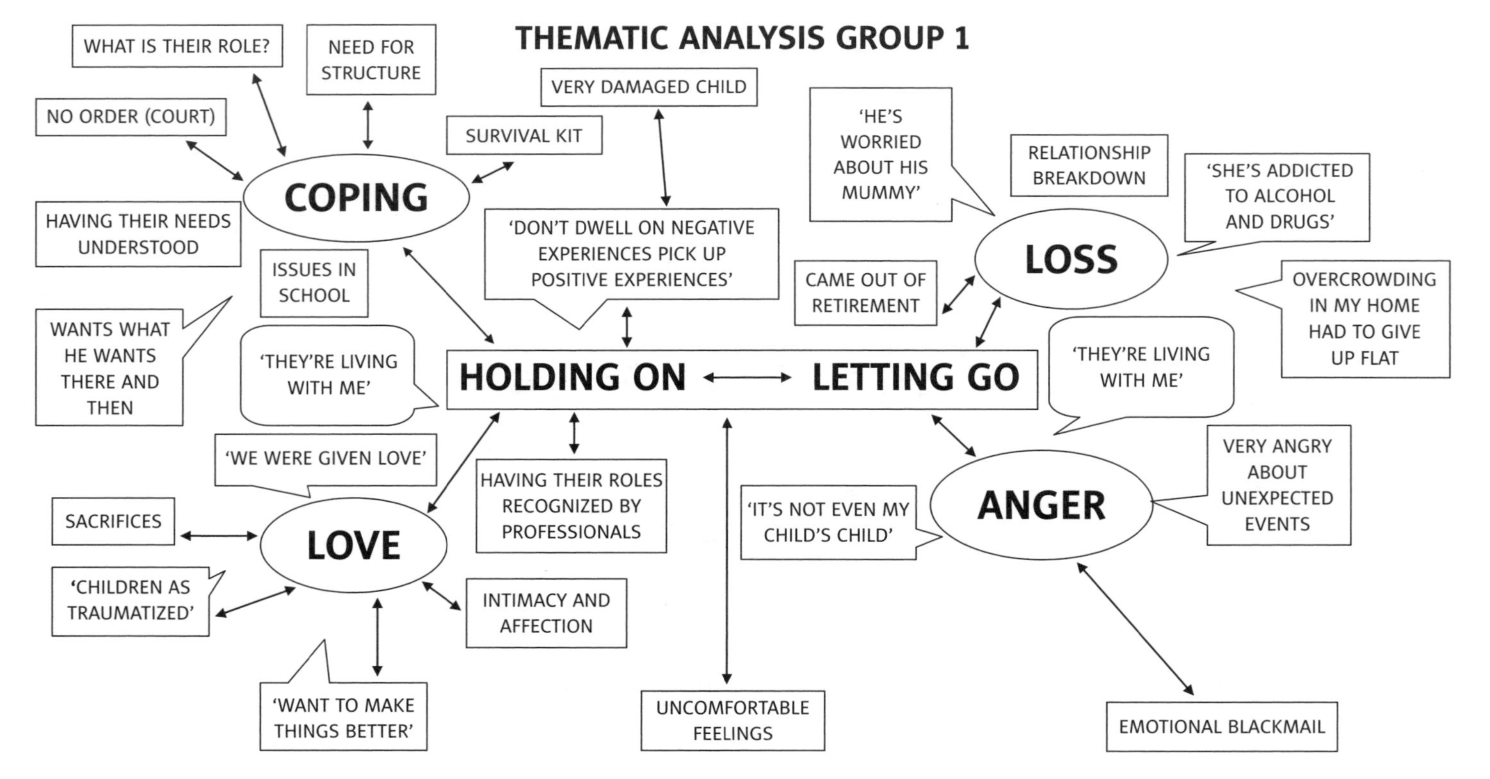

Figure 15.7 Diagram to show the *Holding On* and *Letting Go* themes for Group 1 in the KCTG programme

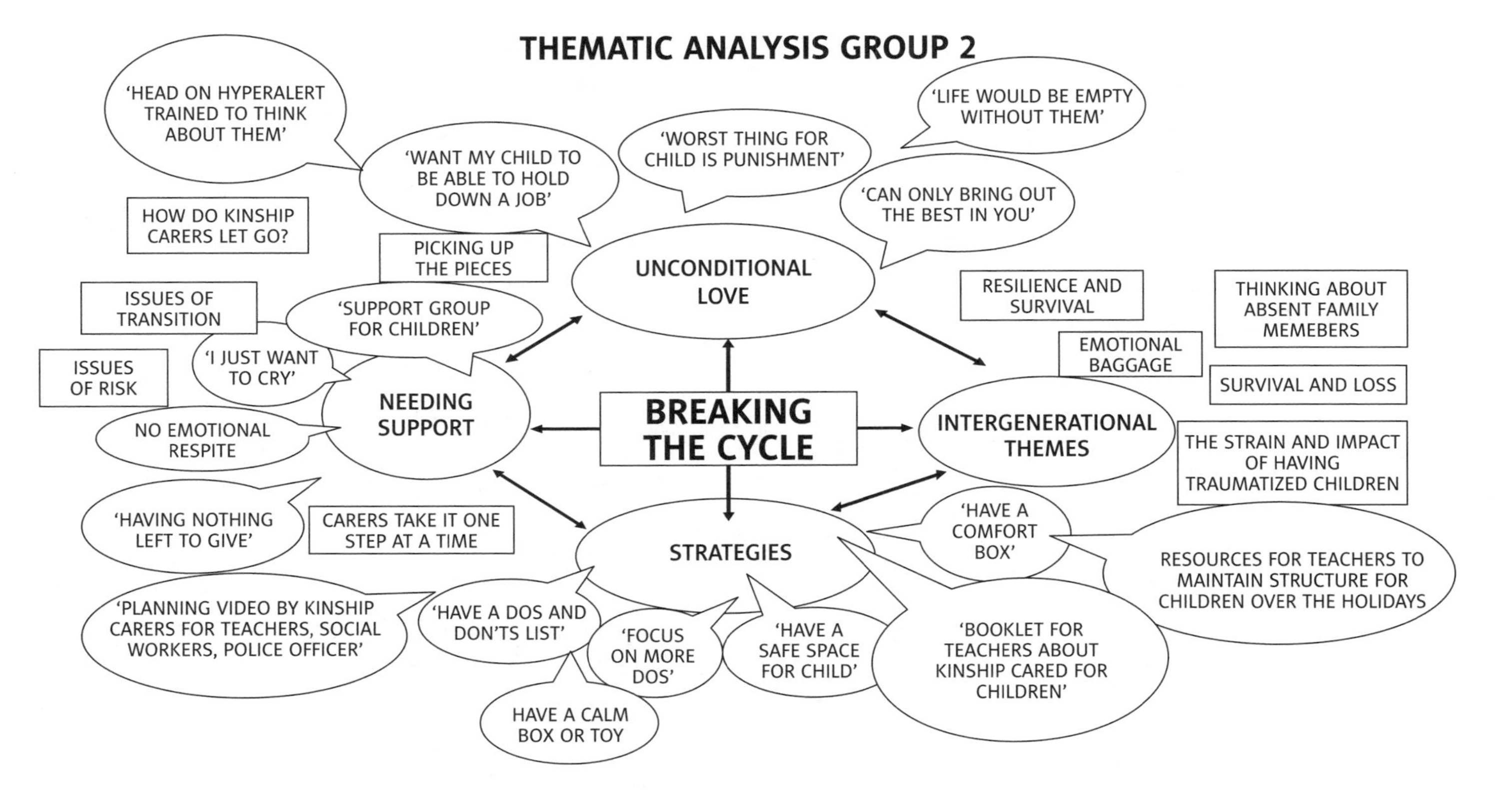

Figure 15.8 Diagram to show the *Breaking the Cycle* theme for Group 2 in the KCTG programme

Conclusions and implications

The strengths of the KCTG were that as researchers and clinicians we were able to capture the uniqueness and dilemmas of kinship care through research, which was also an intervention. There was active participation in constructing the programme in each session, and for both groups this meant that the group deviated from the set programme according to the feedback during the sessions.

The limitation to this study was borne out of the frustrations and tensions of being a researcher-clinician. Discussions around whether to video and tape record the sessions or not were also discussions about how best to study our research sample with minimal disturbance. Writing during the sessions while facilitating meant that the facilitators were hindered in terms of what and how they wrote about how they experienced the group and how the participants experienced them. Although highlighting salient points and pertinent comments, it was not possible to write down conversations verbatim. There may be ways around making the videoing and recording of the group a less stifling and exposing process. Making the video less conspicuous, having discussions about anxiety in the introductory session and using videos and a tape recorder during group activities may be a way to make participants less self-conscious.

The analysis of quantitative and qualitative data provided some evidence that group intervention can offer effective treatment for kinship carers. Kinship carers' individual and collective feedback through the GBOM and thematic analysis highlighted the benefits they derived from the KCTG socially, emotionally and educationally. For the purposes of this service-based research, this seems more relevant than statistically significant change. Unfortunately the design did not allow for a breakdown of the PSI data in order to ascertain how much of the carer's stress was to do with the child or other personal or interpersonal factors.

In relation to the GBOM, this highlighted that the sessions were adequately tailored towards the needs of kinship carers. Thematic analysis further furnished facilitators with insights and knowledge about kinship carers' experiences and needs. What seemed most informative was that kinship carers in both groups rated understanding why their child behaved the way she did as more important than discussing behaviour management strategies.

Jacobson, Follette and Revenstorf (1984, 1986) defined clinically significant change in terms of the way in which therapy moves someone outside the range of the dysfunctional population or within the range of the functional population. What this innovative research has underlined is the viability of practice-based research that can provide a measure of clinical change for a *group* and a rich picture of the therapeutic encounter. Although due to its size, it cannot reach the threshold of being a robust measure of clinical effectiveness, it provides a much-needed springboard for considering clinical significance in a much broader sense.

Chapter 16

Child Sexual Exploitation and Multi-Dimensional Safety for Children in Care

LUCIE SHUKER

Introduction

Detailed knowledge about children who are sexually abused or exploited is always constrained by our awareness of how hard it is for children to disclose their experiences at the time of abuse (Allnock and Miller 2013; Smith, Dogaru and Ellis 2015), and this prevents us being able to speak confidently about who victims are. Although research indicates that most victims of child sexual exploitation are adolescents, female and live at home (Berelowitz *et al.* 2012), we also know that there are additional barriers in identifying those who are boys and young men and/or from Black and Minority Ethnicity (BME) backgrounds (Gohir 2013; Lillywhite and Skidmore 2006). When it comes to looked after children, research suggests a disproportionate number experience sexual exploitation compared with their peers in the general population (Shuker 2013a). This is likely to be related both to the patterns of vulnerability and need that looked after young people carry with them, as well as the ways the care system may compound those vulnerabilities.

Children in care experience poorer educational and life outcomes than peers who live with their birth parents, with only half of all looked after children having emotional and behavioural health that is considered normal (Department for Education 2014c). More generally, victims of sexual exploitation are very often, although not always, also managing a variety of adverse life experiences that include bereavement, domestic violence, physical or sexual abuse and neglect, and the breakdown of family and/or care relationships (Berelowitz *et al.* 2012; Coy 2008; Pearce, Haynes and Bovarnick 2009; Scott and Skidmore 2006). 'Vulnerability' is only relevant insofar as someone decides to takes advantage of it to abuse a young person, but unfortunately perpetrators do target children with experiences that make them more susceptible to being groomed for abuse (Child Exploitation and Online Protection Centre 2011).

It is therefore paramount for those responsible for children in care to be trained both to proactively spot the signs that a child may be exploited, and to respond appropriately to signs and disclosures. The impact of sexual exploitation on victims' physical, mental and emotional health can be severe and long lasting – in terms of direct violence, as well as the harmful coping mechanisms acquired to manage trauma and the social exclusion that result (Chanon Consulting 2014; Department for Children, Schools and Families 2009). A shared, multi-agency approach is ideal for addressing this uncomfortable constellation of issues, but understanding of child sexual exploitation (CSE) among carers and the professionals supporting them remains poor (Shuker 2011 and 2013b).

This chapter outlines the findings from an evaluation of a pilot specialist foster care programme with children in care at risk or victims of sexual exploitation (Shuker 2013b). It identifies the learning that could be shared with other practitioners to improve safeguarding through the development of new theories about providing safe accommodation for sexually exploited young people.

Child sexual exploitation defined

CSE is a form of sexual abuse in which 'young people (or a third person or persons) receive "something" (e.g. food, accommodation, drugs, alcohol, cigarettes, affection, gifts, money) as a result of them performing, and/or another or others performing on them, sexual activities' (Department for Children, Schools and Families 2009, p.9). Those who abuse children in this way often exploit their relative power, using violence, coercion and intimidation to win trust and retain control.

The types and contexts of abuse suffered by children are always evolving, but research has identified a series of forms of sexual exploitation over recent years. Jago *et al.* (2011) found that the 'older boyfriend' or grooming model was the best understood, and was most often identified as a primary form of coercion in sexually exploitative relationships. This involves an adult or peer (working alone or in a group) winning a young person's trust over time to prepare him or her for abuse – in some examples through the young person believing an older person to be his or her boyfriend/girlfriend. Other recurring contexts include sexually harmful norms in peer networks (Firmin 2011), 'party houses', and gangs and organized networks, often facilitated by local businesses (Beckett *et al.* 2012, Berelowitz *et al.* 2012). While some exploitation takes place exclusively online (McGuire and Dowling 2013), practically all is in some way facilitated via technology (Palmer 2015).

Safe accommodation for children in care who are sexually exploited

All care providers have a duty to safeguard children from sexual exploitation, and should be aware of some of the specific risks that can arise to looked after children. Young people in care are three times more likely to run away than those living at home (The Children's Society 2011) and going missing is consistently reported as one of the strongest indicators of risk of CSE (Sharp 2012). It has been suggested that foster care is generally more appropriate for those at risk, or victims, of CSE, but that their 'chaotic behaviour' often leads to young people being disproportionately placed in residential units (Lillywhite and Skidmore 2006; Office of the Children's Commissioner 2012; Shuker 2013a). While residential and secure accommodation can be successfully used to disrupt exploitative relationships, it can also potentially increase the risk of sexual exploitation (Harper and Scott 2005; Jago and Pearce 2008). This is where children encounter situational risks such as peer introduction to exploitative men and lifestyles (Coy 2008; Office of the Children's Commissioner 2012); perpetrators targeting residential homes (Creegan, Scott and Smith 2005; Lillywhite and Skidmore 2006; Munro 2004); the expansion of private care homes that are not well connected to local statutory services; and poor recording of, and responses to, young people going missing (Office of the Children's Commissioner 2012).

As a result of high-profile criminal trials and media attention on statutory responses to CSE there is now much greater awareness of safeguarding children in care from abuse. However, significant challenges remain in relation to recruiting and training appropriate carers, preventing placement instability, and accessing appropriate therapeutic care.

Evaluation of specialist foster placements

The rest of this chapter summarizes key findings from a two-year evaluation (2011–13) of a Barnardo's programme of specialist foster care for children at risk or victims of child sexual exploitation and/or trafficking. Multiple sources of data were gathered as each of the 13 pilot placements progressed, including 87 one-to-one interviews, and 224 weekly monitoring logs. The young people in these placements had multiple vulnerabilities, including abuse and neglect; unstable care histories; low self-esteem; bereavement; domestic abuse; self-harm and poor mental health; disengagement from education; and going missing. Six were known victims of exploitation and the remaining seven were assessed to be at high or medium high risk. Specialist foster carers learned about and employed a range of safety strategies as a result of the training they received, and ongoing support and advice from Barnardo's. Positive outcomes were clearly related to placement length and stability, with greater improvements evident in the nine specialist placements that were stable and did not breakdown during the life of the project. In these placements, young people reported feeling safe and protected from exploitation, their awareness of the difference between exploitative and healthy relationships increased; there was evidence of protective factors in their lives and improvements to their physical, emotional and psychological well-being. Finally, in seven of the nine stable placements, there were either no missing episodes, a reduction in missing episodes, or very few occasions of missing children. For full details of the methodology and outcomes of the evaluation please see Shuker (2013b).

Context and mechanisms of change

Evidence from the evaluation of specialist foster placements showed that warm and trusting relationships were at the heart of placements that had a positive impact on young people, and these relationships contributed to a wider safety and well-being. In this regard, young people's advice to carers was to listen to them, not to judge them and to give them space – practices that are well recognized to be crucial to effective communication. The relationship between a young person and his carer(s) then became a mediating outcome – that is, it created the conditions in which other positive outcomes were more likely.

There are multiple theories of psychological change that highlight the importance of various kinds of context to patterns of behaviour, thought and interaction (see Bateson 1972, 1979). In keeping with such insights, this research sought to reveal which elements of placement context had the most significant influence on the young person's life and safety, and enabled the development of some theories about what underpins effective placements for those at risk or victims of sexual exploitation.

1. Positive and trusting relationships are key to all wider attempts and strategies to improve the young person's safety and well-being. Carers' characteristics are therefore crucial. They need to have confidence, commitment, compassion and the ability to cope with challenging situations. Carers also need intensive and responsive support and training, and to be available for the young person.

2. A shared, multi-agency approach is crucial to the effective use of safeguarding measures to protect children from sexual exploitation. The level of understanding of CSE within children's services, education, police and other relevant agencies directly affects perceptions of risk/need and subsequent action or inaction to protect children.

3. Safety is multi-dimensional. It takes time to progress from short-term physical safety to medium-term positive, trusting relationships, and ultimately a sustainable recovery. Commissioners need to carefully consider placement length and how this will support or undermine relational security for a child.

4. Specialist foster care must give young people a reason to stay and invest in a placement in light of 'pull factors' drawing them elsewhere. Placements must take account of young people having strong attachments to individuals/groups that present a risk to them, as well as the location of such people – in order to prevent young people going missing.

5. Specialist foster placements are likely to be most successful when young people are ready, willing and able to engage in them. Regardless of risk level, a young person's willingness and capacity to engage in a placement is fundamental to its chances of success.

It is shifts and movements in the contexts above that affect the possibility of supportive change in a young person's situation. In the study, carers, professionals and young people described positive outcomes as the result of the following mechanisms of change – themselves the result of supportive contexts. Table 16.1 lists these *mechanisms of change*. For further description and supporting evidence see Shuker (2013b).

Table 16.1 The key mechanisms of change in pilot specialist foster placements for children at risk or victims of sexual exploitation

Mechanism	Associated behaviours and activities of foster carers
Caring: seeing past behavioural challenges to young people's need for compassion and unconditional acceptance	Providing positive attention Persisting without evidence of change Avoiding escalation and placement breakdown Meeting practical needs Noticing and responding to emotional needs
Safeguarding: appropriate sensitivity to risk	Disrupting exploitation e.g. working with police[1] Applying boundaries consistently Making it harder for the young person to run away Monitoring risk and trusting the young person to manage risk
Child-centred: working from the young person's perspective	Making sense of their world Persistently reaching out to the young person Giving the young person control
Communication: sensitive communication	Taking opportunities to discuss risk in everyday life Challenging oppressive assumptions Talking frankly and openly
Relational/family: a non-abusive environment	Including the young person in everyday family life Modelling healthy relationships Facilitating safe friendships
Activity: offering viable alternative activity	Offering activities to promote positive self-esteem Occupying spare time in the early days of a placement Relieving the pressure and intensity of a placement Building relationship through doing things together
Advocacy: representing young people	Gate-keeping and brokering

1 It is worth repeating here that these mechanisms almost exclusively focus on the role of carers. In cases of child sexual exploitation, the police have a statutory responsibility to investigate and disrupt cases of abuse and safeguard children, which is not foregrounded in this list but is crucial.

The multi-dimensional aspects of safety for children in care affected by child sexual exploitation

Data from the specialist foster care evaluation was reviewed in light of previous research literature to develop a multi-dimensional model of safety for children in care affected by sexual exploitation.[2]

- *Physical safety* – we need to make it as hard as possible for perpetrators to access young people, whether on the phone, or online, or in person.
- *Relational safety* – we need to make it easier for young people to experience good, stable relationships that counteract the abuse, and avoid the chronic placement instability that can increase the risk of sexual exploitation.
- *Psychological safety* – we need to help young people find sources of self-identify outside of relationships that harm them.

Physical safety: The young person's level of risk and need must lead the strategies that are adopted to increase his safety. In this research, for example, some carers would not lock the front door at night or during the day, even if there was a high risk of the young person going missing, while others would. Some judged that it was safer to make sure the young person always had credit on their phone in case he was in trouble, while in a number of placements young people had no access to a phone in case they used it to contact those who posed a risk to them. In some placements young people had no access to the internet, no direct access to money, and were accompanied everywhere they went. The length of time such measures were applied varied, but they were often relaxed within a few weeks or months if it was felt that the young person was now at lower risk of harm, and to allow him the opportunity to show he had understood and could manage some of those risks himself.

Relational safety: Even though they may not have shown it, all of the young people consulted as part of this small study described feeling nervous, scared and emotional when they first arrived to a care placement. They felt welcomed when carers took the time to find out

2 This developed learning from the pilot around the need to think beyond achieving immediate physical safety from exploitative relationships and contexts. Instead we could take a more holistic view of safety that comprises these three dimensions.

about them and made sure they had everything they needed; when they were included as 'one of the family'; being talked to with respect and when carers showed concern about where they were if they were out. Interestingly, access to food could be a sign of care, inclusion and feeling 'at home' or could make a young person feel that he was an intruder in the family. Relational safety describes the child's need to access stable, supportive relationships, particularly during transitions between placements. It requires creative and flexible responses to support young people to see their friends safely, especially when they feel isolated and are at risk of going missing in order to visit them.

Psychological safety: There are various experiences that can increase young people's resilience, well-being and sense of a positive self-identity in the face of harmful experiences like exploitation and instability in care (Coy 2008; Gilligan 2006). 'Protective activities' can reduce risk by building self-esteem, introducing young people to alternative social networks, giving them the opportunity to learn new skills and helping them avoid risky situations. Providing positive attention countered some of the negative self-perceptions created by young people's prior experiences in care and at home. This often came in the form of encouragement and consistently positive messages to young people about their value and worth. Other research has suggested that over time this attention can help young people resist relationships that are ultimately harmful and abusive (Scott and Skidmore 2006). Post-abuse recovery is a long-term process and access to appropriate therapy is crucial – another significant reason to prioritize placement stability. A range of therapeutic interventions should be available to sexually exploited young people, including counselling that can be delivered in more informal and flexible ways.

A placement model for keeping young people safe from sexual exploitation

The learning from the evaluation was drawn together into a diagram (Figure 16.1) that attempts to capture how everyone involved in a placement plays their part in effectively safeguarding children from sexual exploitation. It will be evident that this shares the same principles as the model of the protective shield found in Chapter 11 (Guishard-Pine *et al.* 2007).

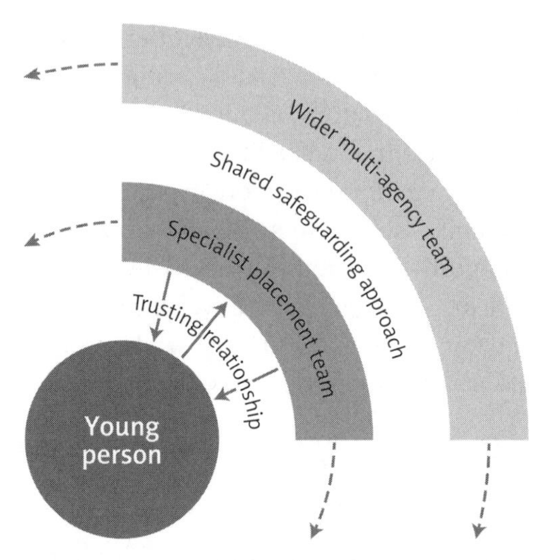

Figure 16.1 Placement model for the Safe Accommodation Project

In this diagram the young person is at the centre, as is recognition of the importance of his autonomy, perspectives and choices. The specialist placement team (specialist foster carer, project worker, fostering social worker) then creates a safe environment around the young person that can 'hold' him in to the placement. This centres on creating the right balance between safeguarding mechanisms and demonstrations of care, through which trusting relationships with the young person are built. The arrows indicate that this safeguarding environment/hold can be more or less restrictive depending on the young person's needs and the risks he faces. Finally, the specialist placement team is supported by a wider team around the child, which is informed about CSE and trafficking, and which reinforces the safeguarding approach within the placement. This team is likely to include representatives from children's services, education, health and the police, among others.

Conclusion

The findings of this evaluation supported existing research that highlights the importance of building and sustaining positive, trusting relationships. However, these take time to build and therefore specialist foster placements should be in place for at least a year. Foster carers can create a safe environment on a day-to-day basis through the provision of practical and emotional support, including the young people in their family environment, and continuing to provide acceptance and warmth if risky behaviour continues. In such a partnership, positive messages about safety and well-being are 'drip-fed' to the young person and reinforced by different people in his life.

Finally, the excerpt below from an interview with 14-year-old 'Briony' captures many of the themes of the research, including the importance of adults holding back judgement, taking time to build their trust and being committed to a relationship with a young person. Other young interviewees stressed that there can be good reasons why young people appear to be 'putting themselves at risk' and they wanted carers to be interested in what those reasons were. They might have appeared dismissive, independent or given the impression they didn't want adults to interfere, but the young people interviewed all wanted to feel cared for. Although they often complained about rules and boundaries, they agreed that these were signs of being cared for – and the worst possible response would be indifference to their safety and their needs:

> Once you get a kid through that door, you know their past on a piece of paper, but you don't know about their rules, like, their view. So, like, you've got to talk to them, you've got to sit down and think 'Mate, I'm gonna put time into this' and after a couple of months, like they're open to you, they'd think 'All right, she's gonna stick around'. Because how many times I thought, 'Mate, you ain't gonna stick around, see you later, I ain't gonna talk to you'. It's like, 'Oh she was this, she was that'. Why was she this? Why was she that? It's just like, you sit there and think, 'Hold on, hold on, you're calling me these names, you ain't made no effort'. If you ask a lot of foster kids, that's what they say. You've got to make effort for them to make effort.

Endnote

It is inevitable that in any publication there will be omissions. We are mindful that the scope of this book has not encompassed the mental health needs of care leavers specifically. We have evidenced clearly the reduced life chances of those who have experienced a sustained period of being looked after in terms of mental health, physical health, educational achievements and income generation throughout the lifespan. One statistic notes that 'a care leaver has a greater chance at 18 of being in prison than attending a university'.[1] The Children (Leaving Care) Act 2000 amends the previous social care provision and details support that a local authority will provide for a care leaver until the age of 21, or in some cases 24. It was a long overdue recognition of unmet need. But in mental health, through the existing child and adolescent specialist services, the provision for support has not been likewise universally extended. As such, a child in care reaching 18 must be transitioned to adult mental health services if he needs continued support. As things are generally, we can say that he will need to have a recognized mental health disorder to be transitioned and that, as many young people in care are frequently seen as having predominantly behavioural or social care issues, rather than mental health difficuties, they are not seen as priorities for transition. For example, while it is our experience that trauma underlies much of their presentation, they may never have been diagnosed as having any type of acute stress disorder. We also know, via anecdotal evidence, that even when they transitioned, the 'culture shock' experienced by these young people on entering treatment-focused adult services means they do not frequently take up offers of support in any case.

It is, in our minds, an unethical and unsustainable position for mental health services to occupy given the profound level of evidence of continued mental health need. It is well known that those leaving care are often developmentally, psychologically and physically younger

1 Creating Chances Trust at http://creating chances.org.uk/children-in-care

than their chronological ages. In short, they are very ill equipped to benefit from adult services as they are currently structured, and to take on an adult role.

While it is often said that this is due to the complexities of breaching funding structures that are designed to cater for divided groups – adults or young people – there are models of service provision in some areas already that have accomplished this, such as some psychosis services that can deliver services from adolescence well into adulthood. It is not, therefore, 'impossible' and one has to think that 'where there is a will, there is a way'. As the 'will' appears to be rather lagging behind the clinical evidence of continued need, the 'way' may need to be a sustained pressure on political structures to review this situation.

List of Contributors

Olatayo Afuape is a child and adolescent psychoanalytic psychotherapist and chartered education and child psychologist. She has previously worked as a senior specialist psychologist on domestic violence projects and as a clinical child psychologist.

Dr Sidra Aslam is an educational and child psychologist working within a large urban local authority. She works as a senior psychologist within children's services, specializing in the development and delivery of psychological support services within adoption and fostering alongside her work within the Educational Psychology Service. Sidra is passionately committed to applying psychology to improve experiences and life chances for children in the care system.

Dr Hannah Baron is a clinical psychologist working with CHUMS mental health service for children and young people in Bedfordshire. She completed her doctoral thesis on the experiences of children and adolescents who are looked after.

Dr Siobain Bonfield is a senior clinical psychologist currently working in adult mental health, and with young people, in Melbourne, Australia. She has previously worked with children and young people in child protection and within the school system. She remains passionate about improving the psychological well-being of vulnerable populations.

Dr Gail Coleman-Oluwabusola is a consultant clinical psychologist and lecturer. She has worked in clinical psychology services since 1996, from innovative community psychology services for BME children and their families to adolescent secure inpatient care. She has focused on the impact of racism on mental health. She is dedicated to working therapeutically at both an individual and organizational level with the impact and issues of child abuse.

Christine Cork is a qualified nurse, midwife, neonatal nurse and health visitor. She has over 40 years' experience of working in the NHS in clinical and managerial positions. She has focused her expertise on promoting the well-being of mothers and young children. She has a master's degree in psychoanalytical observational studies and is currently working in a child and adolescent mental health service in Luton.

Professor Jeune Guishard-Pine OBE is an activist psychologist. Throughout her career in the health, education, social services, voluntary and private sectors she has devoted herself to working with marginalized or disenfranchised groups of people. She is a trained teacher, educational and child psychologist, humanistic psychotherapist and systemic practitioner. She and her husband have six children.

Eleanor Havsteen-Franklin is an art psychotherapist, who has worked in child and adolescent mental health services since 1999. During this time much of her work has been with children and young people in care, offering individual and joint sessions, family work, art psychotherapy groups for children and foster carers and consultation to the wider system.

Dr Zoë Lander is a specialist clinical psychologist with looked after children, working in States Social Care in Guernsey, the Channel Islands. She has worked closely with children who are looked after in different roles, such as social worker and teacher, over a period of 20 years.

Tonie Lawrence-Mahrra is a transpersonal psychotherapist who works with individuals and families. She holds the firm belief that in her work with fragile children she witnesses their true potential and discovers that beneath the shell of that troubled behaviour lies a pearl of who they truly are, just waiting to be found.

Suzanne McCall is a senior accredited counsellor who has worked in child and adolescent mental health services for 15 years, primarily focused on working with looked after adolescents within a specialist team. She previously worked as a social worker working with children in care and child protection. She is an author and also runs her own counselling practice.

Devinia Malcolm is a psychological well-being practitioner at iCope Islington and is currently studying a part-time masters in occupational psychology.

Sheri Mosuro is a psychological well-being practitioner. She delivers cognitive behavioural self-help interventions to people with mild to moderate anxiety difficulties. She is also involved in research around improving mental health care services.

Lisa Robinson is the team lead for a specialist treatment team at a young persons alcohol and drug service. Her experience spans over 15 years, within mental health and social care sectors working with children, young people and families with complex and mental health needs. In addition she is a professional training facilitator for the Luton Safeguarding Children Board, specializing in child sexual exploitation. Lisa enjoys motherhood with her four-year-old son.

Clare Shaw is an educationalist and a writer. As she is a trainer, consultant and project researcher with organizations across the UK, her work is explicitly grounded in academic and professional knowledge, and also in her own experiences of self-injury using mental health services. She is the author of *Otis Doesn't Scratch* (2015); co-editor of *Our Encounters with Self-Harm*; and has published numerous articles and book chapters. Clare is also a Royal Literary Fellow and 'one of Britain's most dynamic and powerful young poets' (Arvon Foundation). With two Bloodaxe collections and several awards to her name, creativity and performance are an important element of her work.

Dr Lucie Shuker is Senior Research Fellow in the International Centre: Researching Child Sexual Exploitation, Violence and Trafficking at the University of Bedfordshire. Her recent research has explored the exploitation of children in care and in gang contexts, as well as evaluations of services designed to support child victims of sexual exploitation.

Dr Sam Warner is a chartered and consultant clinical psychologist (qualifying in 1991), and she holds an honorary lectureship in social sciences at Salford University. Sam works as an academic, consultant, expert witness, researcher, therapist and trainer. Throughout Sam's career she has specialized in sexual violence, child protection, domestic abuse and mental health. Sam has written books and papers on abuse and related issues such as self-harm. Her books include *Understanding the Effects of Child Sexual Abuse: Feminist Revolutions in Theory, Research and Practice* (2009, Routledge), and with Helen Spandler (eds) (2007) *Beyond Fear and Control: Working With Young People Who Self-harm* (PCCS Books). Sam is currently working on a second edition of *Understanding Child Sexual Abuse: Making the Tactics Visible* (PCCS Books) and designing a training manual and DVD pack based on this. Sam has also been engaged by the Department of Health and British Government as an expert in mental health on various national and international sexual violence projects. She is currently providing clinical supervision to Barnardo's Safer Future Services in the North West.

Dr Emily Wilkens is a clinical psychologist currently working for Compass Outreach, an innovative new service for children and their families on the edge of care in Norfolk. She has worked extensively in child protection and child bereavement and has been the clinical lead for a specialist foster care service in Suffolk. She has recently undertaken her hardest challenge yet in becoming a new mum to her daughter, Mia.

References

Aarons, G., Brown, S., Coe, M., Nyers, M. *et al.* (1999) 'Adolescent alcohol and drug abuse and health.' *Journal of Adolescent Health, 24(6)*, 412–421.

Abidin, R. (1992) *The Parenting Stress Index.* Florida: PAR.

Ainsworth, M., Bell, S. and Stayton, D. (1971) 'Individual Differences in Strange-Situation Behaviour of One Year Olds.' In H. Schaffer (ed.) *The Origins of Human Social Relations.* New York: Academic Press.

Aldgate, J. and McIntosh, M. (2006) *Looking After the Family: A Study of Children Looked After in Kinship Care in Scotland.* Edinburgh: Social Work Inspection Agency.

Aldridge, S. and Rigby, S. (eds) (2001) *Counselling Skills in Context.* London: Hodder & Stoughton.

Alessandri, S. and Lewis, M. (1993) 'Parental evaluation and its relation to shame and pride in young children.' *Sex Roles, 29*, 335–343.

Allen, B. and Johnson, J. (2011) 'Utilization and implementation of trauma-focused cognitive-behavioral therapy for the treatment of maltreated children.' *Child Maltreatment 17(1)*, 80–85.

Allen, J. and Vostanis, P. (2005) 'The impact of abuse and trauma on the developing child: an evaluation of a training programme for foster carers and supervising social workers.' *Adoption & Fostering, 29(3)*, 68–81.

Allnock, D., Bunting, L., Price, A., Morgan-Klein, N. *et al.* (2009) *Sexual Abuse and Therapeutic Services for Children and Young People: The Gap Between Provision and Need.* London: NSPCC. Available at www.nspcc.org.uk/globalassets/documents/research-reports/sexual-abuse-therapeutic-services-children-young-people-summary.pdf, accessed on 26 March 2016.

Allnock, D. and Miller, P. (2013) *No One Noticed, No One Heard: A Study of Disclosures of Childhood Abuse.* London: NSPCC.

Angold, A., Costello, E.J. and Erkanli, A. (1999) 'Comorbidity.' *Journal of Child Psychology and Psychiatry, 40*, 57–88.

Antaki, C., Billig, M., Edwards, D. and Potter, J. (2002) 'Discourse analysis means doing analysis: a critique of six analytic shortcomings.' *Daol Discourse Analysis Online [Electronic Version], 1*(1).

Anyan, S. and Pryor, J. (2002) 'What is in a family? Adolescent perceptions.' *Children & Society, 16*, 306–317.

Arcelus, J., Bellerby, T. and Vostanis, P. (1999) 'A mental health service for young people in the care of the local authority.' *Clinical Child Psychology and Psychiatry, 4(2)*, 233–245.

Arnold, L. (1995) *Women and Self-injury: A Survey of 76 Women. A Report on Women's Experience of Self-injury and their Views on Service Provision.* Bristol: Bristol Crisis Service for Women.

Arnold, L. and Magill, A. (2005) *Working with Self-injury.* Abergavenny: The Basement Project.

Aronson, J. (1994) 'A pragmatic view of thematic analysis.' *The Qualitative Report, 2(1).*

Aslam, S. (2012) 'Exploring Looked after children's Experiences of Child And Adolescent Mental Health Services.' Unpublished doctoral thesis, University of Birmingham. Available at http://etheses.bham.ac.uk/3726/1/Aslam_AppliedEdChildPsyD_12.pdf, accessed on 3 February 2016.

Atkin, K. and Rollins, J. (1993) *Community Care in a Multiracial Britain: A Critical Review of the Literature.* London: HMSO.

Atkinson, J.M. and Heritage, J. (1984) *Structures Of Social Action: Studies In Conversation Analysis.* Cambridge: Cambridge University Press.

Atkinson, M., Wilkin, A., Stott, A., Doherty, P. and Kinder, K. (2002) *Multi-Agency Working: A Detailed Study.* Slough: National Foundation for Education Research.

Attride-Stirling, J. (2001) *Thematic Networks: An Analytic Tool For Qualitative Research. Qualitative Psychology: A Practical Guide To Methods.* London: Sage.

Audit Commission (1998) *A Fruitful Partnership: Effective Partnership Working.* London: Audit Commission.

Ayers, M. (2003) *Mother-Infant Attachment and Psychoanalysis: The Eyes of Shame.* Hove: Routledge.

Backhouse, J. and Graham, A. (2009) 'Grandparents raising their grandchildren: an uneasy position.' *Elder Law Review, 6.* Available at http://epub.scu.edu.au.educ_pubs/392

Barnardo's Scotland (2014) *Guidance on Child Sexual Exploitation: A Practitioner's Resource Pack.* Available at www.cne-siar.gov.uk/childProtectionCommittee/documents/guidance%20on%20child%20sexual%20exploitation.pdf, accessed on 26 March 2016.

Baron, H. (2012) 'Experiences of Ending Psychological Therapy: Perspectives of Young People who are Looked After.' DClinPsy Thesis, University of Hertfordshire.

Barrett, K., Zahn-Waxler, C. and Cole, P. (1993) 'Avoiders vs. amenders: implications for the investigation of guilt and shame during toddlerhood.' *Cognition and Emotion, 7,* 481–505.

Barth, R., Crea, T., John, K., Thoburn, J. *et al.* (2005) 'Beyond attachment theory and therapy: towards sensitive and evidence-based interventions with foster and adoptive families in distress.' *Child & Family Social Work, 10(4),* 257–268.

Bateson, G. (1972) *Steps to an Ecology of Mind: Collected Essays in Anthropology, Psychiatry, Evolution and Epistemology.* London: Paladin, Granada.

Bateson, G. (1979) *Mind and Nature: A Necessary Unity* (Advances in Systems Theory, Complexity, and the Human Sciences). Cresskill, NJ: Hampton Press.

Baum, N. (2005) 'Correlates of client's emotional and behavioural responses to treatment termination.' *Clinical Social Work Journal, 33,* 309–326.

Baxter, P. and Jack, S. (2008) 'Qualitative case study methodology: study design and implementation for novice researchers.' *The Qualitative Report, 13(4),* 544–559.

Bazalgette, L., Rahilly, T. and Trevelyan, G. (2015) *Achieving Emotional Wellbeing for Children in Care: A Whole System Approach.* London: NSPCC. Available at www.nspcc.org.uk/globalassets/documents/research-reports/achieving-emotional-wellbeing-for-looked-after-children.pdf, accessed on 3 February 2016.

Bebbington, A. and Miles, J. (1989) 'The background of children who enter local authority care.' *British Journal of Social Work, 19,* 349–68.

Beck, A. (2006) 'User's views of children in care's mental health services.' *Adoption and Fostering Journal, 30(2),* 53–63.

Becker-Weidman, A. and Hughes, D. (2008) 'Dyadic Developmental Psychotherapy: an evidence-based treatment for children with complex trauma and disorders of attachment.' *Child & Family Social Work, 13(3),* 329–337.

Beckett, H., Brodie, I., Factor, F., Melrose, M. *et al.* (2012) *Research into Gang-associated Sexual Exploitation and Sexual Violence: Interim Report.* Available at www.beds.ac.uk/research/iasr/centres/intcent, accessed on 31 January 2016.

Beckett, H. and Warrington, C. (2015) *Making Justice Work: Experiences of Criminal Justice for Children and Young People Affected by Sexual Exploitation as Victims and Witnesses.* University of Bedfordshire Publications. Available at www.beds.ac.uk/__data/assets/pdf_file/0005/461867/Beckett-and-Warrington-2015-Making-Justice-Work-Exec-Summary.pdf, accessed 26 March 2016.

Beecham, J. (2006) *Beyond Boundaries: Citizen-centred Local Services for Wales.* The Beecham Report. Review of local service delivery. Report to the Welsh Assembly Government. Crown Copyright.

Begum, N. (2006) *Doing It For Themselves: Participation and Children in Care and Minority Ethnic Users.* London: Race Equality Unit, SCIE.

Belsky, J. and Domitrovich, C. (1997) 'Temperament and parenting antecedents of individual difference in three year old boys' pride and shame reactions.' *Child Development, 68,* 456–466.

Bennett, D., Sullivan, M. and Lewis, M. (2005) 'Young children's adjustment as a function of maltreatment, shame and anger.' *Child Maltreatment, 10(4),* 311–323.

Bensley, L., Spieker, S., Van Eenwyk, J. and Schoder, J. (1999) 'Self-reported abuse history and adolescent problem behaviors. II. Alcohol and drug use.' *Journal of Adolescent Health, 24(3),* 173–180.

Benward, J. and Densen-Gerber, J. (1971) 'Incest as a causal factor in antisocial behaviour: an explanatory study.' *Contemporary Drug Problems: A Law Quarterly, 1,* 323–340.

Berelowitz, S., Firmin, C., Edwards, G., Gulyurtlu, S. *et al.* (2012) 'I thought I was the only one. The only one in the world.' The Office of the Children's Commissioner's inquiry in to child sexual exploitation in gangs and groups: interim report (PDF). London: Office of the Children's Commissioner.

Berrick, J., Barth, R. and Needell, B. (1994) 'A comparison of kinship foster homes and foster family homes: implications for kinship foster-care as family preservation.' *Children And Youth Services Review, 16,* 33–63.

Biehal, N., Ellison, S., Baker, C. and Sinclair, I. (2009) 'Characteristics, outcomes and meanings of three types of permanent placement – adoption by strangers, adoption by carers and long-term foster care.' Research brief DCSF-RBX-09-11, London: Department for Children, Schools and Families.

Big Step Social Inclusion Partnership (2002) *The Health of Young People in Care and Leaving Care in Glasgow.* Glasgow: The Big Step.

Bion, W. (1961) *Experiences in Groups.* London: Tavistock.

Blos, P. (1967) 'The second individuation process of adolescence.' *Pychoanalytic Study of the Child, 22,* 163–185.

Blower, A., Addo, A., Hodgson, J., Lamington, L. *et al.* (2004) 'Mental health of "looked after" children: a needs assessment.' *Clinical Child Psychology and Psychiatry, 9(1),* 117–129.

Bonfield, S., Collins, S., Guishard-Pine, J. and Langdon, P. (2010) 'Help-seeking by foster carers for their 'looked after' children: the role of mental health literacy and treatment attitudes.' *British Journal of Social Work, 40(5),* 1335–1352.

Bonnet, C. and Welbury, J. (2004) 'Meeting the mental health needs of children in care: an example of routine psychological assessment.' *Adoption & Fostering, 28(3),* 81–82.

Boseley, S. (2014) 'Misjudged Counselling and Therapy Can Be Harmful, Study Reveals.' *The Guardian. 26.05.2014.* Available at www.theguardian.com/society/2014/may/26/misjudged-counselling-psychological-therapy-harmful-study-reveals, accessed on 6 August 2016.

Boss, P. (1999) *Ambiguous Loss.* Cambridge, MA: Harvard University Press.

Bowie, F. (ed.) (2004) *Cross-cultural Approaches to Adoption.* London: Routledge.

Bowlby, J. (1969) *Attachment and Loss: Vol. 1.* New York: Basic Books.

Bowlby, J. (1973) *Attachment and Loss: Vol. 2. Separation: Anxiety and Anger.* London: Hogarth Press.

Bowlby, J. (1977) 'The making and breaking of affectional bonds. I: Aetiology and psychopathology in the light of attachment theory, II: Some principles of psychotherapy.' *British Journal of Psychiatry, 130,* 201–210 and 421–431.

Bowlby, J. (1980) *Attachment and Loss: Vol. 3. Loss: Sadness and Depression.* New York: Perseus Books.

Bowlby, J. (1982) *Attachment.* New York: Basic Books.

Bowlby, J. (1988) *A Secure Base: Parent-Child Attachment and Healthy Human Development.* Tavistock professional book. London: Routledge.

Bowman, A. and SCIE (2007) The Social Care Institute for Excellence's response to *Care Matters* white paper. Available at www.careappointments.co.uk/care-news/england/item/8039, accessed on 6 August 2016.

Boyd, C. (1993) 'The antecedents of women's crack cocaine abuse: family substance abuse, sexual abuse, depression and illicit drug use.' *Journal of Substance Abuse Treatment, 10,* 433–438.

Boyd, L. and Remy, L. (1978) 'Is foster-parent training worthwhile?' *The Social Service Review,* 275–296.

Brandon, M., Sidebotham, P., Bailey, S. and Belderson, P. (2011) 'A study of recommendations arising from serious case reviews' Department for Education RR157. Available at www.education.gov.uk/publications/eOrderingDownload/DFE-RR157.pdf, accessed on 6 August 2016.

Briere, J. and Elliott, D. (1994) 'Immediate and long-term impacts of child sexual abuse.' *The Future of Children, 4(2), Sexual abuse of children* (Summer–Autumn), 54–69.

Briere, J. and Runtz, M. (1987) 'Post sexual abuse trauma: data and implications for clinical practice.' *Journal of Interpersonal Violence, 2(4),* 367–379.

Briggs, A. (2012) *Waiting To Be Found: Papers On Children in Care.* London: Karnac Books.

British Association of Adoption and Fostering (2006) *Attachment Disorders, Their Assessment and Intervention/Treatment. Position Statement 4.* Available at www.baaf.org.uk/webfm_send/2066, accessed on 6 August 2016.

British Association of Adoption and Fostering (2014) *Statistics: England.* Coram BAAF, Adoption and Fostering Academy. Available at www.baaf.org.uk/res/statengland, accessed on 6 August 2016.

Broad, B., Hayes, R. and Rushforth, C. (2001) *Kith and Kin: Kinship Care For Vulnerable Young People.* York: Joseph Rowntree Foundation.

Broad, B. and Skinner, A. (2005) *Relative Benefits: Placing Children In Kinship Care.* London: British Association of Adoption and Fostering.

Brooks-Harris, E. (2008) *Integrative Multitheoretical Psychotherapy.* Boston, MA: Houghton-Mifflin.

Brown, R. and Ward, H. (2013) *Decision-making Within a Child's Timeframe.* London: Childhood Wellbeing Research Centre, Institute of Education.

Burnard, P. (1997) *Effective Communication Skills for Health Professionals.* Gloucestershire: Nelson Thornes.

Burton, M. (2012) *An Illuminative Evaluation of Foster Carers' Experiences of Attending an Attachment Theory and Practice Training Programme Offered by a Child and Adolescent Mental Health Service for Children in Care.* Available at: http://eprints.port.ac.uk/8930, accessed on 6 August 2016.

Butcher, J. and Ryan, M. (2006) *Talking About Alcohol and Other Drugs: A Guide for Looked After Children's Services.* London: National Children's Bureau.

Butler, J. and Vostanis, P. (1998) 'Characteristics of referrals to a mental health service for young people in care.' *Psychiatric Bulletin, 22,* 85–87.

Butler, R.J. and Green, D. (2007) *The Child Within: Taking the Young Person's Perspective by Applying Personal Construct Psychology* (second edition). Chichester: John Wiley & Sons.

Byrne, J. and Byrne, D. (1996) *Counselling Skills for the Health Professionals.* Melbourne: Macmillan Education.

Callaghan, J., Young, B., Pace, F. and Vostanis, P. (2004) 'Evaluation of a new mental health service for children in care.' *Clinical Child Psychology and Psychiatry, 9(1),* 130–148.

Cann, N. (2012) 'The Positive Educational Experiences of 'Looked After' Children and Young People.' Unpublished DEdChPsych dissertation, University of East London. Available at http://roar.uel.ac.uk/1886/1/2012_DEdChPsych_Cann.pdf, accessed on 6 August 2016.

Carmichael, S. and Price, J. (1995) 'Limbic connections of the orbital and medial prefrontal cortex in macaque monkeys.' *Journal of Comparative Neurology, 363,* 615–641.

Carr, A. (1989) 'Countertransference to families where child abuse has occurred.' *Journal of Family Therapy, 11(1),* 87–97.

Carter, R. (2001) 'Back to the future in cultural competence training.' *The Counseling Psychologist, 29(6),* 787–789.

Carter, R.T. (ed.) (2000) *Addressing Cultural Issues in Organizations: Beyond the Corporate Context.* Thousand Oaks, CA: Sage.

Case, C. and Dalley, T. (eds) (2008) *Art Therapy with Children: From Infancy to Adolescence.* London: Routledge.

Case, C. and Dalley, T. (eds) (2014) *The Handbook of Art Therapy.* London: Routledge.

Caw, J. and Sebba, J. (2014) *Team Parenting for Children in Foster Care: A Model for Integrated Therapeutic Care.* London: Jessica Kingsley Publishers.

Cepeda-Benito, A. and Short, P. (1998) 'Self-concealment, avoidance of psychological services, and perceived likelihood of seeking professional help.' *Journal of Counseling Psychology, 45(1),* 58–64.

Chamberlain, P., Price, J., Leve, L.D., Laurent, H. *et al.* (2008) 'Prevention of behaviour problems for children in foster care: outcomes and mediation effects.' *Prevention Science, 9,* 17–27.

Chanon Consulting (2014) 'The range of health impacts which can result from child sexual exploitation.' Available at www.barnardos.org.uk/health_impacts_of_child_sexual_exploitation.pdf, accessed on 30 January 2016.

Child Exploitation and Online Protection Centre (2011) *Out of Mind, Out of Sight: Breaking Down the Barriers to Understanding Child Sexual Exploitation.* Available at www.ceop.police.uk/Documents/ceopdocs/ceop_thematic_assessment_executive_summary.pdf, accessed on 30 January 2016.

Christoffersen, M. and Soothill, K. (2003) 'The long-term consequences of parental alcohol abuse: a cohort study of children in Denmark.' *Journal of Substance Abuse Treatment, 25(2),* 107–116.

Chukwudozie, O. (2014) *'Yarankowane' Children Belong to Everyone: Nigeria Report on Kinship Care.* Save the Children. Available at http://resourcecentre.savethechildren.se/library/yarankowane-children-belong-everyone-nigeria-report-kinship-care.

Ciarrochi, J. and Deane, F. (2001) 'Emotional competence and willingness to seek help from professional and non-professional sources.' *Journal of Guidance and Counselling, 29(2),* 233–246.

Cicchetti, D. and Carlson, V. (1989) *Child Maltreatment: Theory and Research on the Causes and Consequences of Child Abuse and Neglect.* Cambridge: University of Cambridge.

Clausen, J., Ruff, S., Von Wiederhold, W. and Heineman, T. (2013) 'For As Long As It Takes: Relationship-based Therapy for Children in Foster Care.' In K. Baker and V. Brandell (eds). *Child and Adolescent Psychotherapy and Psychoanalysis: One Hundred Years after 'Little Hans'.* Oxfordshire: Routledge.

Claveirole, A. (2004) 'Listening to young voices: challenges of research with adolescent mental health service users.' *Journal of Psychiatric and Mental Health Nursing, 11,* 253–260.

Cleaver, H., Unell, I. and Aldgate, J. (2011) *Children's Needs – Parenting Capacity. Child Abuse: Parental Mental Illness, Learning Disability, Substance Misuse, and Domestic Violence.* London: The Stationery Office.

Cocker, C. (2004) 'An examination of current specialist mental health projects for "looked after" children within England.' *International Journal of Child and Family Welfare, 2014(2–3),* 134–156.

Cocker, C. and Scott, S. (2006) 'Improving the mental and emotional well-being of children in care: connecting research, policy and practice.' *Perspectives in Public Health, 126(1),* 18–23.

Cohen, J. and Mannarino, A. (1996) 'A treatment outcome study for sexually abused preschool children: initial findings.' *Journal of the American Academy of Child and Adolescent Psychiatry, 35(1),* 42–50.

Cohen, J., Berliner, L. and Mannarino, A. (2010) 'Trauma focused CBT for children with co-occurring trauma and behavior problems.' *Child Abuse & Neglect, 34,* 215–224.

Colton, M., Roberts, S. and Williams, M. (2008) 'The recruitment and retention of family foster-carers: an international and cross-cultural analysis.' *British Journal of Social Work, 38(5),* 865–884.

Connolly, A. (2011) 'Healing the wounds of our fathers: intergenerational trauma, memory, symbolization and narrative.' *Journal of Analytic Psychology, 56,* 607–626.

Conway, P. (2009) 'Falling between minds: the effects of unbearable experiences on multi-agency communication in the care system.' *Adoption and Fostering 33(1),* 18–29.

Cooke-Cottone, C. and Beck, M. (2007) 'A model for life-story work: facilitating the construction of personal narrative for foster children.' *Child and Adolescent Mental Health, 12(4),* 193–195.

Cooper, E. (2011) 'Exploring the Personal Constructs of Looked After Children and their Foster Carers: A Qualitative Study.' DClinPsy thesis, University of Hertfordshire.

CoramBAAF (2015) Statistics: UK. Available at http://corambaaf.org.uk/res/statuk, accessed on 23 March 2016.

Courtois, C.A., Ford, J.D., and Cloitre, M. (2009) 'Best Practices in Psychotherapy for Adults.' In C.A. Courtois and J.D. Ford (eds) *Treating Complex Traumatic Stress Disorders: An Evidence-based Guide.* New York: The Guilford Press.

Cowden, S. and Singh, G. (2007) 'The user: friend, foe, or fetish? A critical exploration of user involvement in health and social care practice.' *Critical Social Care Policy, 27(5),* 5–22.

Coy, M. (2008) 'Young women, local authority care and selling sex.' *British Journal of Social Work, 38(7),* 1408–1424.

Creegan, C., Scott, S. and Smith, R. (2005) *The Use of Secure Accommodation and Alternative Provisions for Sexually Exploited Young People in Scotland.* Ilford: Barnardo's.

Crittenden, P. (1997) 'Toward an Integrative Theory of Trauma: A Dynamic-Maturation Approach.' In D. Cicchetti and S.L. Toth (eds) *Rochester Symposium on Developmental Psychopathology: Developmental Perspectives on Trauma.* Rochester, NY: University of Rochester Press.

Currie, D., Small, G. and Currie, C. (2002) *Prevalence and Profiles of Substance and Multisubstance Use Among Adolescents: UK and International Perspectives.* Child and Adolescent Health Research Center, University of Edinburgh.

Dalley, T. (1984) *Art as Therapy: An Introduction to the Use of Art as a Therapeutic Technique.* London: Routledge.

Daly, J., Kellehear, A. and Gliksman, M. (1997) *The Public Health Researcher: A Methodological Approach.* Melbourne: Oxford University Press.

Daly, M. (1984) 'Natural History of the Self.' In A. Stevens *Archetypes: A Natural History of Self.* New York: William Morrow & Co.

Dance, C. and Rushton, A. (2005) 'Joining a new family: the views and experiences of young people placed with permanent families during middle childhood.' *Adoption & Fostering, 29(1),* 18–28.

Davidson, J. and Smith, R. (1990) 'Traumatic experiences in psychiatric outpatients.' *Journal of Traumatic Stress, 3,* 459–475.

Davies, C. and Ward, H. (2012) *Safeguarding Children Across All Services.* London: Jessica Kingsley Publishers.

Davies, J. and Wright, J. (2008) 'Children's voices: a review of the literature pertinent to looked after children's views of mental health services.' *Child and Adolescent Mental Health,13(1),* 26–31.

Davies, J. Wright, J., Drake, S. and Bunting, J. (2009) 'By listening hard: developing a service user feedback system for adopted and fostered children in receipt of mental health services.' *Adoption & Fostering, 33,* 19–33.

Davies, P. Webber, M. and Briskman, J. (2015) 'Evaluation of a training programme for foster carers in an independent fostering agency.' *Practice: Social Work in Action, 27(1),* 35–49.

Davis, S. (1990) 'Chemical dependency in women: a description of its effects and outcome on adequate parenting.' *Journal of Substance Abuse Treatment, 7(4),* 225–232.

Dawson, G. (1994) 'Development of Emotional Expression and Emotion Regulation in Infancy.' In G. Dawson and K. Fischer (eds) *Human Behaviour and the Developing Brain.* New York: Guildford Press.

Day, C. (2008) 'Children's and young people's involvement and participation in mental health care.' *Child and Adolescent Mental Health, 13(1),* 2–8.

Day, C., Carey, M., and Surgenor, T. (2006) 'Children's key concerns: piloting a qualitative approach to understanding their experience of mental health care.' *Clinical Child Psychology and Psychiatry, 11,* 139–155.

Dembo, R., Williams, L., La Voie, L., Berry, E. *et al.* (1989) 'Physical abuse, sexual victimization, and illicit drug use: replication of a structural analysis among a new sample of high-risk youths.' *Violence and Victims, 4(2),* 121–138 (18).

Department for Children, Schools and Families (2006) *Care Matters: Transforming the Lives of Young People* White Paper. London: DCSF.

Department for Children, Schools and Families (2008) *Statistical First Release. Outcome Indicators for Children Looked After: Twelve Months to 30 September 2008, England.* London: DCSF.

Department for Children, Schools and Families (2009) *Safeguarding Children and Young People from Sexual Exploitation: Supplementary Guidance to Working Together to Safeguard Children.* Available at www.gov.uk/government/uploads/system/uploads/attachment_data/file/278849/Safeguarding_Children_and_Young_People_from_Sexual_Exploitation.pdf

Department for Children, Schools and Families and Department of Health (2009) *Promoting the Health of Children in Care. Statutory Guidance on the Planning, Commissioning and Delivery of Health Services for Looked after children.* Nottingham: Crown Copyright.

Department for Education (2000) *The Care Standards Act.* London: DfE.

Department for Education (2011a) *Children Looked After by Local Authorities in England (including adoption and care leavers) – Year Ending 31 March 2011.* Available at www.gov.uk/government/publications/children-looked-after-by-local-authorities-in-england-year-ending-31-march-2011, accessed on 30 January 2016.

Department for Education (2011b) *The Munro Review of Child Protection: Final Report – A Child Centred System.* London. DfE.

Department for Education (2014a) *Mental Health and Behaviour in Schools: Departmental Advice for School Staff, June 2014.* London: DfE.

Department for Education (2014b) *Children Looked After in England (including adoption and care leavers) Year Ending 31 March 2014.* London: DfE. Available at www.gov.uk/government/statistics/children-looked-after-in-england-including-adoption-2014-to-2015, accessed on 3 February 2016.

Department for Education (2014c) *Outcomes for Children Looked After by Local Authorities in England as at 31 March 2014.* Available at www.gov.uk/government/statistics/outcomes-for-children-looked-after-by-local-authorities, accessed on 3 February 2016.

Department for Education (2014d) *Statistical First Release: Outcomes for Children Looked After by Local Authorities in England as at 31 March 2014.* Available at www.gov.uk/government/uploads/system/uploads/attachment_data/file/384781/Outcomes_SFR49_2014_Text.pdf, accessed on 3 February 2016.

Department for Education (2014e) *Children in Care. 2014–2015. Statistical First Release,* 50/2013. Available at www.nao.org.uk/wpcontent/uploads/2014/11/Children-in-care1.pdf, accessed on 3 February 2016.

Department for Education (2015a) *Statistics on Children in Care at Both National and Local Authority Levels for the Financial Year 2014 to 2015. Children Looked After in England Including Adoption: 2014 to 2015.* Available at www.gov.uk/government/statistics/children-looked-after-in-england-including-adoption-2014-to-2015, accessed on 3 February 2016.

Department for Education (2015b) *Working together to safeguard children: A guide to inter-agency working to safeguard and promote the welfare of children.* Available at www.gov.uk/government/uploads/system/uploads/attachment_data/file/419595/Working_Together_to_Safeguard_Children.pdf, accessed on 08 August 2016.

Department for Education and Department of Health (2015) *Promoting the Health and Well-being of Looked After Children. Statutory Guidance for Local Authorities, Clinical Commissioning Groups and NHS England.* London: HMSO. Available at www.gov.uk/government/uploads/system/uploads/attachment_data/file/413368/Promoting_the_health_and_well-being_of_looked-after_children.pdf, accessed on 3 February 2016.

Department for Education and Skills (2003) *Every Child Matters.* London: The Stationery Office.

Department of Health (1989) *An Introduction to the Children Act 1989.* London: The Stationery Office.

Department of Health (1998) *The Quality Protects Programme: Transforming Children's Services, 2001–02.* London: DoH.

Department of Health (2000) *The Children (Leaving Care) Act (2000).* London: DoH.

Department of Health (2002) *The Children Act Report 2001.* London: The Stationery Office.

Department of Health (2004) *National Service Framework: Children, Young People and Maternity Services.* London: DoH. Available at www.gov.uk/government/publications/national-service-framework-children-young-people-and-maternity-services, accessed 26 March 2016.

Department of Health (2009) *Promoting the Health and Wellbeing of Children in Care – Revised Statutory Guidance.* London: DoH.

Department of Health (2010) *Equity and Excellence: Liberating the NHS.* London: DoH.

Department of Health (2012) Response to Consultation: *Liberating the NHS: No Decision About Me, Without Me.* London: Crown Copyright. Available at www.gov.uk/government/uploads/system/uploads/attachment_data/file/216980/Liberating-the-NHS-No-decision-about-me-without-me-Government-response.pdf, accessed on 3 February 2016.

Deykin, E., Levy, C. and Wells, V. (1987) 'Adolescent depression, alcohol and drug abuse.' *American Journal of Public Health, 77(2),* 178–182.

Dickson, K., Sutcliffe, K. and Gough, D. (2009) 'What outcomes matter to Looked After Children and young people and their families and carers? A systematic review of their experience, views and preferences.' Available at www.nice.org.uk/guidance/ph28/documents/looked-after-children-review-e5-qualitative-review-of-experiences-views-and-preferences2, accessed on 3 February 2016.

Dimigen, G., Del Priore, C. and Butler, S. (1999) 'Psychiatric disorder among children at time of entering local authority care: questionnaire survey.' *British Medical Journal, 319,* 675.

Doelling, J. and Johnson, J. (1990) 'Predicting success in foster placement: the contribution of parent-child temperament characteristics.' *American Journal of Orthopsychiatry, 60,* 585–593.

Dorsey, S., Farmer, E., Barth, R., Greene, K. *et al.* (2008) 'Current status and evidence base of training for foster and treatment foster parents.' *Children and Youth Services Review, 30,* 1403–1416.

DosReis, S., Zito, J., Safer, D. and Soeken, L. (2001) 'Mental health services for youths in foster care and disabled youths.' *American Journal of Public Health, 91,* 1094–1099.

Doyle, J. (2007) *Child Protection and Child Outcomes: Measuring the Effects of Foster Care.* Available at www.mit.edu/~jjdoyle/doyle_fosterlt_march07_aer.pdf, accessed on 3 February 2016.

Dube, S., Felitti, V., Dong, M., Chapman, D. *et al.* (2003) 'Childhood abuse, neglect and household dysfunction and the risk of illicit drug use: the adverse childhood experiences study.' *Pediatrics, 111(3),* 564–572.

Duncan, B. and Argys, L. (2007) 'Economic incentives and foster care placement.' *Southern Economic Journal, 74(1)* (July), 114–142.

Earley, J. (2000) *Interactive Group Therapy: Integrating Interpersonal, Action Oriented, and Psychodynamic Approaches.* Philadelphia: Brunner/Mazell (Taylor Francis Group).

Edmonds, K., Sumnall, H., McVeigh, J. and Bellis, M. (2005) *Drug Prevention Among Vulnerable Young People.* Liverpool: National Collaborating Centre for Drug Prevention/Liverpool John Moores University.

Elder, R., Evans, K., Nizette, D. and Trenoweth, S. (2008) *Mental Health Nursing.* London: Churchill and Livingstone.

Ellingsen, I.T., Shemmings, D. and Storksen, I. (2011) 'The concept of "family" among Norwegian adolescents in long-term foster care.' *Child and Adolescent Social Work Journal, 28(4),* 301–318.

Emanuel, L. (1997) 'Facing the damage together.' *Journal of Child Psychotherapy, 23(2),* 279–302.

Emanuel, L. (2002) 'Deprivation X3: the contribution of organisational dynamics to the "triple deprivation" of looked-after-children.' *Journal of Child Psychotherapy, 28,* 163–179.

Emanuel, R. (1984) 'Primary disappointment.' *Journal of Child Psychotherapy, 10(1),* 71–87.

Erikson, E. (1950) *Childhood and Society.* New York: W.W. Norton & Company, Inc.

Erikson, E. (1963) *Childhood and Society* (2nd Edition). New York: W.W. Norton & Company, Inc.

Ernst, J. (1999) 'Whanau Knows Best: Kinship Care in New Zealand.' In R. Hegar and M. Scannapieco (eds) *Kinship Foster Care: Policy, Practice, and Research.* New York: Oxford University Press.

Evans, R., Scourfield, J., Morgan, H., Turley, R. *et al.* (in preparation) *Systematic Review and Meta-analysis of Self-harm and Suicide in Looked after children and Young People.* York: NIHR.

Everson-Hock, E., Jones, R., Guillaume, L., Duenas, A. *et al.* (2009) *Review 2: The effectiveness of training and support for carers/professionals/volunteers working with children in care and young people on the physical and emotional health and well-being of children in care and young people.* ScHARR Public Health Evidence Report 6.2 © 2009 ScHARR (School of Health and Related Research) University of Sheffield, ISBN 190075228X.

Ewers, M. and Havsteen-Franklin, E. (2012) '"You don't know anything about us!" An art psychotherapy group for adolescent girls.' *Art Therapy OnLine, 1(4).*

Famularo, R., Kinscherff, R. and Fenton, T. (1991) 'Post-traumatic stress disorder among children clinically diagnosed as borderline personality disorder.' *Journal of Nervous and Mental Disease 179,* 428–431.

Farmer, E., Burns, B. and Chapman, M. (2001) 'Use of mental health services by youth in contact with social services.' *Social Service Review, 75,* 605–624.

Farmer, E., Lipscombe, J. and Moyers, S. (2005) 'Foster carer strain and its impact on parenting and placement outcomes for adolescents.' *British Journal of Social Work, 35,* 237–254.

Farmer, E. and Moyers, S. (2008) *Kinship Care: Fostering Effective Family and Friends Placement.* London: Jessica Kingsley Publishers.

Felitti, V., Anda, R., Nordenberg, D., Williamson, D. *et al.* (1998) 'Relationship of childhood abuse and household dysfunction to many of the leading causes of death in adults: the Adverse Childhood Experiences (ACE) Study.' *American Journal of Preventative Medicine, 14(4),* 245–258.

Fendrich, M., Mackesy-Amiti, M., Wislar, J. and Goldstein, P. (2011) 'Childhood abuse and the use of inhalants: differences by degree of use.' *American Journal of Public Health, 87(5),* 765–769.

Firmin, C. (2011) *This is It: This is My Life. Female Voice in Violence Final Report: On the Impact of Serious Youth Violence and Criminal Gangs on Women and Girls across the Country.* London: ROTA.

Flynn, R. (2002) 'Kinship foster care: research review.' *Child & Family Social Work, 7(4),* 311–321.

Fonagy, P. (2001) *Attachment Theory and Psychoanalysis.* New York: Sage.

Fonagy, P., Gergely, G., Jurist, E. (2003) *Affect Regulation, Mentalisation and the Development of the Self.* London: Karnac Books.

Ford, T., Vostanis, P., Meltzer, H. and Goodman, R. (2007) 'Psychiatric disorder among British children looked after by local authorities: comparison with children living in private households.' *British Journal of Psychiatry, 190(4),* 319–325.

Fostering Network (2004) *Training for Foster Carers: A Discussion Paper.* Available at www.fostering.net/sites/www.fostering.net/files/public/resources/reports/manifesto_training.pdf, accessed on 3 February 2016.

Fostering Network (2012) *Foster Care Magazine, 151, Autumn.*

Fransella, F. (2005) *The Essential Pratictioner's Handbook of Personal Construct Psychology.* Chichester: John Wiley & Sons Ltd.

Franzén, E., Vinnerljung, B. and Hjern, A. (2008) 'The epidemiology of out-of-home care for children and youth: a national cohort study.' *British Journal of Social Work, 38(6),* 1043–1059.

Frauenholz, S., Conrad-Hiebner, A. and Mendenhall, A. (2015) 'Children's mental health providers' perceptions of mental health literacy among parents and caregivers.' *Journal of Family Social Work, 18(1),* 40–56.

Freud, S. (1918) *Totem and Taboo Resemblance the Psychic Lives of the Savages and Neurotics.* New York: Moffat Yard and Co.

Freud, S. (1921) *Dream Psychology: Psychoanalysis for Beginners.* New York: The James A. McCann Company.

Freud, S. (1922) *Group Psychology and the Analysis of the Ego.* (Translated by James Strachey.) New York: Boni and Liviright.

Friedlaender, E., Rubin, D., Alpern, E., Mandell, D. *et al.* (2005) 'Patterns of health care use that may identify young children who are at risk for maltreatment.' *Pediatrics, 116(6),* 1303–1308.

Frye, M. and Webb, A. (2002) *Effective Partnership Working.* London: HM Treasury.

Furnivall, J., McKenna, M., McFarlane, S. and Grant, E. (2012) *Attachment Matters for All – An Attachment Mapping Exercise for Children's Services in Scotland.* Strathclyde: CELCIS.

Garland, A., Landsverk, J., Hough, R. and Ellis-MacLeod, E. (1996) 'Type of maltreatment as a predictor of mental health service use for children in foster care.' *Child Abuse and Neglect, 20,* 675–688.

Gianino, A. and Tronick, E.Z. (1988) 'The Mutual Regulation Model: The Infant's Self and Interactive Regulation Coping and Defense.' In T. Field, P. McCabe and N. Schneiderman (eds) *Stress and Coping.* Hillsdale, NJ: Erlbaum.

Gibbs, I., Sinclair, I. and Wilson, K. (2004) *Foster Placements: Why They Succeed and Why They Fail.* London: Jessica Kingsley Publishers.

Gilbert, P., McEwan, K., Mitra, R., Franks, L. *et al.* (2008) 'Feeling safe and content: a specific affect regulation system? Relationship to depression, anxiety, stress, and self-criticism.' *Journal of Positive Psychology, 3(3),* 182–191.

Giles, L.D. (2003) *'Use of Drawings and Reflective Comments in Family Construct Development.'* Unpublished PhD thesis, University of British Columbia, Canada.

Gilligan, R. (2000) 'The importance of listening to the child in foster care.' In G. Kelly and R. Gilligan (eds) *Issues in Foster Care: Policy, Practice and Research.* London: Jessica Kingsley Publishers.

Gilligan, R. (2006) 'Creating a warm place where children can blossom.' *Social Policy Journal of New Zealand, 28 (July),* 36–45.

Goeders, N. (2003) 'The impact of stress on addiction.' *European Neuropsychopharmocology, 13(6),* 435–441.

Goelet, P. and Kandel, E. (1986) 'Tracking the flow of learned information from membrane receptors to genome.' *Trends in Neuroscience, 9,* 492–499.

Gohir, S. (2013) *Unheard Voices: The Sexual Exploitation of Asian Girls and Young Women.* Birmingham: Muslim Women's Network.

Golding, K. (2003) 'Helping foster carers, helping children: using attachment theory to guide practice.' *Adoption & Fostering, 27(2),* 64–73.

Golding, K. (2010) 'Multi-agency and specialist working to meet the mental health needs of children in care and adopted.' *Clinical Child Psychology and Psychiatry, 15(4),* 573–587.

Golding, K.S., Dent, H.R., Nissim, R. and Stott, L. (2006) 'Being Heard: Listening to the Voices of Young People and their Families.' In K. Golding, H.R. Dent and L. Stott (eds) *Thinking Psychologically About Children who are Looked After and Adopted: Space for Reflection.* Chichester: John Wiley & Sons.

Golding, K. and Hughes, D. (2012) *Creating Loving Attachments.* London: Jessica Kingsley Publishers.

Golding, K. and Picken, W. (2004) 'Group work for foster carers caring for children with complex problems.' *Adoption and Fostering, 28(1),* 25–37.

Goldney, R., Dal Grande, E. and Fisher, L. (2002) 'Population attributable risk of major depression for suicidal ideation in a random and representative community sample.' *Australian and New Zealand Journal of Psychiatry, 34,* 98–106.

Goodman, R. (1997) 'The Strengths and Difficulties Questionnaire: a research note.' *Journal of Child Psychology and Psychiatry, 38*, 581–586.

Goodman, R., Ford, T., Simmons, H., Gatward, R. *et al.* (2000) 'Using the Strengths and Difficulties Questionnaire (SDQ) to screen for child psychiatric disorders in a community sample.' *British Journal of Psychiatry, 177*, 534–539.

Goodyear-Brown, P. (ed.) (2012) *Handbook of Child Sexual Abuse: Identification, Assessment and Treatment.* Hoboken, NJ: Wiley.

Gonzalez, J., Alegria, M. and Prihoda, T. (2005) 'How do attitudes toward mental health treatment vary by age, gender, and ethnicity/race in young adults?' *Journal of Community Psychology, 33(5)*, 611–629.

Granville, J. and Langton, P. (2002) 'Working across boundaries: systemic and psychodynamic perspectives on multi-disciplinary and inter-agency practice.' *Journal of Social Work Practice 16(1)*, 23–27.

Greef, R. (ed.) (1999) *Fostering Kinship: An International Perspective on Kinship Foster Care.* Aldershot: Arena.

Green, Y. and Gray, M. (2013) 'Lessons learned from the kinship education and support program (KEPS): developing effective support groups for formal kinship caregivers.' *Social Work with Groups, 36(1)*, 27–42.

Greenspan, S. (2002) *The Secure Child: Helping Children Feel Safe and Confident in a Changing World.* New Caledonia: Perseus Books.

Grubbs, G. (1994) 'An abused child's use of sandplay in the healing process.' *Clinical Social Work Journal, 22(2)*, 193–209.

Grubbs, J. (1995) 'A comparative analysis of the sandplay process of sexually abused and non-clinical children.' *The Arts in Psychotherapy, 22(5)*, 429–446.

Guerra, L. (2015) *Preventing Suicide Among Lesbian, Gay and Bisexual Young People: A Toolkit for Nurses.* Public Health England. PHE publications gateway number: 2014800.

Guishard, J. and Malcolm L. (1993) 'They know why the caged bird sing: the behaviour of abused girls.' *DECP Newsletter.* British Psychological Society.

Guishard-Pine, J. (2013) *10th Annual Report of the Service to Children Requiring Intensive Psychological Therapies (SCRIPT).* Luton: Family Consultation Service.

Guishard-Pine, J., McCall, S. and Hamilton, L. (2007) *Understanding Looked After Children. An Introduction to Psychology for Foster Care.* London: Jessica Kingsley Publishers.

Guishard-Pine, J., McCall, S., Havsteen-Franklin, E., Afuape, O. *et al.* (2013) *Fierce Commitment: A Two-Day Course for Foster Carers. (SCRIPT).* Luton: Family Consultation Service.

Hackett, S., Masson, H. and Phillips, S. (2006) 'Exploring concensus in practice with youth who are sexually abusive: findings from a Delphi study of practitioner views in United Kingdom and the Republic of Ireland.' *Child Maltreatment, 11(2)*, 146–156.

Hagell, A. (2013) Adolescent Self-harm. Association for Young People's Health. Available at www.ayph.org.uk/publications/316_RU13%20Self-harm%20summary.pdf, accessed on 3 February 2016.

Halfron, N., Berkowitz, G. and Klee, L. (1992) 'Mental health utilization by children in foster care in California.' *Paediatrics, 89*, 1238–44.

Hammill, P. and Boyd, B. (2001) 'Rhetoric or reality? Interagency provision for young people with challenging behaviour.' *Emotional and Behavioural Difficulties, 6(3)*, 135–149.

Hampson, R. (1985) 'Foster Parent Training: Assessing its Role in Upgrading Foster Home Care.' In M.J. Cox and R.D. Cox (eds) *Foster Care: Current Issues, Policies and Practices.* Norwood, NJ: Ablex.

Hampson, R., Schulte, M. and Ricks, C. (1983) 'Individual vs. group training for foster parents: Efficiency/effectiveness evaluations.' *Family Relations, 32(2)*, 191–202.

Happer, H., McCreadie, J. and Aldgate, J. (2006) *Celebrating Success: What Helps Looked After Children Succeed?* Edinburgh: Social Work Inspection Agency. Available at www.gov.scot/Resource/Doc/129024/0030718.pdf, accessed on 3 February 2016.

Harber, A. and Oakley, M. (2012) *Fostering Aspirations: Reforming the Foster Care System in England and Wales.* London: Policy Exchange Unit. Available at www.policyexchange.org.uk/images/publications/fostering%20ambitions%20-%20jan%2012.pdf, accessed on 3 February 2016.

Hargreaves, J. and Page, L. (2013) *Reflective Practice.* Oxford: Polity Press.

Harden, A. (1997) *Formal And Informal Kinship Care.* Chicago: Chapin Hall.

Harker, R., Dobel-Ober, D., Akhurst, S. and Berridge, D. (2004a) 'Who takes care of education 18 months on? A follow-up study of looked after children's perceptions of support for educational progress.' *Child and Family Social Work, 9,* 273–284.

Harker, R., Dobel-Ober, D., Berridge, D. and Sinclair, R. (2004b) 'More than the sum of its parts? Inter-professional working in the education of children in care.' *Children and Society, 18(3),* 179–193.

Harker, R., Dobel-Ober, D., Lawrence, J., Berridge, D. and Sinclair, R. (2003) 'Who takes care of education? Looked after children's perceptions of support for educational progress.' *Child and Family Social Work, 8,* 89–100.

Harker, L., Jütte, S., Murphy, T., Bentley, H., Miller, P. and Fitch, K. (2013) *How Safe Are Our Children?* NSPCC. Available at www.nspcc.org.uk/globalassets/documents/research-reports/how-safe-children-2013-report.pdf.

Harlow, E. and Frost, N. (2007) 'Reforming the care system: New Labour and corporate parenting.' *Social Work and Social Sciences Review, 13(2),* 7–17.

Harper, Z. and Scott, S. (2005) *Meeting the Needs* of *Sexually Exploited Young People in London.* Ilford: Barnardo's.

Harrison, P., Fulkerson J. and Beebe, T. (1997) 'Multiple substance use among adolescent physical and sexual abuse victims.' *Child Abuse & Neglect, 21(6),* 529–539.

Hawkins, J., Catalano, R. and Miller, J. (1992) 'Risk and protective factors for alcohol and other drug problems in adolescence and early adulthood: implications for substance abuse prevention.' *Psychological Bulletin, 112(1),* 64–105.

Hawton, K., Zahl, D. and Weatherall, R. (2003a) 'Suicide following deliberate self-injury: long-term follow-up of patients who presented to a general hospital.' *British Journal of Psychiatry, 182,* 537–542.

Hawton, K., Hall, S., Simkin, S., Bale, L. *et al.* (2003b) 'Deliberate self-harm in adolescents: a study of characteristics and trends in Oxford, 1990–2000.' *Journal of Child Psychology and Psychiatry, Nov, 44(8),* 1191–1198.

Haydon, D. (2003) *Teenage Pregnancy Amongst Children in Care/Care Leavers.* Available at www.law.qub.ac.uk/schools/SchoolofLaw/Research/ResearchProjects/ChildhoodTransitionandSocialJusticeInitiative/FileStore/Filetoupload,414900,en.pdf, accessed on 3 February 2016.

Hayslip, B. and Kaminski, P. (2005) 'Grandparents raising their grandchildren.' *Marriage & Family Review, 37,* 147–169.

Hegar, R. (1999) 'The Cultural Roots of Kinship Care.' In R. Hegar and M. Scannapieco (eds) *Kinship Foster Care: Policy, Practice, and Research.* New York: Oxford University Press.

Herrenkohl, T., Hong, S., Klika, B., Herrenkohl, R. *et al.* (2013) 'Developmental impacts of child abuse and neglect related to adult mental health, substance use, and physical health.' *Journal of Family Violence, 28(2),* doi: 10.1007/s10896-012-9474-9

Herriott, R. and Firestone, W. (1983) 'Multisite qualitative policy research: optimising description and generalisability.' *Educational Researcher, 12,* 14–19.

Heslop, P. and MacCaulay, F. (2009) *Hidden Pain? Self Injury and People with Learning Disabilities.* Available at www.selfinjurysupport.org.uk/files/docs/hidden-pain/hidden-pain-full-report.pdf, accessed on 3 February 2016.

Hicks, L., Simpson, D., Mathews, I., Koorts, H. *et al.* (2012) *Communities in care: a scoping review to establish the relationship of community community to the lives of looked after children and young people.* Available at http://eprints.lincoln.ac.uk/6066/1/Communities_in_care_-_A_scoping_review.pdf, (2012), accessed on 27 March 2016.

Hill, C. (1992) 'Research on therapist techniques in brief individual therapy implications for practitioners. *The Counseling Psychologist 20(4),* 689–711. doi: 10.1177/0011000092204012.

Hill-Tout, J., Pithouse, A. and Lowe, K. (2003) 'Training foster carers in a preventative approach to children who challenge: mixed messages from research.' *Adoption & Fostering, 27(1),* 47–56.

Hinshelwood R.D. (1991) 'Psychodynamic formulation in assessment for psychotherapy.' *British Journal of Psychotherapy, 8(2),* 166–174.

Hirsch, D. (2008) *Estimating The Costs Of Child Poverty.* York: Joseph Rowntree Foundation.

Hodges, J., Steele, M., Hillman, S., Henderson, K. *et al.* (2003) 'Changes in attachment representations over the first year of adoptive placement: narratives of maltreated children.' *Clinical Child Psychology and Psychiatry, 8,* 351–367.

Holmes, J. (2013) *John Bowlby and Attachment Theory* (2nd edn). London: Routledge.
Honey, K., Rees, P. and Griffey, S. (2011) 'Investigating self-perceptions and resilience in children in care.' *Educational Psychology in Practice, 27,* 37–52.
Horwath, J. and Morrison, T. (2007) 'Collaboration, integration and change in children's services: Critical issues and key ingredients.' *Child Abuse & Neglect, 31,* 55–69.
House of Commons Children, Schools and Families Committee (2009) Third Report of Session 2008–09: *Looked after children, Volume I.* Available at www.publications.parliament.uk/pa/cm200809/cmselect/cmchilsch/111/11102.htm, accessed on 3 February 2016.
House of Commons Education Committee (2013) *Children First: The Child Protection System in England Fourth Report of Session 2012–13 Volume I.* London: The Stationery Office Limited. Available at www.publications.parliament.uk/pa/cm201213/cmselect/cmeduc/137/137.pdf, accessed on 3 February 2016.
Howe, D. and Fearnley, S. (2003) 'Disorders of attachment in adopted and fostered children: recognition and treatment.' *Clinical Child Psychology and Psychiatry, 8,* 369–387.
Howe, D., Feast, J. and Coster, D. (2002) *Adoption, Research and Reunion: The Long-term Experience of Adopted Adults.* London: The Children's Society.
Hughes, D. (2004) *Building the Bonds of Attachment: Awakening Love in Deeply Troubled Children.* Maryland: Aronson.
Hughes, D. (2005) 'An attachment treatment for foster and adoptive families.' *Service and Practice Update, 4,* 26–28.
Hunt, J. (2003) *Family And Friends As Carers.* London: Department Of Health.
Hunt, L. (2011) 'Preventing placement breakdown among looked after children with complex mental health needs.' *Community Care online.* 27 October. Available at www.communitycare.co.uk/2011/10/27/preventing-placement-breakdown-among-looked-after-children-with-complex-mental-health-needs, accessed on 3 February 2016.
Hunt, J., Waterhouse, S. and Lutman, E. (2008) *Keeping Them in The Family: Outcomes For Children Placed in Kinship Care Through Care Proceedings.* London: British Association For Adoption And Fostering.
Hunter, M. (2001) *Psychotherapy with Young People in Care: Lost and Found.* Hove: Brunner-Routledge.
Improving Access to Psychological Therapies (2012) *Improving Access to Psychological Therapies Newsletter, December 2012.* Available at www.cypiapt.org/docs/cyp-iapt-newsletter-3-december-2012.pdf, accessed on 3 February 2016.
Ince, L. (2009) *Kinship Care: An Afro-centric Perspective.* PhD, University of Birmingham.
Indyk, S. (2015) *Emotional and Psychological Well-Being of Children in Foster Care.* Available at www.nccwe.org/downloads/info-packs/ShoshanaIndyk.pdf, accessed on 3 February 2016.
Ineichen, B. (2008) 'Suicide and attempted suicide among South Asians in England: who is at risk?' *Mental Health Family Medicine, 5,3,* 135–138.
IRISS (Institute for Research and Innovation in Social Services) (2013) 'Understanding suicide and self-harm amongst children in care and care leavers.' IRISS. Available at www.iriss.org.uk/sites/default/files/iriss-insight-21.pdf, accessed on 3 February 2016.
Ironside, L. (2004) 'Living a provisional existence: thinking about foster carers and the emotional containment of children placed in their care.' *Adoption & Fostering, 28(4),* 39–49.
Jackson, C. (2012) 'What do young people want?' *Therapy Today, 23(2).* Available at www.therapytoday.net/article/show/2957/what-do-young-people-want, accessed on 3 February 2016.
Jackson, C. (2015) 'News focus: when therapy does harm.' *Therapy Today, 26(5),* 8–9.
Jacobson, N., Follette, W. and Revenstorf, D. (1984) 'Psychotherapy outcome research: methods for reporting variability and evaluating clinical significance.' *Behavior Therapy, 15,* 336–352.
Jacobson, N., Follette, W. and Revenstorf, D. (1986) 'Toward a standard definition of clinically significant change.' *Behavior Therapy, 17,* 308–311.
Jacobsen, H., Ivarsson, T., Wentzel-Larsen, T., Smith, L. *et al.* (2014) 'Attachment security in young foster children: continuity from 2 to 3 years of age.' *Attachment and Human Development, 16(1),* 42–57.
Jacobson, N. and Truax, P. (1991) 'Clinical significance: a statistical approach to defining meaningful change in psychotherapy.' *Journal of Consulting and Clinical Psychology, 59,* 12–19.

Jago, S. and Pearce, J. (2008) *Gathering Evidence of the Sexual Exploitation of Children and Young People: A Scoping Exercise.* Available at www.beds.ac.uk/__data/assets/pdf_file/0018/40824/Gathering_evidence_final_report_June_08.pdf, accessed on 3 February 2016.

Jago, S., Arocha, L., Brodie, I., Melrose, M. *et al.* (2011) *What's Going on to Safeguard Children and Young People from Sexual Exploitation? How Local Partnerships Respond to Child Sexual Exploitation.* Luton: University of Bedfordshire.

James, B. (1994) *Handbook for Treatment of Attachment-trauma Problems in Children.* New York: Lexington.

Janoff-Bulman, R. (1992) *Shattered Assumptions: Towards a New Psychology of Trauma.* New York: Free Press.

Johns, C. (2013) *Becoming a Reflective Practitioner.* London: Wiley.

Johnson, P. and Richter, L. (2002) 'The relationship between smoking, drinking, and adolescents' self-perceived health and frequency of hospitalization: analyses from the 1997 National Household Survey on Drug Abuse.' *Journal of Adolescent Health, 30(3),* 175–183.

Jones-Smith, E. (2012) *Theories of Counselling and Psychotherapy: An Integrative Approach.* Thousand Oaks, CA: Sage.

Jorm, A.F. (2000) 'Mental health literacy: public knowledge and beliefs about mental disorder.' *British Journal of Psychiatry, 17,* 396–401.

Jorm, A., Korten, A., Jacomb, P., Christensen, H. *et al.* (1997) 'Mental health literacy: a survey of the public's ability to recognise mental disorders and their beliefs about the effectiveness of treatment.' *The Medical Journal of Australia,166,* 182–186.

Jütte, S., Bentley, H., Miller, P. and Jetha, N. (2015) *How Safe Are Our children? The Most Comprehensive Overview of Child Protection in the UK.* London: NSPCC.

Kalivas, P. and Kuffy, P. (1989) 'Similar effects of daily cocaine and stress on mesocorticolimbic dopamine neurotransmission in the rat.' *Biological Psychiatry, 25,* 913–928.

Kalland, M., Sinkkonen, J., Gissler, M., Meriläinen, J. *et al.* (2006) 'Maternal smoking behaviour, background and neonatal health in Finnish children subsequently placed in foster care.' *Child Abuse & Neglect, 30(9),* 1037–1047.

Kane, E. (1989) *Recovering from Incest: Imagination and the Healing Process.* Boston, MA: Sigo Press.

Kataoka, S., Zhang, L. and Wells, K. (2002) 'Unmet need for mental health care among U.S. children: variation by ethnicity and insurance status.' *American Journal of Psychiatry, 159(9),* 1548–1555.

Kaufman, G. (1989) *The Psychology of Shame.* New York: Springer.

Kay, J. (2003) *Protecting Children: A Practical Guide.* London: Continuum International Publishing Limited.

Kelly, A. and Achter, J. (1995) 'Self-concealment and attitudes toward counseling in university students.' *Journal of Counseling Psychology, 42(1),* 40–46.

Kelly, G.A. (1955) *The Psychology of Personal Constructs,* Volumes 1 and 2. New York: Norton.

Kelly, C., Allan, S., Roscoe, P. and Herrick, E. (2003) 'The mental health needs of children in care: an integrated multi-agency model of care.' *Clinical Child Psychology and Psychiatry, 8(3),* 323–335.

Kendall-Tackett, K. (2002) 'The health effects of childhood abuse: four pathways by which abuse can influence health.' *Child Abuse & Neglect, 26 (6–7),* 715–729.

Kenrick, J. (2000) '"Be A Kid": the traumatic impact of repeated separations on children who are fostered or adopted.' *Journal of Child Psychopathology, 26(3),* 393–412.

Kenrick, J., Lindsey, C. and Tollemache, L. (eds) (2006) *Creating New Families: Therapeutic Approaches to Fostering, Adoption and Kinship Care* (The Tavistock Clinic Series). London: Karnac Books.

Kerker, B. and Dore, M. (2006) 'Mental health needs and treatment of foster youth: barriers and opportunities.' *American Journal of Orthopsychiatry, 76(1),* 138–147.

Kernberg, O. (1965) 'Notes on countertransference.' *Journal of the American Psychoanalytic Association, 13,* 38–56.

Khantzian, E. (1997) 'The self-medication hypothesis of substance use disorders: a reconsideration and recent applications.' *Harvard Review of Psychiatry, 4(5),* 231–244.

Kilpatrick, D., Ruggiero, K., Acierno, R., Saunders, B. *et al.* (2003) 'Violence and risk of PTSD, major depression, substance abuse/dependence and comorbidity: results from the National Survey of Adolescents.' *Journal of Consulting and Clinical Psychology, 71(4),* 692–700.

Kinsey, D. and Schlösser, A. (2013) 'Interventions in foster and kinship care: a systematic review.' *Clinical Child Psychology and Psychiatry, 18(3),* 429–463.

Kirton, D. (2001) 'Love and money: payment, motivation and the fostering task.' *Child & Family Social Work, 6(3),* 199–208.

Kirton, D., Beecham, J. and Ogilvie, K. (2007) 'Gaining satisfaction? An exploration of foster-carer's' attitudes to payment.' *British Journal of Social Work, 37(7),* 1205–1224.

Klass, D., Silverman, P. and Nickman, S. (1996) *Continuing Bonds: New Understandings of Grief.* Abingdon: Taylor & Francis.

Knox, S., Adrians, N., Everson, E., Hess, S. *et al.* (2011) 'Client's perspectives of therapy termination.' *Psychotherapy Research, 21,* 154–167.

Kohut, H. (1971) *The Analysis of the Self: A Systematic Approach to the Psychoanalytic Treatment of Narcissistic Personality Disorders.* New York: International Universities Press.

Laming, H. (2011) *Care Matters: Placements Working Group Report.* Department for Education and Science. Available at http://dera.ioe.ac.uk/id/eprint/8068, accessed on 3 February 2016.

Lancashire Care Foundation Trust (2012) *Clinical Risk Assessment and Management in Mental Health Services Policy.* Lancashire: LCFT.

Lauber, C., Nordt, C., Falcato, L. and Rössler, W. (2003) 'Do people recognise mental illness?' *European Archives of Psychiatry and Clinical Neuroscience, 253(5),* 248–251.

Law, D. (2013) *Goal-based Outcome Measures.* London: CAMHS Press.

Lawrence-Mahrra, T. (2014) 'Your World, My World, Our World: Through Who's Eyes? Let's Dance.' Unpublished dissertation for MA in Transpersonal Child, Adolescent and Family Therapy.

Lear, J. (2005) *Freud (The Routledge Philosophers).* Abingdon: Routledge.

Lee, J. and Holland, T. (1991) 'Evaluating the effectiveness of foster parent training.' *Research on Social Work Practice, 1(2),* 162–174.

Lee, R. and Whiting, J. (2007) 'Foster children's expressions of ambiguous loss.' *American Journal of Family Therapy, 35(5),* 417–428.

Leslie, L., Landsverk J., Ezzet-Lofstrom R., Tschann J. *et al.* (2000) 'Children in foster care: factors influencing outpatient mental health service use.' *Child Abuse & Neglect, 24,* 465–476.

Lewis, C. (2011) 'Providing therapy to children and families in foster care: a systemic-relational approach.' *Family Process, 50(4),* 436–452.

Lewis, C. (2015) *Young People's Statistics from the National Drug Treatment Monitoring System (NDTMS): 1 April 2013 to 31 March 2014.* London: Public Health England.

Lewis, H. (1971) *Shame and Guilt in Neurosis.* New York: International Universities Press.

Lewis, M. (1992) *The Exposed Self.* New York: Free Press.

Lewis, M., Alessandri, S. and Sullivan, M. (1992) 'Differences in pride and shame as a function of children's gender and task difficulty.' *Child Development, 63,* 630–638.

Liebschutz, J., Savetsky, J., Saitz, R., Horton, N. *et al.* (2002) 'The relationship between sexual and physical abuse and substance abuse consequences.' *Journal of Substance Abuse Treatment, 22(3),* 121–128.

Lilliengren, P. (2011) 'Patient Attachment to Therapist Rating Scale.' Unpublished manual, Department of Psychology, Stockholm University, Sweden.

Lilliengren, P., Werbart, A., Mothander, P.R., Ekström, A., Sjögren, S., and Ögren, M.-L. (2014) 'Patient attachment to therapist rating scale: development and psychometric properties.' *Psychotherapy Research, 24,* 184–201.

Lilliengren, P., Falkenström, F., Sandell, R., Risholm, P. and Werbart, A. (2015) 'Secure attachment to therapist, alliance, and outcome in psychoanalytic psychotherapy with young adults.' *Journal of Counseling Psychology, 62(1),* 1–13. Available at http://dx.doi.org/10.1037/cou0000044, accessed on 3 February 2016.

Lillywhite, R. and Skidmore, P. (2006) 'Boys are not sexually exploited? A challenge to practitioners.' *Child Abuse Review, 15(5),* 351–361.

Linares, L., Montalto, D., Li, M. and Oza, V. (2006) 'A promising parenting intervention in foster care.' *Journal of Consulting and Clinical Psychology, 74,* 32–41.

Lloyd, C. (1998) 'Risk factors for problem drug use: identifying vulnerable groups.' *Drugs, Education, Prevention and Policy, 5(3),* 217–232.

Lloyd, G., Stead, J. and Kendrick, A. (2001) *Hanging On In There: A Study of Interagency Work to Prevent School Exclusion in Three Local Authorities.* London: Joseph Rowntree Foundation with National Children's Bureau Enterprise.

Loader, P. (1998) 'Such a shame: a consideration of shame and shaming mechanisms in families.' *Child Abuse Review, 7,* 44–57.

Logan, D. and King, C. (2001) 'Parental facilitation of adolescent mental health service utilisation: a conceptual and empirical review.' *Clinical Psychology: Science and Practice, 8(3),* 319–333.

Lynch, M. (2012) 'Factors influencing successful psychotherapy outcomes.' *Master of Social Work Clinical Research Papers.* Paper 57. Available at http://sophia.stkate.edu/msw_papers/57, accessed on 3 February 2016.

Macdonald, G. and Turner, W. (2005) 'An experiment in helping foster carers manage challenging behaviour.' *British Journal of Social Work, 35,* 1265–1282.

MacKay, T. and Greig, A. (2007) 'Editorial.' *Educational and Child Psychology, 24(1),* 4–6.

Maguire, S. (2005) 'Mental Health Literacy and Attitudes in Foster Carers: Identification of Factors that Influence Help-seeking.' Unpublished DclinPsy dissertation, University of East Anglia.

Malinowski, B. (1929) *The Sexual Lives of Savages in North Western Melanesia: An Ethnographic Account of Courtship, Marriage, and Family Life Among the Natives of the Trobriand Islands, British New Guinea.* New York: Eugenics Publishing Company.

Mann, K. (2005) 'Looked After Adolescents' Experiences of Mental Health Services.' Unpublished doctoral thesis, University of Hertfordshire, Hertfordshire, UK.

Margison, F., McGrath, G., Barkham, M., Mellor Clark, J. *et al.* (2000) 'Measurement and psychotherapy: evidence-based practice and practice-based evidence.' *British Journal of Psychology, 177,* 123–130.

Mason, B. (1993) 'Towards positions of safe uncertainty.' *Human Systems: Journal of Therapy, Consultation and Training, 4(3–4),* 189.

Masten, A. (2001) 'Ordinary magic: resilience processes in development.' *American Psychologist, 56,* 227–238.

Matsumoto, D. (1996) *Culture and Psychology.* Pacific Grove, CA: Brooks/Cole.

McAuley, C. and Davis, T. (2009) 'Emotional well-being and mental health of children in care in England.' *Child & Family Social Work, Special Issue: High Risk Youth: Evidence on Characteristics, Needs and Promising Interventions, 14(2),* 147–155.

McCall, S. and Guishard-Pine, J. (2011) *Counselling Skills for Foster Carers. (SCRIPT).* Luton: Family Consultation Clinic.

McCann, I.L. and Pearlman, L. (1990) 'Vicarious traumatization: a framework for understanding the psychological effects of working with victims.' *Journal of Traumatic Stress, 3(1),* 131–149.

McCann, J., James, A., Wilson, S. and Dunn, G. (1996) 'Prevalence of psychiatric disorders in young people in the care system.' *British Medical Journal, 313,* 1529–1530.

McCarthy, G., Janeway, J. and Geddes, A. (2003) 'The impact of emotional and behavioural problems on the lives of children growing up in the care system.' *Adoption & Fostering, 27(3),* 14–19.

McEvoy, M. (1990) 'Repairing Personal Boundaries: Group Therapy with Survivors of Sexual Abuse.' In T.A. Laidlaw and C. Malmo (eds) *Healing Voices: Feminist Approaches to Therapy with Women.* San Francisco, CA: Jossey-Bass.

McEwen, B. (2006) 'Protective and damaging effects of stress mediators: central role of the brain.' *Dialogues Clinical Neuroscience, 8(4),* 367–381.

McEwen, B. and Gianaros, P. (2010) 'Central role of the brain in stress and adaptation: links to socioeconomic status, health and disease.' *Annals NY Academy Sciences, 1186,* 190–222.

McGuire, M. and Dowling, S. (2013) 'Cyber crime: A review of the evidence.' Research Report 75 Chapter 3: Cyber-enabled crimes – sexual offending against children. London: Home Office. Available at www.gov.uk/government/uploads/system/uploads/attachment_data/file/246754/horr75-chap3.pdf, accessed on 3 February 2016.

Mead, M. (1928) *Coming of Age in Samoa.* New York: William Morrow Paperbacks.

Meadowcroft, P. and Trout, B. (1990) *Troubled Youth in Treatment Homes: A Handbook of Therapeutic Foster Care.* Washington DC: Child Welfare League of America.

Melrose, M. and Pearce, J. (eds) (2013) *Critical Perspectives on Child Sexual Exploitation and Related Trafficking.* Basingstoke: Palgrave Macmillan.

Meltzer, D. (1998) 'On Aesthetic Reciprocity.' In D. Meltzer and M. Harris Williams, *The Apprehension of Beauty.* Strath Tay: Clunie Press.

Meltzer, H., Gatward, R., Goodman, R. and Ford, T. (2000) *Mental Health of Children and Adolescents in Great Britain.* London: The Stationery Office.

Meltzer, H., Corbin, T., Gatward, R., Goodman, R. and Ford, T. (2003) *The Mental Health of Young People Looked After by Local Authorities in England.* London: The Stationery Office.

Mental Health Foundation (2002) *The Mental Health of Children in Care. Bright Futures: Working with Vulnerable Young People.* London: Mental Health Foundation.

Middleman, R. and Wood, G. (1990) *Skills for Direct Practice in Social Work.* New York: Columbia University Press.

Miller, A. (2008) *The Drama of Being a Child: The Search for the True Self.* London: Virago Press.

Mills, R. (2003) 'Possible antecedents and developmental implications of shame in young girls.' *Infant and Child Development, 12,* 329–349.

Millward, R., Kennedy, E., Towlson, K. and Minnis, H. (2006) 'Reactive attachment disorder in looked after children.' *Emotional and Behavioural Difficulties, 11(4),* 273–279.

Ministry of Justice (2015) *Voice of the Child: Children to be More Clearly Heard in Decisions About their Future.* Available at www.gov.uk/government/news/voice-of-the-child-children-to-be-more-clearly-heard-in-decisions-about-their-future, accessed on 27 March 2016.

Minnis, H. and Del Priore, C. (2001) 'Mental health services for children in care: implications from two studies.' *Adoption & Fostering, 25(4),* 27–38.

Minnis, H. and Devine, C. (2001) 'The effect of foster care training on the emotional and behavioural functioning of children in care.' *Adoption & Fostering, 25(1),* 44–54.

Minnis, H., Everett, K., Pelosi, A., Dunn, J. *et al.* (2006) 'Children in foster care: mental health, service use and costs.' *European Journal of Child and Adolescent Psychiatry, 15,* 63–70.

Minnis, H., Pelosi, A., Knapp, M. and Dunn J. (2001) 'Mental health and foster carer training.' *Community Child Health, Public Health and Epidemiology. Archives of Disease in Childhood, 84,* 302–306.

Mirza, K., McArdle, P., Crome, I. and Gilvarry, E. (eds) (2008) *The Role of CAMHS and Addiction Psychiatry in Adolescent Substance Misuse Services.* London: National Treatment Agency for Substance Misuse.

Montgomery, C. (2002) 'Role of dynamic group therapy in psychiatry.' *Advances in Psychiatric Treatment, 8(1),* 34–41.

Moran, H. (2010) 'Clinical observations of the differences between children on the autism spectrum and those with attachment problems: the Coventry Grid.' *Good Autism Practice, 11(22),* 49–59.

Morgan, R., Ness, D. and Robinson, M. (2003) 'Students' help-seeking behaviours by gender, racial background, and student status.' *Canadian Journal of Counselling, 37,* 151–166.

Moroz, K. (2005) *The Effects of Psychological Trauma on Children and Adolescents. Vermont Agency of Human Services.* Department of Health, Division of Mental Health, Child, Adolescent and Family Unit. Available at http://mentalhealth.vermont.gov/sites/dmh/files/report/cafu/DMH-CAFU_Psychological_Trauma_Moroz.pdf, accessed on 3 February 2016.

Morris, J. (2003) *Children on the Edge of Care.* Available at http://disability-studies.leeds.ac.uk/files/library/morris-children-on-the-edge-of-care.pdf, accessed on 26 March 2016.

Morrison, T. (1996) 'Partnership and collaboration: rhetoric and reality.' *Child Abuse & Neglect, 20(2),* 127–140.

Mosuro, S., Malcolm, D. and Guishard-Pine, J. (2014) 'Mental health awareness and coping in foster carers: the impact of a counselling skills intervention.' *Educational and Child Psychology. Child Abuse and Protection, 31(3),* 64–70.

Mulvihill, D. (2005) 'The health impact of childhood trauma: an interdisciplinary review, 1997–2003.' *Issues in Comprehensive Pediatric Nursing, 28(2),* 115–136.

Munro, C. (2004) 'Scratching the Surface…What we know about the abuse and sexual exploitation of young people by adults targeting residential and supported accommodation units.' Glasgow: Barnardo's Street Team. Available at www.barnardos.org.uk/scratching_the_surface.pdf, accessed on 31 January 2016.

Murphy, M. and Fonagy, P. (2012) 'Mental Health Problems in Children and Young People.' Chapter 10 in Department of Health Annual Report of the Chief Medical Officer: *Our Children Deserve Better: Prevention Pays.* Available at www.gov.uk/government/uploads/system/uploads/attachment_data/file/252660/33571_2901304_CMO_Chapter_10.pdf, accessed on 3 February 2016.

Nandy, S., Selwyn, J., Farmer, E. and Vaisey, P. (2004) 'The Buttle Report': *Spotlight on Kinship Care: Using Census Microdata to Examine the Extent and Nature of Kinship Care in the UK at the Turn of the Twentieth Century.* Available at www.bristol.ac.uk/media-library/sites/sps/migrated/documents/finalkinship.pdf, accessed on 27 March 2016.

National Institute for Clinical Excellence (2002) *Scoping document for self-harm: the short-term physical and psychological management and secondary prevention of intentional self-harm in primary and secondary care.* London: NICE.

National Treatment Agency (2012) *Statistics from the National Drug Treatment Monitoring System (NDTMS) 1 April 2011–31 March 2012.* Vol. 1: The Numbers. London: National Treatment Agency for Substance Misuse.

National Working Group on Sexually Exploited Children and Young People (2008) *How Is Child Sexual Exploitation Defined?* Available at www.nwgnetwork.org/who-we-are/what-is-child-sexual-exploitation, accessed on 3 February 2016.

Needell, B. and Barth, R. (1998) 'Infants entering foster care compared to other infants using birth status indicators.' *Child Abuse & Neglect, 22(12),* 1179–1187.

Neimeyer, G. and Hudson, J. (1985) 'Couple's Constructs: Personal Systems in Marital Satisfaction.' In D. Bannister (ed.) *Issues and Approaches in Personal Construct Theory.* London: John Wiley & Sons.

Neumann, E. (1988) *The Child: Structure and Dynamics of the Nascent Personality.* London: Karnac Books.

Newburn, T. and Pearson, G. (2002) *Drug Use Among Young People in Care.* Sheffield: Youth Citizenship and Social Change Programme.

Newbury-Birch, D., Walker, J., Avery, L., Beyer, F. *et al.* (2009) *Impact of Alcohol Consumption on Young People: A Systematic Review of Published Reviews.* Newcastle University: DCSF.

NHS (National Health Service) Health Advisory Service (1996) 'Children and young people: substance misuse services; the substance of young needs; commissioning and providing services for children and young people who use and misuse substances.' In R. Williams, J. Christian, M. Gay and E. Gilvarry (eds). London: HMSO.

NHS (National Health Service) National Treatment Agency for Drugs Misuse (2007) *The Role of CAMHS and Addiction Psychiatry in Adolescent Substance Misuse Services.* Available at www.nta.nhs.uk/uploads/yp_camhs280508.pdf, accessed on 3 February 2016.

NICE (National Institute for Health and Clinical Excellence) (2007a) *Community-based Interventions to Reduce Substance Misuse Among Vulnerable and Disadvantaged Children and Young People.* London: NICE.

NICE (National Institute for Health and Clinical Excellence) (2007b) *Drug Misuse: Psychosocial Interventions.* NICE clinical guideline 51. London: NICE.

NICE (National Institute for Health and Clinical Excellence) (2010) *Looked After Children and Young People. PH28.* Refreshed May 2015. Available at www.nice.org.uk/guidance/ph28, accessed on 3 February 2016.

NICE (National Institute for Health and Care Excellence) (2013) *Children's Attachment* draft scope. Available at http://guidance.nice.org.uk/CG/Wave0/675/ScopeConsultation/DraftScope/pdf/English, accessed on 25 March 2015.

NICE (National Institute for Health and Care Excellence) (2015) *Children's Attachment: Attachment in Children and Young People who are Adopted from Care, in Care or at High Risk of Going into Care.* Available at www.nice.org.uk/guidance/ng26, accessed on 3 February 2016.

Nitter, A. and Onate, S. (2013) *Kinship Care Album: Researching Kinship Care in West and Central Africa.* Save the Children. Available at http://resourcecentre.savethechildren.se/library/kinship-care-album-researching-kinship-care-west-and-central-africa, accessed on 3 February 2016.

Norcross, J.C. (ed.) (2011) *Psychotherapy Relationships That Work* (2nd edn). New York: Oxford University Press.

Norcross, J. and Prochaska, D. (1988) 'A study of eclectic (and integrative views) revisited.' *Professional Psychology: Research and Practice, 19(2),* 170–174.

NSPCC (2014) *What Works in Preventing and Treating Poor Mental Health in Looked After Children?* Available at www.nspcc.org.uk/globalassets/documents/evaluation-of-services/preventing-treating-mental-health-looked-after-children-report.

O'Brien, F. (2008) 'Attachment Patterns Through the Generations: Internal and External Homes.' In C. Case and T. Dalley (eds) *Art Therapy with Children: From Infancy to Adolescence.* London: Routledge.

O'Connor, T. and Zeanah, C. (2003) 'Attachment disorders: assessment strategies and treatment approaches.' *Attachment & Human Development, 5(3),* 223–244.

O'Neil, C. (2004) '"I remember the first time I went into foster care – it's a long story": children, permanent parents and other supportive adults talk about the experience of moving from one family to another.' *Journal of Family Studies, 10(2),* 205–219.

O'Neill, S., Holland, S. and Rees P. (2013) *In Good Hands. Scoping Study: Transforming the Outcomes for Children in Care in Wales.* Available at www.biglotteryfund.org.uk/-/media/Files/Programme%20Documents/In%20Good%20Hands/In%20Good%20Hands%20Scoping%20report.pdf, accessed on 2 February 2015.

Oaklander, V. (1997) 'The therapeutic process with children and adolescents.' *Gestalt Review, 1(4),* 292–317.

Oatley, K. (1984) *Selves in Relation: An Introduction to Psychotherapy and Groups.* London: Methuen Inc.

Obholzer, A. (ed.) (1994) *The Unconscious at Work: Individual and Organizational Stress in the Human Services.* London: Routledge.

Office of the Children's Commissioner (2012) *Briefing for the Rt. Hon Michael Gove MP, Secretary of State for Education, on the Emerging Findings of the Office of the Children's Commissioner Inquiry into Child Sexual Exploitation in Gangs and Groups with a Special Focus on Children in Care, July 2012.* London: OCC. Available at www.childrenscommissioner.gov.uk/content/publications/content_580, accessed on 3 February 2016.

Oliver, C. (2010) *Children's Views and Experiences of their Contact with Social Workers: A Focused Review of the Evidence.* London: Children's Workforce Development Council (CWDC). Available at http://dera.ioe.ac.uk/518/1/Children_s_views_and_experiences_of_contact_with_social_workers_report_July_2010.pdf, accessed on 3 February 2016.

Oosterman, M., Schuengel, C., Wim Slot, N., Bullens, R. *et al.* (2007) 'Disruptions in foster care: a review and meta-analysis.' *Children and Youth Services Review, 29,* 53–76.

Ostrea, E., Chavez, C. and Strauss, M. (1976) 'A study of factors that influence the severity of neonatal narcotics withdrawal.' *Journal of Paediatrics, 88,* 642–645.

Owens, D., Horrocks, J. and House, A. (2002) 'Fatal and non-fatal repetition of self-harm: systematic review.' *British Journal of Psychiatry, 181,* 193–199.

Paley, G. and Lawton, D. (2001) 'Evidence-based practice: accounting for the importance of the therapeutic relationship in UK National Health Service therapy provision.' *Counselling and Psychotherapy Research: Linking Research with Practice, 1(1),* 12–17.

Palmer, T. (2015) *Digital Dangers: The Impact of Technology on the Sexual Abuse and Exploitation of Children and Young People.* Ilford: Barnardo's.

Parliament UK (2015) Education and Adoption Bill. Available at www.publications.parliament.uk/pa/cm201516/cmpublic/educationadoption/memo/educ03.htm, accessed on 3 February 2016.

Partridge, E. (1992) *The Dictionary of Catchphrases: American and British from the Sixteenth Century to the Present Day.* Maryland: Scarborough House.

Pasztor, E. and Evans, R. (1992) *Evaluation of Foster Parent Training: Literature Review.* Report to Evaluation Work Group, Illinois Department of Child and Family Services Comprehensive competency-based foster parent training project. Washington DC: Child Welfare League of America.

Pavis, S., Constable, H. and Masters, H. (2003) 'Multi-agency, multi-professional work: experiences from a drug prevention project.' *Health Education Research Theory & Practice, 18(6),* 717–728.

Pavis, S., Cunningham-Burley, S. and Amos, A. (1997) 'Alcohol consumption and young people: exploring meaning and social context.' *Health Education Research, 12(3),* 311–322.

Pearce, J., Hynes, P. and Bovarnick, S. (2009) *Breaking the Wall of Silence: Practitioners' Responses to Trafficked Children and Young People.* London: NSPCC.

Pearce, J., Hynes, P. and Bovarnick, S. (2013) *Trafficked Young People: Breaking the Wall of Silence.* London: Routledge.

Peck, E., Trowell, D. and Gulliver, P. (2001) 'The meanings of "culture" in health and social care: a case study of the combined Trust in Somerset.' *Journal of Interprofessional Care, 15(4),* 321–327.

Pecora, P. (2010) 'Why current and former recipients of foster care need high quality mental health services.' *Administration and Policy in Mental Health, 37(1–2),* 185–90.

Pecora, P., Jensen, P., Jackson, L. *et al.* (2009) 'Mental health services for children placed in foster care: an overview of current challenges.' *Child Welfare, 88(1),* 5–26.

Pembroke, L. (2000) 'Damage limitation.' *Nursing Times, 96(34),* 34.

Pembroke, L. (2007) 'Harm Minimisation: Limiting the Damage of Self-injury.' In H. Spandler and S. Warner (eds) (2007) *Beyond Fear and Control: Working with Young People who Self-harm.* Ross-on-Wye: PCCS Books.

Perez-del-Aguila, R., Holland, S., Faulkner, A., Connell, D. *et al.* (2003) *Overview and survey of effectiveness of interventions to promote stability and continuity of care for looked after children. National Assembly for Wales sponsored project.* Cardiff: University School of Social Sciences, University of Wales College of Medicine, Morgannwg Health Authority.

Perry, B., Pollard, R., Blakley, T., Baker, W. *et al.* (1995) 'Childhood trauma, the neurobiology of adaptation, and "use-dependent" development of the brain: how "states" become "traits".' *Infant Mental Health Journal, 16(4),* 271–291.

Perry, B. and Szalavitz, M. (2006) *The Boy Who was Raised as a Dog...and Other Stories From a Child Psychiatrist's Notebook.* New York: Basic Books.

Petrowski, K., Pokorny, D., Nowacki, K. and Buchheim, A. (2013) 'The therapist's attachment representation and the patient's attachment to the therapist.' *Psychotherapy Research, 23,* 25–34.

Phillips, J. (1997) 'Meeting the psychiatric needs of children in foster care: social workers' views.' *Psychiatric Bulletin, 21,* 609–611.

Piescher, K. (2013) 'Evidence based practice in foster parent training and support.' Center for Advanced Studies in Child Welfare. Available at http://cascw.umn.edu/wp-content/uploads/2013/12/EBPFPTrainingSupportComplete.pdf, accessed on 3 February 2016.

Pithouse, A., Hill-Tout, J. and Lowe, K. (2002) 'Training foster carers in challenging behaviour: a case study in disappointment?' *Child and Family Social Work, 7(3),* 203–214.

Potter-Efron, R. and Potter-Efron, P. (1989) *Letting Go Of Shame: Understanding How Shame Affects Your Life.* Center City, MN: Hazelden.

Prior, D. and Paris, A. (2005) *Preventing Children's Involvement in Crime and Anti-Social Behaviour: A Literature Review.* Research Report 623. Nottingham: Department for Education and Skills.

Public Health England (2008) Everybody's Business – learning and training. Available at www.chimat.org.uk/camhs/everybodysbusiness, accessed on 3 February 2016.

Public Health England (2015) *Mental Health: Children in Care.* Available at www.chimat.org.uk/default.aspx?QN=MENT_CHILDINCARE, accessed on 3 February 2016.

Puckering, C., Connolly, B., Werner, C., Toms-Whittle, L. *et al.* (2011) 'Rebuilding relationships: a pilot study of the effectiveness of the Mellow Parenting Programme for children with reactive attachment disorder.' *Clinical Child Psychology and Psychiatry, 16(1),* 73–87.

Racker, H. (1957) 'The meaning and uses of countertransference.' *Psychoanalytic Quarterly, 56,* 303–357.

Radford, L., Corral, S., Bradley, C., Fisher, H. *et al.* (2011) *Child Abuse and Neglect in the UK Today.* NSPCC: London.

Ratnayake, A., Bowlay-Williams, J. and Vostanis, P. (2014) 'When are attachment difficulties an indication for specialist mental health input?' *Adoption & Fostering, 38(2),* 159–170.

Rich, P. (2011) *Understanding, Assessing and Rehabilitating Juvenile Sexual Offenders* (2nd edn). New Jersey: John Wiley.

Richards, A. (2001) *Second Time Around: A Survey Of Grandparents Raising Their Children.* London: Family Rights Group.

Richards, A. and Tapsfield, R. (2003) *Family And Friends Care: The Way Forward.* London: Family Rights Groups.

Richardson, H. (2015) 'Mental health services "turning care children away".' BBC News 17.12.2015. Available at www.bbc.co.uk/news/education-35113899, accessed on 3 February 2016.

Richardson, J. and Joughin, C. (2000) *The Mental Health Needs of Looked After Children.* London: Royal College of Psychiatry.

Richardson, J. and Lelliot, P. (2003) 'Mental health of children in care.' *BJPsych Advances, 9,* 249–256.

Ringrose, J., Gill, R., Livingstone, S. and Harvey, L. (2012) *A Qualitative Study of Children, Young People and 'Sexting': A Report Prepared for the NSPCC.* Available at www.nspcc.org.uk/globalassets/documents/research-reports/qualitative-study-children-young-people-sexting-report.pdf, accessed on 17 November 2015.

Roberts, V. (2003) 'The Self Assigned Impossible Task.' In A. Obholzer and V. Roberts (eds) *The Unconscious At Work: Individual and Organizational Stress In Human Services.* Abingdon: Taylor and Francis.

Robson, L. (2014) 'Psychotherapy With Children in Care: Some Common Themes and Technical Interventions.' Unpublished doctoral thesis, Birkbeck University, London.

Robson, S. and Briant, N. (2009) 'What did they think? An evaluation of the satisfaction and perceived helpfulness of a training programme developed as an indirect intervention for foster carers.' *Adoption and Fostering, 33(2),* 34–44.

Rocco-Briggs, M. (2008) '"Who owns my pain?" An aspect of the complexity of working with children in care.' *Journal of Child Psychotherapy, 34 (2),* 190–206.

Rock S., Michelson, D., Thomson, S. and Day, S. (2013) 'Understanding foster placement instability for looked after children: a systematic review and narrative synthesis of quantitative and qualitative evidence.' *British Journal of Social Work, (Impact Factor: 1.19). 01/2013; 45(1),* 177–203.

Rodrigues, V. (2004) 'Health of children looked after by the local authorities.' *Public Health, 118,* 370–376.

Roesch-Marsh, A. (2012) *Behaviour as Communication: Understanding the Needs of Neglected and Abused Adolescents.* Stirling: With Scotland.

Rogers, C. (1961) *On Becoming a Person: A Therapist's View of Psychotherapy.* New York: Houghton Mifflin.

Rogers, C. (1980) *A Way of Being.* New York: Houghton Mifflin.

Rohsenow, D., Corbett, R., and Devine, D. (1988) 'Molested as children: a hidden contribution to substance misuse?' *Journal of Substance Abuse Treatment, 5,* 13–18.

Rostill-Brookes, H., Larkin, M., Toms, A. and Churchman, C. (2011) 'A shared experience of fragmentation: making sense of foster placement breakdown.' *Clinical Child Psychology and Psychiatry, 16,* 103–127.

Roth, A. and Fonagy, P. (2004) *What Works for Whom? A Critical Review of Psychotherapy Research* (2nd edn). Hove: Guildford.

Roth, D. and Ashley, C. (2010) *Family and Friends Care: A Guide To Good Practice For English Local Authorities: Summary of Key Points.* London: Family Rights Group.

Royal College of Paediatrics and Child Health (RCPCH) (2015) *Looked After Children: Knowledge, Skills and Competences of Health Care Staff: Intercollegiate Role Framework.* Available at: www.rcpch.ac.uk/sites/default/files/page/Looked%20After%20Children%202015.pdf, accessed on 3 February 2016.

Rubin, J. (1999) *Art Therapy: An Introduction.* Philadelphia: Taylor and Francis.

Ruegger, M. and Rayfield, L. (1999) 'The Nature and Dilemmas of Fostering in the 90s.' In A. Wheal (ed.) *The RHP Companion to Fostering.* Dorset: Russell House.

Russell, L. (1972) *This Masquerade.* Shelter Records.

Rustin, M. and Quagliata, E. (1994) *Assessment in Child Psychotherapy.* London: Gerald Duckworth and Co Ltd.

Rustin, M. and Quagliata, E. (2000) *Assessment in Child Psychotherapy.* London: Karnac Books.

Rutter, M. (1990) 'Psychosocial resilience and protective mechanisms.' In J. Rolf, A. Masten, D. Cicchetti, K. Nuechterlein and S. Weintraub (eds) *Risk and Protective Factors in the Development of Psychopathology.* New York: Cambridge University Press.

Runyan, A. and Fullerton, S. (1981) 'Foster care provider training: a preventive program.' *Children and Youth Services Review, 3,* 127–141.

Sanders, P. (2007) *Using Counselling Skills on the Telephone and in Computer-mediated Communication* (3rd edn). Ross-on-Wye: PCCS Books.

Saunders, L. and Broad, R. (1997) *The Health Needs of Young People Leaving Care.* Leicester: Centre for Social Action.

Saunders, H. and Selwyn, J. (2008) 'Supporting informal kinship care.' *Adoption & Fostering, 32,* 31–42.

Save the Children (1995) *Towards a Children's Agenda.* London: Save the Children.

Schnider, A. and Ptak, R. (1999) 'Spontaneous confabulators fail to suppress currently irrelevant memory traces.' *Nature Neuroscience, 2,* 677–681.

Schofield, G. and Beek, M. (2005a) 'Risk and resilience in long-term foster care.' *British Journal of Social Work, 35,* 1283–1301.

Schofield, G. and Beek, M. (2005b) 'Providing a secure base: parenting children in long-term foster care.' *Attachment & Human Development, 7,* 3–26.

Schofield, G. and Beek, M. (2009) 'Growing up in foster care: providing a secure base through adolescence.' *Child and Family Social Work, 14(3),* 255–266.

Schön, D. (1984) *The Reflective Practitioner: How Professionals Think in Action.* New York: Perseus.

Schonert-Reichl, K.A. and Muller, J.R. (1996) 'Correlates of help-seeking in adolescence.' *Journal of Youth and Adolescence, 25(6),* 705–731.

Schore, A. (1994) *Affect Regulation and the Origin of the Self: The Neurobiology of Emotional Development.* Hillsdale, NJ: Erlbaum.

Schore, A. (1997) 'Early organization of the nonlinear right brain and development of a predisposition to psychiatric disorders.' *Development and Psychopathology, 9,* 595–631.

Schore, A. (1998) 'Early Shame Experience and Infant Brain Development.' In P. Gilbert and B. Andrews (eds) *Shame: Interpersonal Behaviour, Psychopathology, and Culture.* New York: Oxford University Press.

Schore, A. (2000) 'Attachment and the regulation of the right brain.' *Attachment and Human Development, 2(1),* 23–47.

Schore, A. (2001) 'The effects of relational trauma on right brain development, affect regulation, and infant mental health.' *Infant Mental Health Journal, 22,* 201–269.

Schore, A. (2012) *The Science of the Art of Psychotherapy.* New York: W.W. Norton and Company, Inc.

Schwartz, T., White, G.M. and Lutz, C.A. (1992) *New Directions in Psychological Anthropology.* Cambridge: Cambridge University Press.

Scott, S. and Skidmore, P. (2006) *Reducing the Risk: Barnardo's Support for Sexually Exploited Young People: A Two-year Evaluation.* Ilford: Barnardo's.

Scottish Government (2009) *Moving Forward In Kinship And Foster Care, Getting It Right For Every Child In Kinship And Foster Care Reference Group.* Edinburgh: Scottish Government. Available at www.gov.scot/Publications/2009/02/27085637/0, accessed on 3 February 2016.

Seiffge-Krenke, I. (1989) 'Problem Intensity and the Disposition of Adolescents to Take Therapeutic Advice.' In M. Bramring, F. Losel and H. Skowronek (eds) *Children at Risk: Assessment, Longitudinal Research, and Intervention.* Berlin: De Gruyter.

Self-harm UK (2015) 'The facts: who self-harms?' Self-harm UK website, www.selfharm.co.uk, accessed on 3 February 2016.

Selwyn, J., Frazer, L. and Quinton, D. (2006) 'Paved with good intentions: the pathway to adoption and the costs of delay.' *British Journal of Social Work, 36,* 561–576.

Selwyn, J., Harris, P., Quinton, D., Nawaz, S. *et al.* (2008) *Pathways to Permanence for Black, Asian and Mixed Ethnicity Children: Dilemmas, Decision Making and Outcomes.* Nottingham: DCSF.

Selwyn, J. and Saunders, H. (2006) *Greenwich Kinship Care Team: An Evaluation of the Team's Work. Report to Greenwich Council.* Bristol: The Hadley Centre, School for Policy Studies, University of Bristol.

Sempik, J., Ward, H. and Darker, I. (2008) 'Emotional and behavioural difficulties of children and young people at entry into care.' *Clinical Child Psychology and Psychiatry, 13(2),* 221–233.

Sharp, N. (2012) *Still Missing.* London: Missing People. Available at www.missingpeople.org.uk/about-us/about-the-issue/research/12-missing-people-research.html, accessed on 27 March 2016.

Shaw, C. and Shaw, T. (2007) 'A Dialogue of Hope and Survival.' In H. Spandler and S. Warner (eds) *Beyond Fear and Control: Working with Young People who Self-harm.* Ross-on-Wye: PCCS Books.

Shaw, S. (2006) 'Certainty, revision and ambivalence: a qualitative investigation into women's journeys to stop self-injuring.' *Women and Therapy, 29,* 153–177.

Shonkoff, J., Garner, A., Siegel, B., Dobbins, M. *et al.* (2012) 'The lifelong effects of early childhood adversity and toxic stress.' *Pediatrics, 129(1),* 232–246.

Shuker, L. (2011) 'Safe accommodation for sexually exploited and trafficked young people: briefing paper.' University of Bedfordshire. Available at www.beds.ac.uk/__data/assets/pdf_file/0020/203591/Safe-Accommodation-for-Sexually-Exploited-and-Trafficked-Young-People-Dr-Lucie-Shuker.pdf, accessed on 31 January 2016.

Shuker, L. (2013a) 'Constructs of Safety for Children in Care Affected by Sexual Exploitation.' In M. Melrose (ed.) *Critical Perspectives on Child Sexual Exploitation and Trafficking.* London: Palgrave Macmillan.

Shuker, L. (2013b) *Evaluation of Barnardo's Safe Accommodation Project for Sexually Exploited and Trafficked Young People.* Luton: University of Bedfordshire. Available at www.barnardos.org.uk/barnardo27s-sa-project-evaluation-full-report__3_.pdf, accessed on 31 January 2016.

Siegel, D. and Hartzell, M. (2014) *Parenting From The Inside Out.* London: Scribe Publications. (Original work published 2004.)

Simkiss, D., Spencer, N., Stallard, N. and Thorogood, M. (2012) 'Health service use in families where children enter public care: a nested case control study using the General Practice Research Database.' *BMC Health Services Research, 12,* 65.

Simon, R.D. and Simon, D.K. (1982) 'The effect of foster parent selection and training on service delivery.' *Child Welfare, 61(8),* 515–524.

Simpson, T. and Miller, W. (2002) 'Concomitance between childhood sexual and physical abuse and substance use problems: a review.' *Clinical Psychology Review, 22(1),* 27–77.

Sinclair, I. (2005) *Fostering Now: Messages From Research.* London: Jessica Kingsley Publishers.

Sinclair, I. (2008) *Stability and Well-being in the Care System.* NICE Expert Paper, EP2 – LAC 2.4, London: National Institute for Health and Clinical Excellence. Available at www.nice.org.uk/guidance/ph28/evidence/ep2-stability-and-wellbeing-in-the-care-system-ian-sinclair-430039981, accessed on 27 March 2016.

Sinclair I., Baker C., Wilson K. and Gibbs I. (2005) *Foster Children: Where They Go and How They Get On.* London: Jessica Kingsley Publishers.

Sinclair, I., Gibbs, I. and Wilson, K. (2004) *Foster Carers: Why They Stay and Why They Leave.* London: Jessica Kingsley Publishers.

Sinclair, I. and Wilson, K. (2003) 'Matches and mismatches: the contribution of carers and children to the success of foster placements.' *British Journal of Social Work, 33,* 871–884.

Singer, E., Doornenbal, J. and Okma, K. (2004) 'Why do children resist or obey their foster parents? The inner logic of children's behaviour during discipline.' *Child Welfare, 83, 6,* 581–610.

Singer, M., Petchers, M. and Hussey, D. (1989) 'The relationship between sexual abuse and substance abuse among psychiatrically hospitalized adolescents.' *Child Abuse and Neglect, 13(3),* 319–325.

Skills for Care (2012) *Counselling Skills Make the Difference.* Available at www.skillsforcare.org.uk/Document-library/NMDS-SC,-workforce-intelligence-and-innovation/Workforce-integration/7CounsellingSkills.pdf, accessed on 3 February 2016.

Skoll, G. (2012) 'Ethnography and psychoanalysis.' *Human and Social Studies: Research and Practice, 1(1),* 29–50.

Smallwood, S. and Wilson, B. (2007) *Focus On Families.* Office for National Statistics. London: Palgrave Macmillan.

Smith, N., Dogaru, C. and Ellis, F. (2015) *Hear Me. Believe Me. Respect Me. A Survey of Adult Survivors of Child Sexual Abuse and their Experiences of Support Services.* University Campus Suffolk and Survivors in Transition.

Social Care Institute for Excellence (2005) *Preventing Teenage Pregnancy in Children in Care.* Briefing 9, London: Social Care Institute for Excellence.

Social Care Institute for Excellence (2010) 'Help-seeking by foster-carers for their "looked after" children: the role of mental health literacy and treatment attitudes. Available at www.scie-socialcareonline.org.uk/help-seeking-by-foster-carers-for-their-looked-after-children-the-role-of-mental-health-literacy-and-treatment-attitudes/r/a1CG0000000GUsHMAW, accessed on 3 February 2016.

Social Exclusion Task Force (2008) *Families At Risk Review.* London The Cabinet Office.

Social Exclusion Unit (1998) *Truancy and School Exclusion.* London: Stationery Office.

Social Exclusion Unit (2003) *A Better Education for Children in Care.* London: Author.

Solis, J., Shadur, J., Burns, A. and Hussong, A. (2012) 'Understanding the diverse needs of children whose parents abuse substances.' *Current Drug Abuse Review, 5(2),* 135–147.

Solomon, J., George, C. and De Jong, A. (1995) 'Children classified as controlling at age six: evidence of disorganized representational strategies and aggression at home and school.' *Development and Psychopathology*, 7, 447–464.

Spandler, H. (1996) *Who's Hurting Who? Young People, Self-harm and Suicide* (reprint). Gloucester: Handsell Publishing Ltd.

Spandler, H. and Warner, S. (eds) (2007) *Beyond Fear and Control: Working with Young People Who Self-harm.* Ross-on-Wye: PCCS Books.

Spencer-Oatey, H. (2008) *Culturally Speaking: Culture, Communication and Politeness Theory* (2nd edn). London: Continuum.

Spencer-Oatey, H. (2012) *What is Culture? A Compilation of Quotations.* GlobalPAD Core Concepts. Available at www2.warwick.ac.uk/fac/soc/al/globalpad/openhouse/interculturalskills/global_pad_-_what_is_culture.pdf, accessed on 3 February 2016.

Spinelli, E. (2005) *The Interpreted World: An Introduction to Phenomenological Psychology.* London: Sage.

Sprang, G. (2009) 'The efficacy of a relational treatment for maltreated children and their families.' *Child and Adolescent Mental Health, 14,* 81–88.

Sprince, J. (2000) 'Towards an integrated network.' *Journal of Child Psychotherapy, 26 (3),* 413–431.

Stanley, N. and Manthorpe, J. (2002) *Students' Mental Health Needs: Problems and Responses.* London: Jessica Kingsley Publishers.

Stanley, N., Riordan, D. and Alaszewski, H. (2005) 'The mental health of children in care: matching response to need.' *Health and Social Care in the Community, 13(3),* 239–248.

Stein, E., Evans, B., Mazumdar, R. and Rae-Grant, N. (1996) 'The mental health of children in foster care: a comparison with community and clinical samples.' *Canadian Journal of Psychiatry, 41,* 385–391.

Stein, M. (2002) 'Leaving Care.' In D. McNeish, T. Newman and H. Roberts (eds) *What Works for Children?* Buckingham: Open University Press.

Stendhal, R. (2002) *The Red and the Black.* London: Penguin.

Stenner, P. (1993) 'Discoursing Jealousy.' In E. Burman and I. Parker (eds) *Discourse Analytic Research: Repertoires and Readings of Texts in Action.* London: Routledge.

Stern, D. (1977) *The First Relationship: Infant and Mother, The Developing Child.* Glasgow: Fontana/Open Books Original.

Stern, D. (1985) *The Interpersonal World of the Infant.* New York: Basic Books.

Stern, D. (1998) *The Motherhood Constellation: A Unified View of Parent-Infant Psychotherapy.* London: Karnac Books.

Stewart, O. (2008) 'User participation in health care services.' *London Race Equality Foundation, (7),* 1–7.

Stewart, S. (1996) 'Alcohol abuse in individuals exposed to trauma: a critical review.' *Psychological Bulletin, 120(1),* 83–112.

Stiles, W., Shapiro, D. and Elliott, R. (1986) 'Are all psychotherapies equivalent?' *American Psychologist, 41,* 165–180.

Stipek, D. (1995) 'The Development of Pride and Shame in Toddlers.' In J.P. Tangney and K.W. Fischer (eds) *Self-Conscious Emotions: The Psychology of Shame, Guilt, Embarrassment and Pride.* New York: Guilford Press.

Stovall, K. and Dozier, M. (1998) 'Infants in foster care: an attachment perspective.' *Adoption Quarterly, 2(1),* 55–87.

Stovall-McClough, K. and Dozier, M. (2004) 'Forming attachments in foster care: infant attachment behaviours during the first 2 months of placement.' *Development and Psychopathology, 16,* 253–271.

Strauss, A. and Corbin, J. (1998) *Basics of Qualitative Research: Techniques and Procedures for Developing Grounded Theory.* Thousand Oaks, CA: Sage.

Street, C. (2004) 'In-patient mental health services for young people: changing to meet new needs?' *Perspectives in Public Health,124(3),* 115–118.

Strijker, J., van Oijen, S. and Knot-Dickscheit, J. (2011) 'Assessment of problem behaviour by foster parents and their foster children.' *Child & Family Social Work, 16,* 93–100.

Strozier, A (2012) 'The effectiveness of support groups in increasing social support for kinship caregivers.' *Children and Youth Services Review, 34(5),* 876–881.

Sue, D.W., Bernier, J.B., Duran, M., Feinberg, L., Pedersen, P. *et al.* (1982) Position paper: 'Cross-cultural counseling competencies.' *The Counselling Psychologist, 10(2),* 45–52.

Sutton, S. (2014) '*Being Taken In.*' British Association for Counselling and Psychotherapy, Children and Young People, December 2014.

Swain, V. (2007) *Can't Afford to Foster: A Survey of Fee Payments to Foster Carers in the UK.* London: The Fostering Network.

Tangney, J., Miller, R., Flicker, L. and Barlow, D. (1996a) 'Are shame, guilt, and embarrassment distinct emotions?' *Journal of Personality and Social Psychology, 70(6),* 1256–1269.

Tangney, J., Wagner, P., Barlow, D., Marschall, D. and Cramzow, R. (1996b) 'The relation of shame and guilt to constructive vs. destructive responses to anger across the life span.' *Journal of Personality and Social Psychology, 70,* 797–809.

Tangney, J.P. (1999) 'The Self-conscious Emotions: Shame, Guilt, Embarrassment and Pride.' In T. Dalgleish and M. Power (eds) *Handbook of Cognition and Emotion.* Chichester: Wiley.

Tarren-Sweeney, M. (2008) 'Retrospective and concurrent predictors of the mental health of children in care.' *Children & Youth Services Review, 30,* 1–25.

Taylor, G. and Ussher, J.M. (2001) 'Making sense of S&M: a discourse analytic account.' *Sexualities, 4(3),* 293–314.

Teets, J. (1990) 'What women talk about: sexuality issues among chemically dependent women.' *Journal of Psychosocial Nursing, 28(12),* 4–7.

The Children's Society (2011) *Make Runaways Safe Launch Report.* London: TCS. Available at www.childrenssociety.org.uk/sites/default/files/tcs/make_runaways_safe_report.pdf, accessed on 3 February 2016.

The NHS Confederation (2011) *Involving Children and Young People in Mental Health Services.* The NHS Confederation.

Tomlinson, K. (2003) *Effective Interagency Working: A Review of the Literature and Examples from Practice.* Local Government Association Research Report 40. Slough: NFER.

Trevithick, P. (2005) 'The knowledge base of groupwork and its importance within social work.' *Groupwork, 15(2),* 80–107.

Trevithick, P. (2008) 'Revisiting the knowledge base of social work: a framework for practice.' *British Journal of Social Work, 38,* 1212–1237.

Tritter, J. and McCallum, A. (2006) 'The snakes and ladders of user involvement.' *Health Policy, 76,* 156–168.

Tronick, E. (2007) 'Of Course All Relationships Are Unique: How Co-creative Processes Generate Unique Mother-infant and Patient-therapist Relationships and Change Other Relationships.' In E. Tronick *Neurobehavioral and Social Emotional Development of Infants and Children.* (Norton Series on Interpersonal Neurobiology). New York: Norton.

Tronick, E. and Beeghly, M. (2011) 'Infants' meaning-making and the development of mental health problems.' *American Psychologist, 66(2),* 107–119. Available at www.ncbi.nlm.nih.gov/pmc/articles/PMC3135310, accessed on 3 February 2016.

Turner, W., Macdonald, G. and Dennis, J.A. (2007) 'Behavioural and cognitive behavioural training interventions for assisting foster carers in the management of difficult behaviour.' *Cochrane Database of Systematic Reviews.* Issue 1. Art. No.CD003760.

UNICEF (1989) *The Convention on the Rights of the Child.* New York: UNICEF.

UNICEF (2000) *The State of the World's Children.* New York: UNICEF.

Utting, W., Baines, C., Stuart, M., Rolands, J. *et al.* (1997) *People Like Us: The Report of the Review of the Safeguards for Children Living Away from Home.* London: The Stationery Office.

Vanderfaeillie, J., Van Holen, F. and Coussens, S. (2008) 'Why foster care placements breakdown? A study into the factors influencing foster care placement breakdown in Flanders.' *Outcome Network.* Available at www.outcome-network.org/paper/159:why_foster_care_placements_breakdown_a_study_into_the_factors_influencing_foster_care_placement_breakdown_in_flanders, accessed on 3 February 2016.

Verhulst, F. and van der Ende, J. (1997) 'Factors associated with child mental health service use in the community.' *Journal of the American Academy of Child and Adolescent Psychiatry, 36,* 901–909.

Verny, T. with P. Weintraub (2002) *Tomorrow's Baby: The Art and Science of Parenting from Conception Through Infancy.* New York: Simon & Schuster.

Vogel, D. and Wester, S. (2003) 'To seek help or not to seek help: the risks of self-disclosure.' *Journal of Counseling Psychology, 50(3),* 351–361.

Vostanis, P. (2010) 'Mental health services for children in public care and other vulnerable groups: implications for international collaboration.' *Clinical Child Psychology and Psychiatry, 15(4),* 555–571.

Wade, J., Dixon, J. and Richards, A. (2010) *Special Guardianship In Practice.* London: British Association for Adoption and Fostering.

Wakelyn, J. (2008) 'Transitional psychotherapy for looked after children in "short-term" foster care.' *Journal of Social Work Practice, 22, 1,* 27–36.

Walsh-Burke, K. (1992) 'Family communication and coping with cancer: impact of the We Can Weekend.' *Journal of Psychosocial Oncology, 10(1),* 63–81.

Ward, H., Jones, H., Lynch, M. and Skuse, T. (2002) 'Issues concerning the health of children in care.' *Adoption &Fostering, 26, 4,* 1–11.

Ward, H., Munro, E., Dearden, C. and Nicholson, D. (2003) *Outcomes for Looked after children: Life Pathways and Decision-Making for Very Young Children in Care.* Loughborough: Loughborough University Centre for Child and Family Research.

Warmington, P., Daniels, H., Edwards, A., Brown, S. *et al.* (2004) *Interagency Collaboration: A Review of the Literature.* University of Bath: Learning In and For Interagency Working Project.

Warner, S. (2009) *Understanding the Effects of Child Sexual Abuse: Feminist Revolutions in Theory, Research and Practice.* London: Routledge.

Warner, S. (in press) *Understanding Child Sexual Abuse: Making the Tactics Visible* (2nd edn). Ross-on-Wye: PCCS Books Ltd.

Warner, S. and Spandler, H. (2012) 'New strategies for practice-based evidence: a focus on self-harm.' *Qualitative Research in Psychology, 9, 1,* 13–26.

Waterhouse, S. and Brocklesby, E. (1999) 'Placement Choice for Children – Giving More Priority to Kinship Placements?' In R. Greef, (ed.) *Fostering Kinship: An International Perspective on Kinship Foster Care.* Aldershot: Arena.

Watson, N. (2010) 'User Engagement and African Caribbean Experience in Child and Family Care Service.' In J. Guishard-Pine (ed.) *Psychology, Race Equality and Working with Children.* Stoke: Trentham.

Wearmouth, J. (2004) '"Talking Stones": an interview technique for disaffected students.' *Pastoral Care, June,* 7–13.

Webb, R. and Vulliamy, G. (2001) 'Joining up the solutions: the rhetoric and practice of inter-agency cooperation.' *Children and Society, 15 (5),* 315–332.

Weinberg, N., Rahdert, E., Colliver, J. and Glantz, M. (1998) 'Adolescent substance abuse: a review of the past 10 years.' *Journal of American Academic Child and Adolescent Psychiatry, 37(3),* 252–261.

Weiss, J. (1993) *How Psychotherapy Works.* New York: Guilford.

Welland, S. and Wheatley, B. (2010) *What If We Said No? Survey Findings Report.* London: Grandparent Plus.

Wertheimer, M. (1924) *Gestalt Theory* (translated by Willis D. Ellis). New York: Harcourt Brace.

Western, D. (1991) 'Social cognition and object relations.' *Psychological Bulletin, 109(3),* 429–455.

Wheelan, S. (2005) *Group Processes: A Developmental Perspective* (2nd edn). Boston, MA: Pearson Education, Inc.

White, E.B. (1952) *Charlotte's Web.* New York: Harper & Brothers.

Widom, C. (1989) 'The cycle of violence.' *Science, 244,* 160–166.

Wigley, V., Preston-Shoot, M., McMurray, I. and Connolly, H. (2012) 'Researching young people's outcomes in children's services: findings from a longitudinal study.' *Journal of Social Work, 12(6),* 573–594.

Williams, G. (1974) 'Doubly deprived.' *Journal of Child Psychotherapy, 3(4),* 15–28.

Williams, M. (2011) 'The changing roles of grandparents raising grandchildren.' *Journal of Human Behavior in the Social Environment, 21(8),* 948–962.

Williams, J., Jackson, S., Maddocks, A., Cheung, W-Y. *et al.* (2001) 'Case–control study of the health of those looked after by local authorities.' *Archives of Disease in Childhood, 85,* 280–285.

Wilson, K. and Evetts, J. (2006) 'The professionalisation of foster carers.' *Adoption & Fostering 30(1),* 39–47.

Wilson, K., Sinclair, I., Taylor, C., Pithouse, A. and Sellick, C. (2004) *Fostering Success: An Exploration of the Research Literature in Foster Care.* Social Care Institute for Excellence. Bristol: Policy Press.

Winnicott, D. (1965) 'The maturational processes of the facilitating environment: studies in the theory of emotional development.' *International Journal of Psycho-Analysis, 64,* 1–276.

Winnicott, D. (1971) *Playing and Reality.* London: Penguin.

Wiseman, H. and Tishby, O. (2014) 'Client attachment, attachment to the therapist and client-therapist attachment match: how do they relate to change in psychodynamic psychotherapy?' *Psychotherapy Research, 24,* 392–406.

Wolpert, M. and Wilson, P. (2003) 'Child and adolescent mental health services: million dollar question.' *Young Minds Magazine, 65,* 28–29.

World Bank (2000) *Listening to the Voices of the Poor.* Washington, DC: World Bank.

World Health Organization (2014) *Preventing Suicide: A Global Imperative.* World Health Organization. Available at www.who.int/mental_health/suicide-prevention/world_report_2014/en, accessed on 3 February 2016.

Wosket, V. (1999) *The Therapeutic Use of Self: Counselling Practice, Research and Supervision.* London: Routledge.

Yalom, I. (1980) *Existential Psychotherapy.* New York: Basic Books.

Yalom, I. (1985) *The Theory and Practice of Group Psychotherapy* (3rd edn). New York: Basic Books.

Yalom, I. and Leszcz, M. (2005) *The Theory and Practice of Group Psychotherapy* (5th edn). New York: Basic Books.

Yardley, A., Mason, J. and Watson, E. (2009) *Kinship Care In N.S.W.: Finding A Way Forward.* Sydney: University of Western Sydney.

Yin, R. (2009) *Case Study Research* (4th edn). Thousand Oaks, CA: Sage.

Young, E. (1990) 'The role of incest issues in relapse.' *Journal of Psychoactive Drugs, 22(2),* 249–258.

Young Minds (2007) *Looking After Looked After Children: Sharing Emerging Practice.* London: Young Minds.

Young Minds (2012) *Improving the Mental Health of Looked After Young People: An Exploration of Mental Health Stigma.* Available at www.youngminds.org.uk/assets/0000/1440/6544_ART_FINAL_SPREADS.pdf, accessed on 3 February 2016.

Zahner, G. and Daskalakis, C. (1997) 'Factors associated with mental health, general health, and school-based service use for child psychopathology.' *American Journal of Public Health, 87(9),*1440–1448.

Zayed, Y. and Harker, R. (2015) *Children in Care: Statistics.* House of Commons Briefing Paper. 5 October 2015. Available at: www.google.co.uk/url?sa=t&rct=j&q=&esrc=s&source=web&cd=1&ved=0ahUKEwi70rGclObKAhWDGp AKHWzHB kEQFggcMAA&url=http%3A%2F%2Fwww.parliament.uk%2Fbriefing-papers%2Fsn04470.pdf&usg=AFQjCNFXUJO4mO_v0s15gCB bVRPdJvrzIg&bvm=bv.113370389,d.ZWU, accessed on 3 February 2016.

Ziegler, M. (1996) 'At the edge of a cliff: excerpts from a therapist's journal.' *Treating Abuse Today, 5(6)–6(1),* 31–37.

Ziegler, M. and McEvoy, M. (2000) 'Hazardous Terrain: Countertransference Reactions in Trauma Groups.' In R.H. Klein, V. L. Schermer (eds) *Group Psychotherapy for Psychological Trauma.* New York: Guilford Press.

Zilberstein, K. and Popper, S. (2016) 'Clinical competencies for the effective treatment of foster children.' *Clinical Child Psychology and Psychiatry, 21(1),* 32–47.

Zima, B., Budding, M., Yang, X. and Belin, T. (2000) 'Help-seeking steps and service use for children in foster care.' *Journal of Behavioural Health Services and Research, 27(3),* 271–285.

Zlotnick, Y., Wright, M., Cox, K., Te'o, I. and Stewart-Felix, P. (2000) 'The family empowerment club: parent support and education for related caregivers.' *Child and Youth Care Forum, 29(2),* 97–112.

Zukoski, M. (1999). 'Foster Parent Training.' In I. Silver, B. Amster and T. Haecker (eds) *Young Children and Foster Care: A Guide for Professionals.* London: Paul H. Brookes..

Subject Index

Author Index